Windows 98
including Internet Explorer

Jim Muir

Lecturer in Computing
Bournemouth University

Letts
1998

Acknowledgements

The computer program Windows 98 is copyrighted by the Microsoft Corporation, all rights reserved. Screen displays from Windows 98 are reprinted by permission. Windows 98, Internet Explorer, FrontPage Express and Outlook Express are registered trademarks of the Microsoft Corporation.

A CIP record for this book is available from the British Library

ISBN 1 85805 3781

Editorial and production services: Genesys Editorial Limited

Typeset by Kai, Nottingham

Printed in Great Britain by Martins the Printers, Berwick upon Tweed

Contents

About this book

Aims

This book is intended for any new user of Windows 98, whether or not they have used a previous version of Windows. It is aimed at the non-technical user who wants a clear and practical guide to using Windows 98. This book assumes no technical knowledge and is suitable for use at college, work or home.

Structure

The features of Windows 98 are introduced as a series of practical tasks; theory is supported with ample opportunities for independent practice and consolidation.

The book is divided into 13 units which have the following features:

- short tasks guiding the user step-by-step through the necessary skills
- independent activities to be completed with minimal support from the book
- tips and troubleshooting sections offering advice on what to do if an operation doesn't work.

A note to lecturers and students

This learning material requires little, if any, input by lecturers and can therefore be used on programmes of independent learning. A disk containing the files used in the book is available free to lecturers adopting the book as a course text.

Extra material in this edition

If you have used the earlier book 'Windows 95' you will find that the structure of Part 1, covering the Windows 98 operating system, is basically unchanged. Part 2, however, which covers Internet Explorer and the Web, is entirely new. There are four units dealing with browsing and searching the Web, creating your own Web pages, and using email and newsgroups. Aspects of Web security are also covered.

What is the Windows 98 operating system?

To many users, Windows is just the desktop – what you see when the computer has started up. They use it to start up an application such as a word processor and have no interest in it beyond that. However, whenever you are using your applications Windows is working away in the background, controlling the basic actions of the computer 'hardware' – the keyboard, screen, main memory, disk drive etc. As an operating system, Windows also loads up applications (software programs), saves files and prints, so you can think of it as a bridge between you, your hardware and your programs. It translates your commands into a form that the computer can understand. As well as this central core Windows has many other features. These include:

- file management, e.g. Explorer
- utility programs to, e.g., back up your files or compress your disk
- internet and Web applications e.g., to browse the Web and create Web pages and email.

Microsoft Windows is the standard operating system used on nearly all PC's. Its operating environment of mouse, menus and dialog boxes has become the standard way of working for PC users. This standardisation extends not only to Microsoft's own range of products, such as Microsoft Office, but to most new software applications.

Conventions

In this book, 'Windows' means 'Windows 98' ; any references to earlier versions of Windows are specifically identified.

Unless otherwise stated 'click' means click the left mouse button once (see Unit 1, Task 2 for a full list of mouse commands).

The following conventions have been adopted to distinguish between the various objects on the screen.

- Dialog box names, menu items and commands are shown as **File-Exit**, which means choose the **File** menu and then select the option **Exit** from that menu.
- Buttons, tabs and icons are shown in bold inside shaded rectangles, e.g. **Cancel**
- Keys are shown in underlined italics e.g. *Ctrl*
- Filenames are shown in bold e.g. **Accounts**
- Text you type yourself is shown in bold italic, e.g. enter ***yahoo***.

Indicates text that gives a definition of a term. Note that all definitions are also included in the Glossary.

Indicates a tip providing a helpful hint.

Indicates a cautionary note.

Indicates a cross reference.

95 ⇨ 98, Indicates "new features".

About Windows 98

Changes since Windows 3.1

Windows 95 was the first major re-design of Windows since its launch in the 1980's. All the standard elements of the Graphical User Interface were still present – windows, mouse, icons, pull-down menus etc. – but they were radically redesigned. There were also many technical changes 'behind the scenes' that were not so immediately apparent. These are briefly explained below.

The Start Button and the desktop replace Program Manager The **Start** button opens the **Start** menu, which provides a single starting point for all Windows features. The Task bar indicates which applications are running, avoiding the need to have multiple windows open.

The Run Command is now located on the **Start** menu and can be used as before to start programs, open folders etc.

Windows Explorer and My Computer replace File Manager File management tasks, e.g. finding, copying or deleting files, are now performed by these two utilities.

Control Panel controls all the computer settings.

Printers Folder controls printing.

Finding files and running programs The Find and Quick View features make it easier to search for and locate files.

Window Close Button The **Close** button closes an open window, supplementing the **Minimize**, **Maximize** and **Restore** buttons,

Customising Windows Various ways to tailor Windows to individual needs are provided – shortcuts to applications, setting up different user profiles and altering how applications run.

MS-DOS was no longer needed Windows 95 no longer required the MS-DOS operating system in order to run; it was a complete operating system in its own right and could still run older DOS and Windows 3.1 programs.

Improved multitasking Microsoft described Windows 95 as a pre-emptive multithreading, multitasking operating system. *Multitasking* means that more than one program or application can run at once (as they could in Windows 3.1). *Pre-emptive multithreading* means very simply that different sections or threads of different programs can be run at the same time, thereby improving memory usage and processing speed.

Longer file names File names can be up to 255 characters long. Previously the limit was eight characters followed by an optional extension of up to three characters.

Support for networks The built-in networking features make it easier to communicate with other computers and share files.

New and improved applications An improved built-in word processor and paint program were provided, the file display and backup were also improved. New features included fax, electronic mail, a phone dialler, and a disk compressor and defragmenter.

Plug and Play This is an industry-wide standard; Windows 95 automatically detects when new peripherals such as disk drives, adapters, CD-ROMS, and sound cards are plugged in and reconfigures the PC to manage the new component.
The devices can be 'played' straight away without the user needing to go through complex set up routines.

Changes since Windows 95

Windows 98 is an update to Windows 95, not a radical re-design; the most significant developments are integration with the Internet and the World Wide Web.

Getting connected to the Internet Windows 98 includes tools to connect to the Internet, and choose an Internet Service Provider (ISP), with electronic mail (email) and meetings services.

Built-in Web browser Microsoft Internet Explorer allows you to 'browse' or 'surf' the World Wide Web (WWW or the Web).

Downloading from Web sites Windows 98 will automatically check nominated web sites for updated information and transfer (download) it to your computer. You can also save on connect time by storing a Web page, disconnecting from the Internet and reading it later 'offline'.

Improved toolbars and taskbar **Forward** and **Back** buttons have now been added to other Windows features, such as folders and documents. You can also add buttons to the Toolbar that allow you go directly to the Desktop, your email or the Internet.

Improved search The **Find** menu now allows you to to locate information on the Internet as well as on your own computer system.

Improved Help Troubleshooters, accessible through Windows Help or Microsoft's own Website, answer problems you may have with your computer. Updates to the Windows 98 operating system can also be downloaded via the Net.

Improved reliability New tools allow you to check and back up your files more quickly, diagnose system faults and tune up your system to run more efficiently. You can schedule these and other tasks to run at regular intervals.

Diskettes needed

For some of these units you will need two, three and a half inch, high density diskettes (floppy disks), preferably new ones that do not contain any files as the Format and Delete commands will erase any information stored on them.
If you use a brand new disk it will need to be formatted before it can be used – consult Unit 3, Task 1 if necessary.

Section 1

Introduction to Windows 98

unit 1

Windows 98 – Introductory essentials

Introduction

In this unit you will learn such essential preliminaries as starting up Windows 98, finding your way around the main desktop and taskbar, opening and closing windows and using Help. Don't be tempted to skip these activities if you are fairly new to Windows. They lay the foundation for more advanced skills and they give you a general understanding of what Windows is and how it works.

If you already know Windows 3.1 or Windows 95

Many readers will already be familiar with previous Windows versions. If so you will find using Windows 98 fairly straightforward. To help you, brief notes, labelled as follows, explain the differences between new and old versions.

95 ➪ 98, or
3.1 ➪ 98

New features have an icon  in the margin.

What you should know already

No previous knowledge is needed.

What you will learn in this unit

By the end of this unit you will be able to:

- identify the main features of the Windows desktop
- use the main features of Windows, dialog boxes and menus
- arrange Windows on the desktop
- use Windows Help facilities
- perform mouse actions
- check some standard Windows settings.

Task 1: The Windows 98 opening screen

Windows is a Graphical User Interface (GUI). This means that you use graphical or picture-based methods to carry out operations on your computer rather than typing commands.

When you turn on your PC you are taken directly to the Windows desktop. Let's identify the basic components first. They are labelled on Figure 1.1 - don't worry if your layout differs from this.

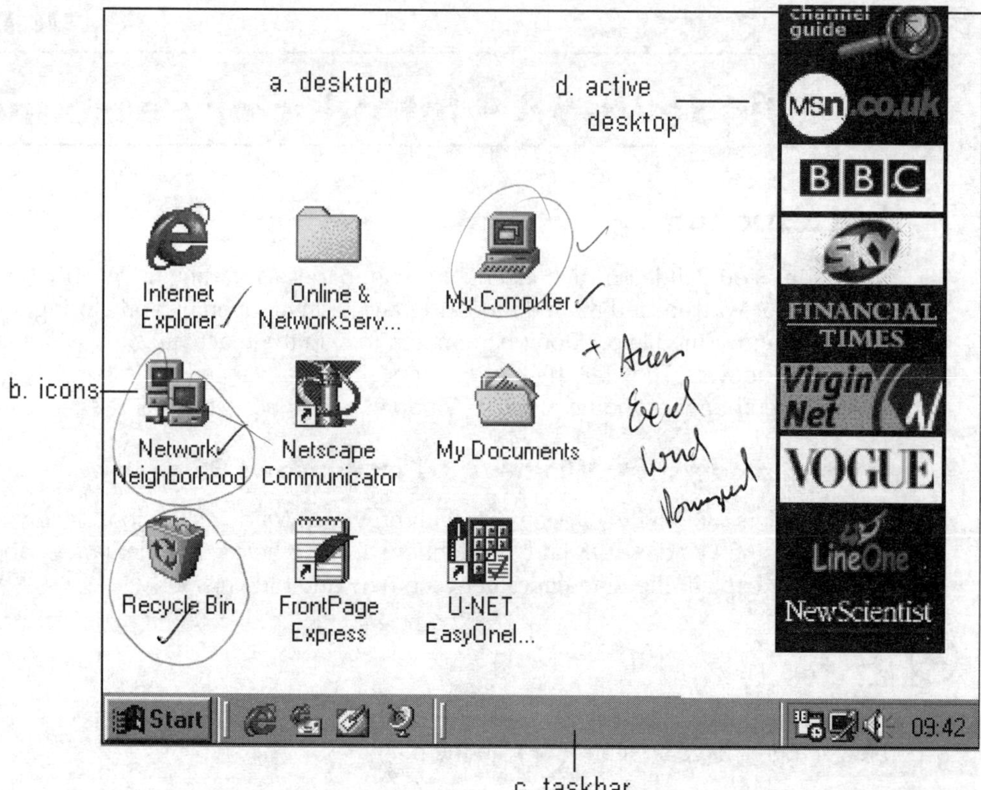

Figure 1.1

a The *desktop* is the background area of the screen which may be plain or patterned. It is used as a working area to open windows, work with them and close them when no longer needed. Nearly all your tasks – viewing documents, running programs, using the Internet or email – start from the desktop.

b Various *icons* are displayed. These are small pictures or graphic images. They represent programs, files or computer hardware – more about these later.

c The *taskbar* is displayed along the bottom of the screen. If you are not using any program or file then it will display the **Start** button, time, and probably some **Quick Launch** buttons for the Internet. The taskbar remains visible no matter what is happening on the rest of the desktop.

d The *Active Desktop* may be displayed to the right of your screen. It displays information channels on the World Wide Web that you can subscribe to – news, entertainment etc. We will turn it off in the next section as we will not be using it in this part of the book.

3.1 ⇨ 98 All the standard windows of Windows 3.1 – Main, Program Manager, File Manager etc. – have been replaced. Don't worry, you can achieve the same tasks more simply in Windows 98.

1 First we will make sure that you are using the same desktop settings as this book.

- If someone else has been using the computer before you, you may find the opening screen is overlaid by some other windows or the Welcome Screen. If so proceed as follows. Move the mouse – the pointer on the screen moves. In the top right hand corner of an open window are three small icons (see Figure 1.5). Move the pointer onto the one marked with a cross and press the left hand button of the mouse. The window will close.
- If one icon is lying on top of another move the mouse on top of the icon, press down the left mouse button and move the mouse to drag it away.
- Click the *right* mouse button on any empty part of the desktop – a pop-up menu will appear.

  Move the mouse pointer onto the **Active Desktop** option and a further menu appears – see Figure 1.2.

Figure 1.2

If the '**View as Web Page**' option is ticked then move the mouse pointer onto it and click it with the *left* mouse button to de-select it. This is an example of a toggle option that can be selected or de-selected by clicking. Try this twice more, ending up by deselecting the **Active Desktop** option.

- Look at the icons on the desktop; if the text is underlined, they have been set to a web-style interface, i.e. they open with a single rather than double click of the left mouse button. I shall be using the double click standard.

  Left-click the **Start** button on the Taskbar - the **Start** menu opens.

  Move the mouse pointer onto the **Settings** option and click **Folder Options** – see Figure 1.3.

Figure 1.3

The **Folder Options** dialog box opens. Move the mouse pointer onto the radio button next to the **Classic style** option and left click to select it – see Figure 1.4.

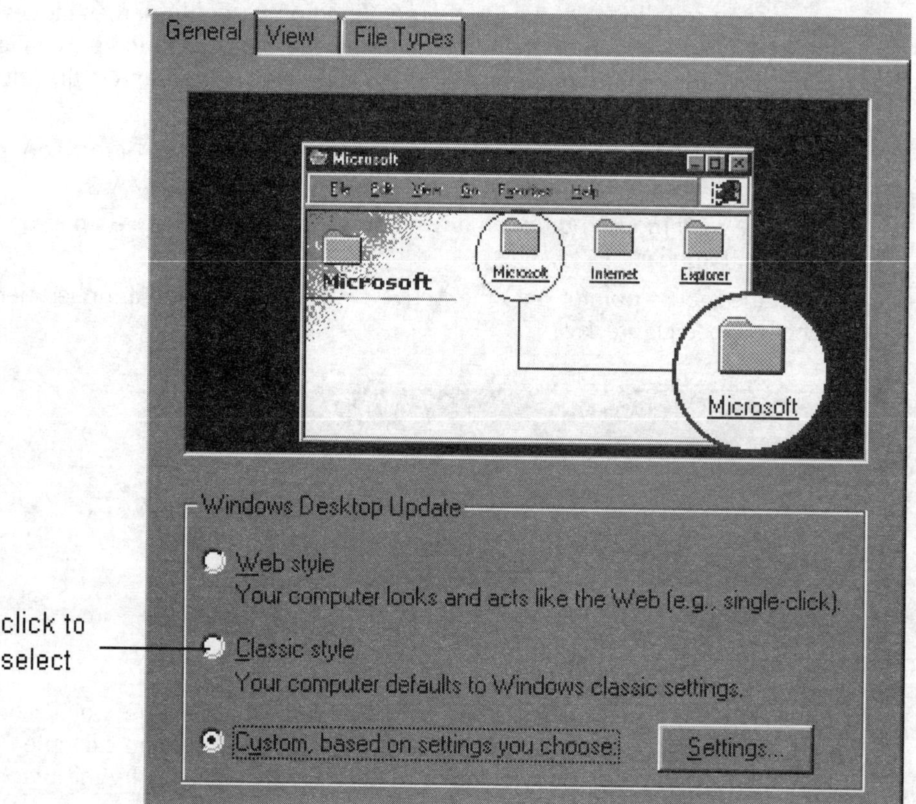

Figure 1.4

Click the **OK** button and you are returned to the desktop.

The default for the desktop should now be set to the one used in this book, i.e. icons not underlined, and the active desktop hidden. This default will be used in all the units in Part 1 of this book. Task 5 in Unit 2 explores some of these settings further.

2 Now, to change the default, move the screen pointer onto the **My Computer** icon. It may have been re-named: if so, identify it by the icon – a picture of a PC (see Figure 1.1)

Press the left button on the mouse twice in quick succession. The icon opens up into a window – try again if it doesn't work.

A window is simply a rectangular area that displays further information – icons, folders or files. At the moment it shows details of the PC's resources – disk drives, printers etc. The My Computer window also contains the Control Panel. You can use it to work with files and drives, e.g. view, sort, copy, rename and delete files.

3 We will use the My Computer window to identify the main components of a window and then try some of them out. Keep referring to Figure 1.5 if necessary. Again, don't worry if your window is different to the one shown.

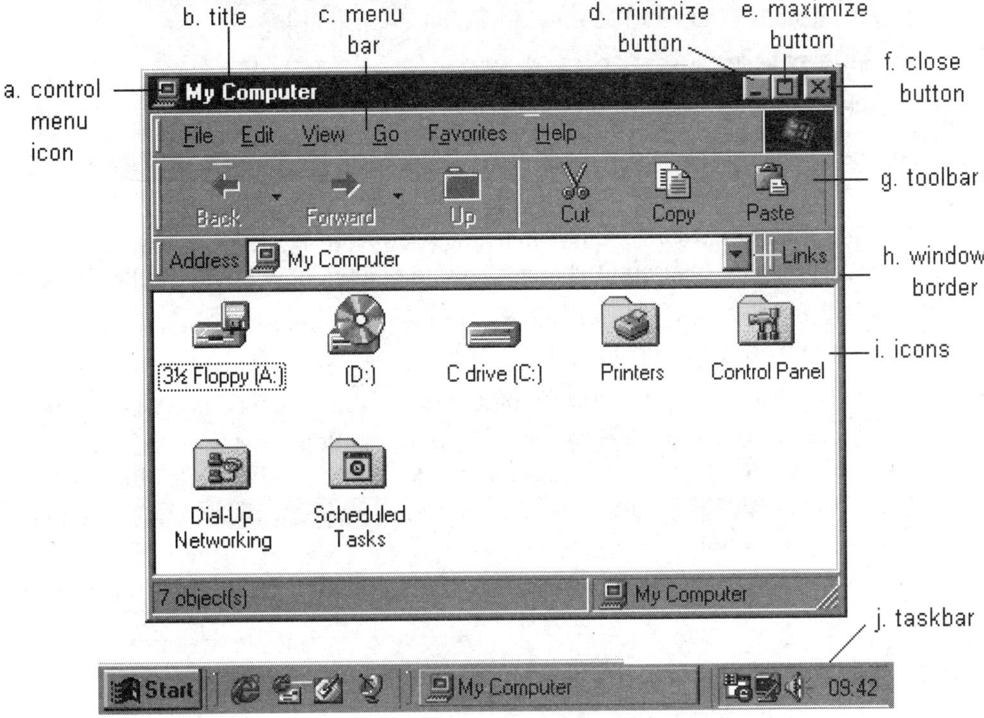

Figure 1.5

a *The Control-menu icon* is in the top left-hand corner of every window. The icon varies, depending on the application. It allows you to close, move and alter the sizes of windows.

b *Title and Title Bar* Every window has these. Depending on the type of window the title can be the name of an application (program), a file or a group of resources, as in the case of My Computer. If there are several windows open then the title bar of the active window – the one that you are using – appears as a deeper colour than the others, usually blue.

c *The Menu Bar* appears just below the Title Bar and shows a list of menus – **File**, **Edit**, **View** etc. These menus will vary from one window to another. Using a menu is the main method of issuing commands and involves two steps, opening the menu then selecting an option from it. Each menu contains a list of related options or commands.

d *The* **Minimize** *button* is in the top right hand corner of every window. It allows you to shrink the window to a button on the taskbar when you are not using it.

e *The* **Maximize** *button* (immediately to the right of the **Minimize** button) allows you to enlarge the window to the full size of the screen. This gives you more room to work if needed. If the screen is already maximised then the **Maximize** button is replaced by a double-squared **Restore** button that restores the window to its previous size (see next task).

f *The* **Close** *button* is used when you no longer need a window, e.g. you have finished with a word processed document or using a program.

d. g *The Toolbar* displays various buttons – **Back**, **Forward**, **Up** etc. These are extra commands and supplement those on the menu bar.

h *The Window Border* is a line enclosing each window. The sides and corners of the border can be used to change the size of a window as we shall see later.

i *Icons* represent windows which aren't being used at the moment – they can be opened by double clicking.

d. j *The Taskbar* is always visible at the bottom of the screen while Windows 98 is running. It shows the **Start** button, plus a button for every task you have started, e.g. program running or document open. So in Figure 1.5 the taskbar shows the **Start** button and a button for **My Computer** indicating that this task is running.

The My Computer window also shows a taskbar reporting '7 objects', i.e. seven items in this window.

3.1 ⇨ 98 You will recognise these standard Windows features; the main changes are the addition of a **Close** button, plus minimised windows being displayed on the taskbar as buttons.

Task 2: Re-sizing and closing windows

Now that we've identified some of the basic Windows components, let's try some of them out; keep referring to Figure 1.5 if necessary.

1 *Maximising and minimising windows* often causes frustration when you start out; typical problems are a window suddenly enlarging, shrinking, disappearing or overlying another.

Make sure that the My Computer window is still open – is the window filling the whole screen? If so, click the **Restore** button and the window reduces to a smaller size in the centre of the screen.

If not, move the screen pointer onto the **Maximize** button and click once. The window enlarges to fill the whole screen and the **Maximize** button is replaced by the **Restore** button.

Now click the **Minimize** button. The My Computer Window shrinks to a button on the taskbar as the application is still running as a 'task'.

Click the button on the taskbar and the My Computer window opens again.

2 To Close a window, click the **Close** button. The window is completely closed – there is no button on the Taskbar as the application is no longer running.

Open it again by moving the screen pointer onto the **My Computer** icon and double-clicking.

---

3 To make finer adjustments to window size we must use the window border. You cannot do this while the window is maximised so click the **Restore** button if necessary.

Move the screen pointer to the bottom right-hand border of the window – the screen pointer changes to a double-headed arrow when correctly located.

Now press down the left mouse button *and keep it pressed down.*

Drag the mouse so that the edge of the worksheet moves diagonally towards the top left of the screen. Release the button when the My Computer window measures about 10 centimetres square.

Your window will now resemble Figure 1.6.

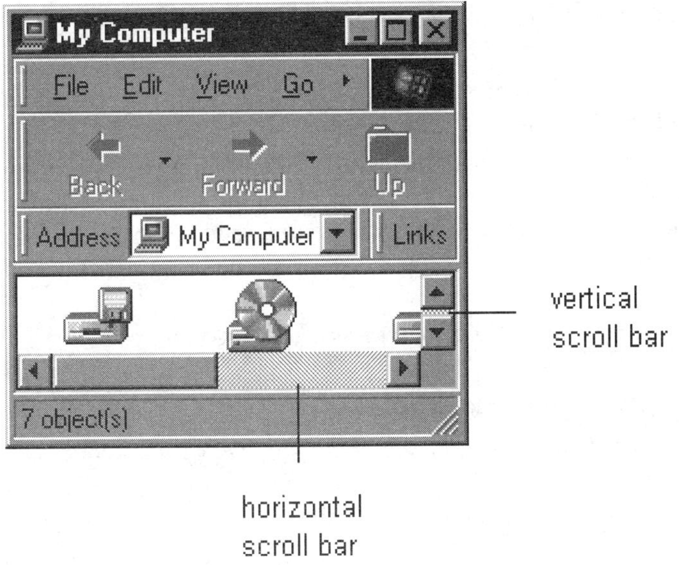

Figure 1.6

Three main changes have taken place – compare your re-sized window with Figure 1.6. First, the Title, Tool and Menu Bars are much shortened.

Secondly, some or all of the icons seem to have disappeared.

Thirdly, two new Windows features have appeared – horizontal and vertical scroll bars; if you don't have both sets of scroll bars then make the window even smaller until they appear.

Scroll bars are permanent features of some windows, but with windows such as My Computer they will only appear if the window is too small to show all the icons.

4 To scroll, move the screen pointer onto the **Up** and **Down** arrow buttons of the vertical scroll bar and hold the mouse button down. The window scrolls, revealing some of the concealed icons.

Now move the screen pointer onto the left and right arrow buttons of the horizontal scroll bar and hold down the mouse button; as before the rest of the icons scroll into view.

Finally enlarge the window again by dragging the border of the window diagonally to the bottom right of the screen.

If all the icons are in view again then the scroll bars will have disappeared (they are not needed).

5 To move windows, move the mouse pointer onto the title bar of the window and drag. The window can be moved around the desktop.

6 You have now learnt three of the four basic mouse actions.

Clicking – locate screen pointer, press left mouse button once

Double clicking – locate screen pointer and press left mouse button twice in quick succession

Dragging – locate screen pointer, hold down left button while moving the mouse, then release button.

Right clicking is the fourth action – locate the screen pointer and press the right mouse button once. When you click an object with the right mouse button it either opens up a pop-up menu, letting you perform actions on the object, or it lets you obtain further information about it. You will be using right click in the next task.

From now on these names will be used to refer to these actions.

Task 3: Working with multiple windows

Confusion often arises when you have more than one window open at once; try out the following tasks.

1 If you are starting a new Windows session make sure that only the My Computer window is open – see Task 2 above. Make sure that it is not maximised.

2 Enlarge the size of the window and use the scroll bars if necessary so that all the icons are visible – see Task 2 above.

3 Now move the screen pointer onto the **Control Panel** icon and double click. The window opens.

4 Now find the **Fonts** icon in the Control Panel window and double click it – this window is now opened.

A further group of icons are displayed in the Fonts window, representing different fonts. Buttons are displayed on the Taskbar, indicating that the applications Control Panel and Fonts are running.

If you can only see one window first check the taskbar, it should show at least two tasks – Control Panel and Fonts.

5 Click anywhere on the Control Panel window – this will make it overlie the Fonts window. Double click on the **Find Fast** icon.

Your desktop should now display three windows and resemble Figure 1.7. Don't worry if the relative positions and sizes of your windows vary from this.

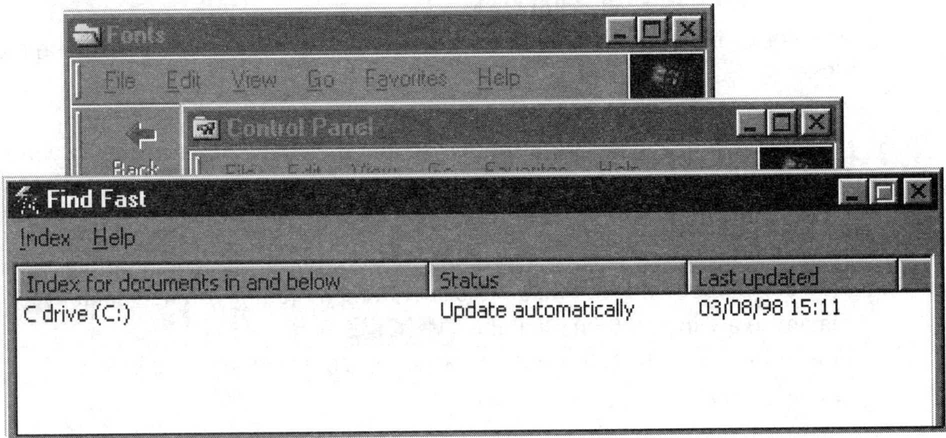

Figure 1.7

6 It is now easy to see how working with multiple windows can cause confusion; one window overlies another, often hiding the title and the icons it contains. Let's experiment with moving and re-sizing these windows.

7 For the purposes of the tasks that follow, we will need to make each window fairly small so that they overlie each other. Re-size and move the windows (see Task 2) so that they resemble Figure 1.7 above. It doesn't matter which window is on top for the moment.

8 We can re-arrange the windows on the desktop.

Move the screen pointer onto a blank area on the taskbar (i.e. not on a task button). Right click. A shortcut menu opens revealing a number of options (see Figure 1.8).

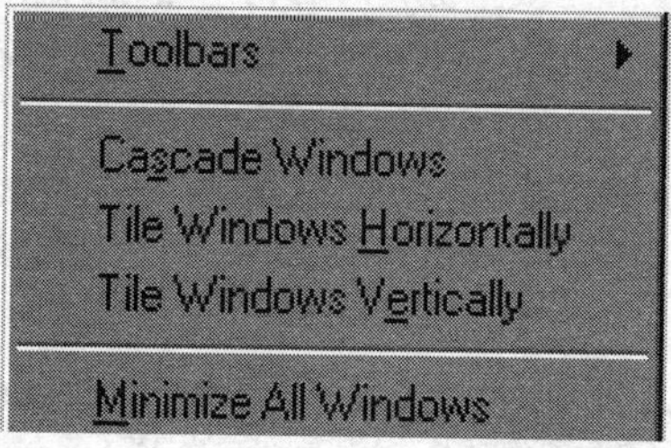

Figure 1.8

9 To move and arrange windows, move the screen pointer onto the menu option **Tile Windows Vertically** and click.

The command is executed and the windows are arranged side by side on the desktop.

Open the menu again and this time choose the option **Cascade Windows**. This command displays the windows so that they overlap, keeping the window titles visible.

Now try the third option, **Tile Windows Horizontally**.

Now drag the three windows to new positions: place the screen pointer on the Title Bar of the window, click it to select it, then drag (if you accidentally maximise a window then click the **Restore** button).
Repeat the **Tile** commands and the windows are re-arranged as before.

Finally select the **Cascade Windows** option.

10 To move between windows, click anywhere on the Fonts window, then anywhere on the Control Panel window. You will notice that clicking a window selects it so that it overlies the others and becomes the 'active' window. This is also confirmed by the title bar changing colour, usually to blue. Other windows are called inactive windows.

11 To bring a window to the top, click each button on the taskbar. The appropriate window moves to the top, although the tiled arrangement is changed.

If you can't see a window always check the taskbar for its related button to ensure that it is still open. If so, click the button and the window will appear on top of the others.

12 Now we will experiment using the **Maximize**, **Minimize** and **Close** buttons. See previous task if necessary.

First maximise the Control Panel window: it fills the whole screen and hides the other two windows, causing beginners to wonder where they have gone!

Now click the **Fonts** button on the taskbar – it overlies the Control Panel window. Minimise the Control Panel window. The window seems to disappear altogether; in fact it has become a button on the taskbar and the Control Panel application is still running.

Click on the **Control Panel** button displayed on the taskbar so that the window fills the whole screen again. Use the **Restore** button to return it to its previous size.

Right click a blank area of the taskbar; the menu appears as before.

This time select the option **Minimize all Windows**. They are all reduced to buttons on the taskbar.

3.1 ➪ 98 Minimised (but not closed) windows appear as buttons on the taskbar. This makes it easier to open a minimised window; in Windows 3.1 a minimised window icon was often hidden by an open window.

13 Click on the three buttons to open the windows again.

The three windows that we have been using are group windows as they contain further groups of icons rather than being applications in their own right.

Close the topmost window using the **Close** button – it no longer appears on the taskbar as a button.

We can also close a window using the **Control-menu** box in the top left hand corner of the window (see Figure 1.9 below). This can be useful if other parts of the window are hidden.

Click the **Control menu** icon on another window and a menu is opened as in Figure 1.9.

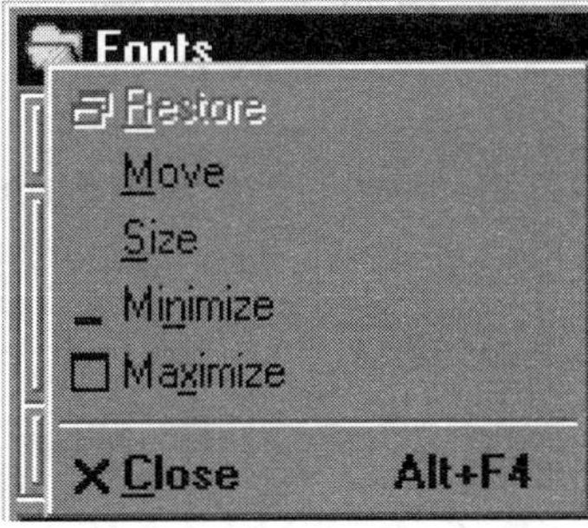

Figure 1.9

The top group of options duplicate ones we have already learnt.

Click the **Close** option and the active window is closed.

Repeat for any windows remaining open (hint: double clicking the **Control menu** icon closes the window in one operation without the need to use the menu).

14 You will have noticed that making windows smaller means that some of the icons may disappear from view. You can rearrange the icons to avoid this.

Open the My Computer window again.

Move the screen pointer onto the menu bar of the My Computer window and click the word **View** – the **View** menu opens.

Click the **Arrange Icons** option to select it: a second menu opens (see Figure 1.10.)

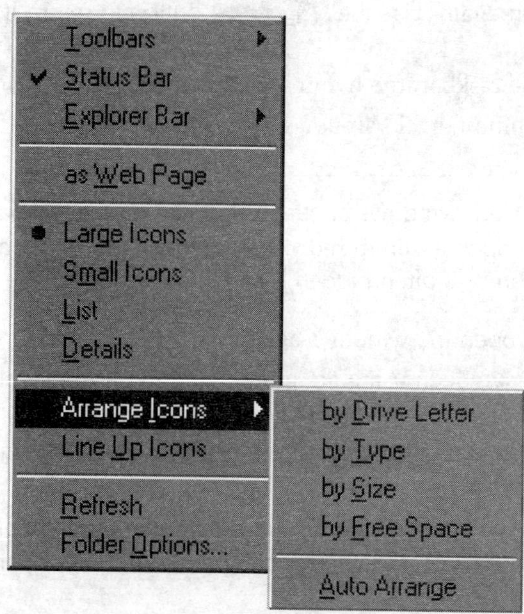

Figure 1.10

Make sure that the **Auto Arrange** option is off, i.e. if it is ticked then click it to de-select the option.

This command is an example of a toggle or switch option – it can be set on or off by clicking it, 'on' being indicated by a tick or check mark next to the option.

You can also right click an empty area of the window to call up the **Arrange Icons** command.

15 Now alter the size of the window so it resembles Figure 1.11. You can see that the window is just too narrow to display all the icons. The presence of scroll bars tell you that there are icons currently not in view.

16 Note that the icons do not spread out to fill all the available space in the window.

Now open the **View** menu and select the **Arrange Icons** option again.

Make sure that the **Auto Arrange** option is on, i.e. it is ticked.

When the **Auto Arrange** command is turned on, any icons that have been compressed together will spread out to fill the space available.

17 You can re-arrange icons to your own taste simply by dragging them, using the left mouse button. This will only work if AutoArrange is set off.

Try this now.

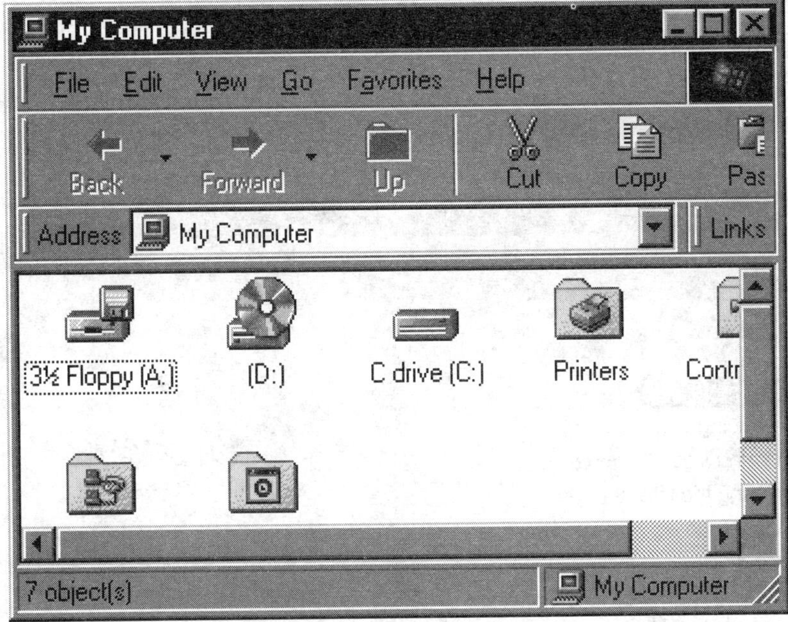

Figure 1.11

18 You will notice that each menu on the My Computer menu bar has one letter underlined, e.g. File, Edit, View etc.. If you hold down the *Alt* key and type the appropriate letter the command is executed. These short-cut keys allow menu commands to be issued from the keyboard, rather than using a mouse.

Try the following.

Hold down the *Alt* key and press the *V* key on the keyboard - the **View** menu opens; keeping the *Alt* key pressed down press the *I* key: a second menu level opens.

With the *Alt* key still pressed down press the *A* key: the AutoArrange command is executed.

In these units we will be using the mouse, not the keyboard equivalent, but it is useful to know that the shortcut keys are available.

19 Close the My Computer window.

Task 4: Using Help

Windows offers good help and tutorial facilities on basic commands, operations, concepts and technical information. There are two main ways to start Help:

- main desktop – click the **Start** button on the taskbar then click **Help**
- from a window – click the **Help** option on the menu bar.

Either way will take you to the same list of topics.

1 Click the **Start** button on the taskbar. A menu appears.
Click the **Help** option. A dialog box appears showing a list of help topics.
In Windows 98 various Web-like features have been added to the Help display, e.g. **Forward** and **Back** buttons – see Figure 1.12.

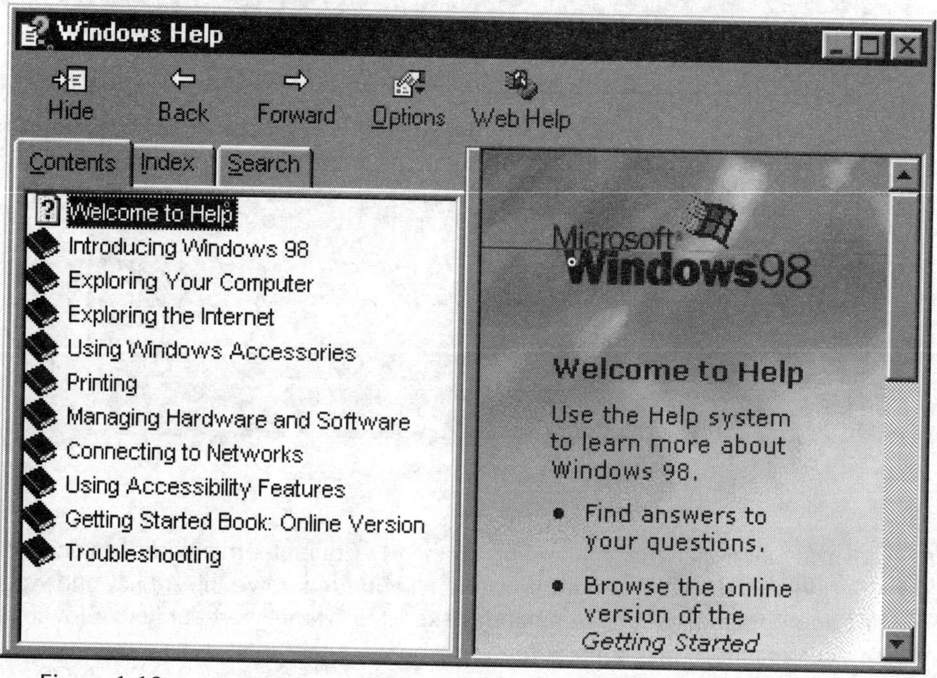

Figure 1.12

2 The Help window is an example of a dialog box. A dialog box either contains a message or asks you to supply some information.
Look at the top left hand corner of the dialog box; three choices are shown as 'tabs': **Contents**, **Index** and **Search**. Click each tab in turn and a new dialog box is shown. Tabs are a common feature of dialog boxes.

3 Finally click the **Contents** tab. 'Contents' is organised like a book's table of contents. It is divided into topics or 'chapters', each of which is divided into further subtopics.
Click on **Introducing Windows 98**; the book icon is now open showing four further subtopics – see Figure 1.13.

4 Click on the **What's New in Windows 98** topic and a further list of subtopics is displayed; you can tell the levels by the indentation of the icons.

5 Next click the topic **Improved Reliability**.
Now that you have reached the third level specific information pages are offered – see Figure 1.14.

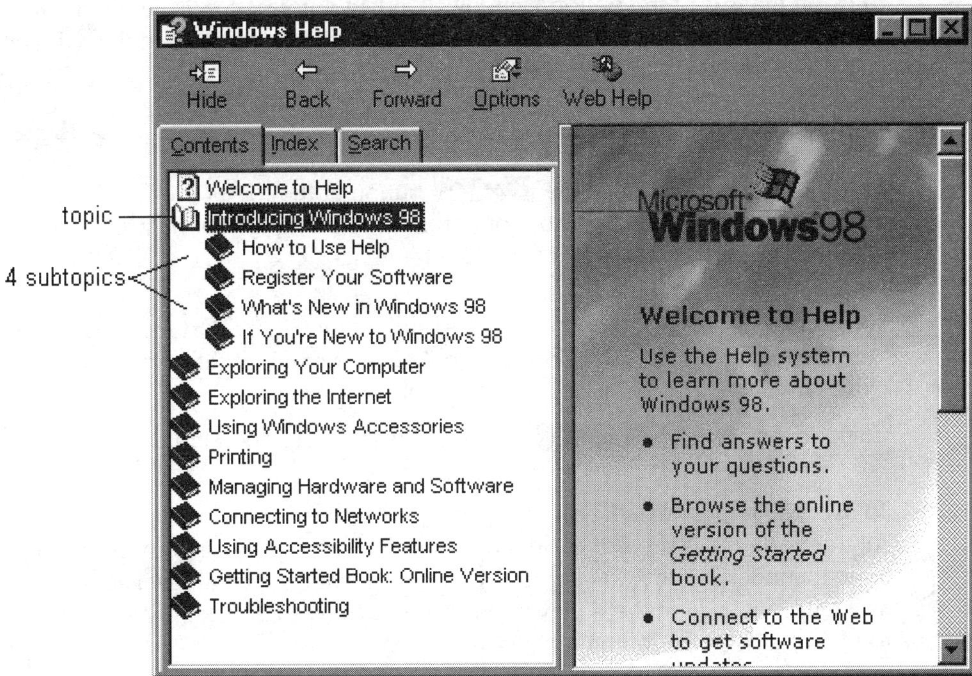

Figure 1.13

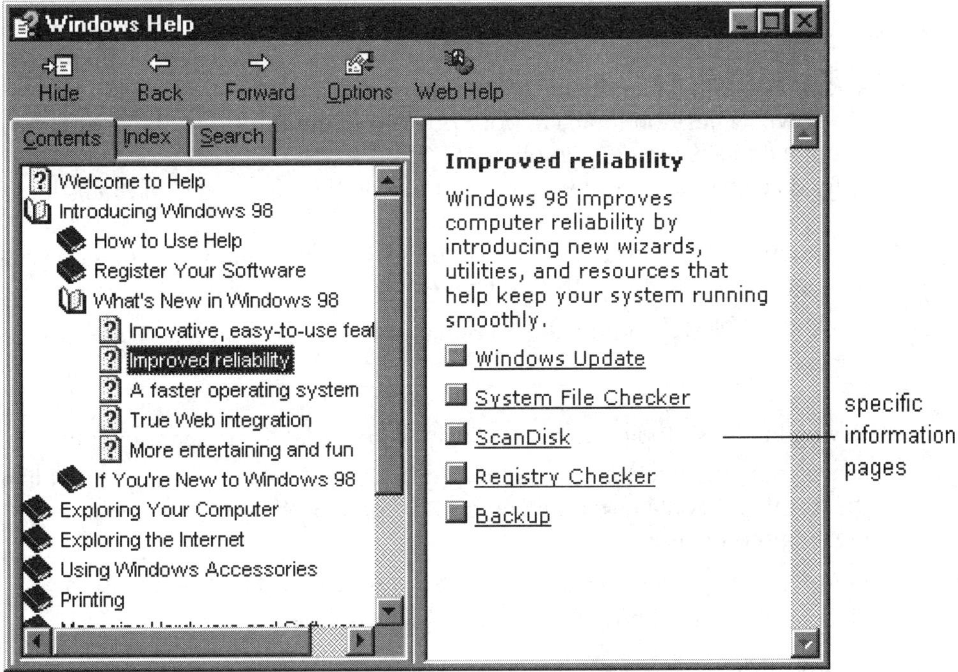

Figure 1.14

6 Click on the text of the option Windows Update. Information is given in a new window. Take time to review it and the other information topics in this window.

Use the **Back** and **Forward** buttons at the top of the window to go from topic to topic.

7 To print a Help topic, click the **Options** button at the top of the window; a menu appears. It offers a number of options, including **Print** which is useful if you wish to print off Help text for future reference.

8 Some of the topics listed in the left hand side of the Help window show an 'open book' icon (see Figure 1.14 above). Simply click on any of them that you wish to close – try this.

Click on the **Welcome to Help** icon to close all the open icons.

9 To use the Help Index, click the **Index** tab at the top left of the Help window. All the Help topics are listed alphabetically. Provided you are fairly sure of your topic the index can be quicker to use than negotiating several levels of contents as we have just done. Let's view the index topics. We can take this opportunity to try out different scrolling techniques.

- *Slow scrolling* Position the screen pointer on the up or down arrow on the scroll bar and click once; the text scrolls line by line.
- *Continuous scrolling* Position the screen pointer on the up or down arrow on the scroll bar and keep the mouse button pressed down; the text scrolls continuously.
- *Rapid scrolling*; Identify the scroll box on the scroll bar (see Figure 1.15 below); its position indicates your position in the list. Click above or below it and the topics move up in blocks.
  Try dragging this box now; you can move to the start or end of the list quickly.

10 To choose a Help topic, scroll down to the topic **My Computer** and choose the subtopic **Creating Shortcuts** (see Figure 1.15).

Click the **Display** button at the bottom of the window and the Help text appears.

11 Keying in a Help topic is a quicker way than scrolling through a long list.

Move your cursor to the start of the text box and if necessary drag to highlight the text that it contains e.g in Figure 1.15 opposite the text 'My Computer, creating short cuts'.

Now type in the letters ***taskb*** – the index moves to this section of topics.

Find **Taskbar** and choose the subtopic **Shortcut menus**.

Finally click the **Close** button to close the Help window.

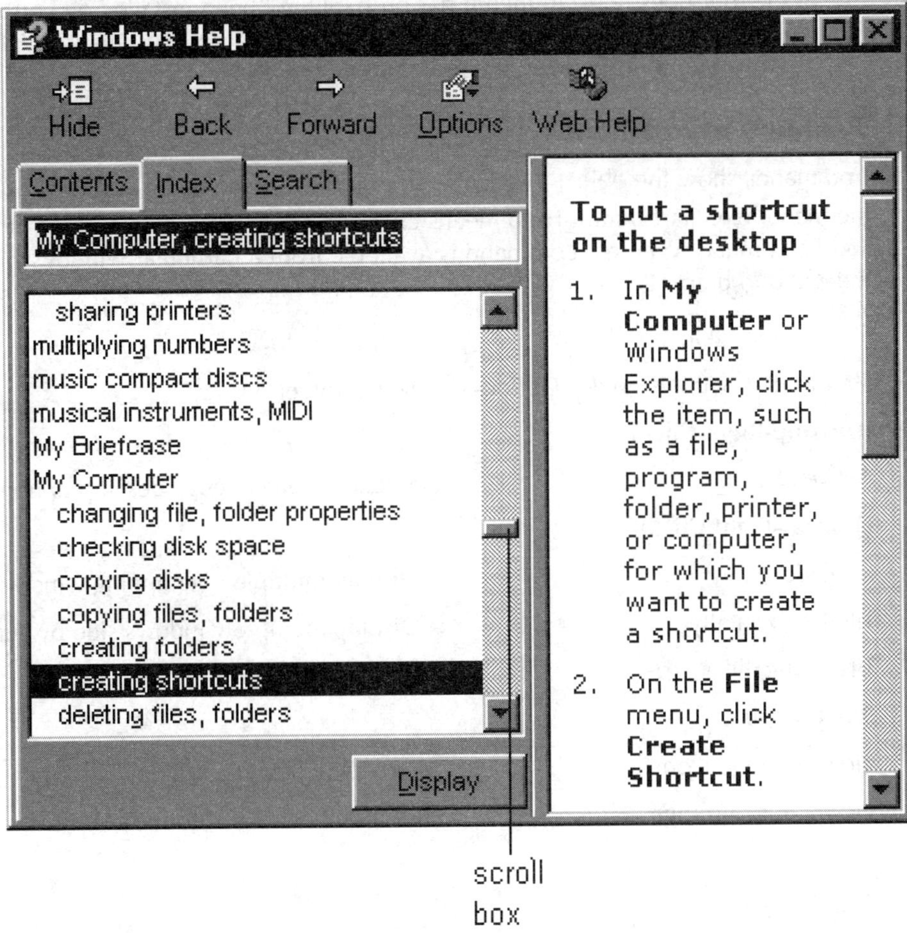

Figure 1.15

12 a Open Help again and use the Help Index feature to locate help on the following:

- Year 2000
- Help overview.

Use the Help Search feature to locate help on the following:

- Screen savers
- Internet – connecting to.

b If you are new to computing and/or Windows you may like to try 'Welcome to Windows', an interactive guide to the essentials of computing and the features of Windows 98.

Click the **Start** button on the taskbar and click **Run**.

A dialog box opens; type ***tour98*** in the **Open:** box and then click the **OK** button (tour98 should be typed with no spaces).

If the tour does not start then it has probably not been installed on your computer system. If you have access to the Windows 98 installation CD then insert it into the CD drive; it can be run from there.

Summary of commands

Commands show the object to select first, followed by the command to choose from the menu, e.g. Start Button-Help means click the **Start** Button and select the **Help** command. Where a command is available from a particular window this is indicated in brackets.

Start Button-Help	Call up Help
Start Button-Settings-Folder Options	Select folder display
(Desktop-Right Click)	
Active Desktop	Select/Deselect active desktop options
(Taskbar-Right Click)	
Cascade	Display multiple overlapping windows
Tile Horizontally	Display multiple windows side by side
Tile Vertically	Display multiple windows vertically
(My Computer)	
View- Arrange icons	Arrange icons in a window
View - Auto Arrange	Re-arrange icons automatically

unit 2

Applications and files

Introduction

In this unit you will be creating a set of files to use in later tasks. You will be using two standard Windows applications, Notepad and Wordpad, to do this. You will also learn how to save different versions of a file under different names and how to view the files you have created on disk.

What you should know already

How to use the standard Windows components – see Unit 1.

What you need

A new blank diskette.

What you will learn in this unit

By the end of this unit you will be able to:

- use the Start menu
- run and exit Applications
- check which applications are running
- create and save text files
- view files using My Computer
- customise windows
- reset the date and time.

Task 1: Running an application from the Start menu

The **Start** button is always displayed at the bottom of the screen and can be used at any time. It is the gateway to all the essential Windows tasks such as starting programs, finding files, getting help and exiting Windows.

3.1 ⇨ 98 In Windows 3.1 you used Program Manager or a group window to run a program. In Windows 98 you can run programs from the **Start** menu.

You will need a suitable diskette (floppy disk) for this task, preferably a new one that does not contain any files. A brand new disk needs to be formatted before it can be used – consult Unit 3, Task 1 if necessary.

In this task we will use the **Start** menu to run an application. An application is any program (or set of programs) that carries out a particular job, e.g. Web browsing or word processing. We are going to use Notepad as our first example application. It is a text editor, (rather like a very simple word processor) and we will use it to create some short text files.

1 Click the **Start** button at the bottom left of the taskbar. A menu opens. Move the pointer onto the **Programs** option.

A further menu opens, move the pointer onto the **Accessories** option and a third menu opens – see Figure 2.1.

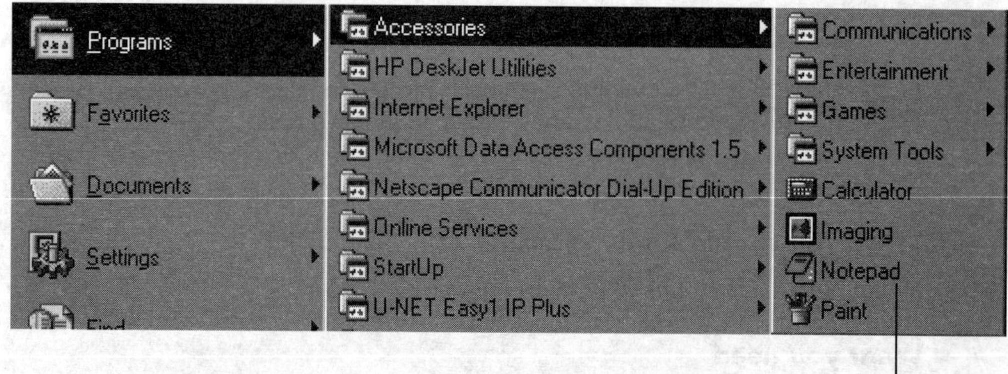

Figure 2.1

Find the icon labelled **Notepad** on the third menu and click it.

The application then loads (i.e. Windows looks for the application program on the hard disk and loads it into the computer's main memory)

(!) If you open the wrong menu click elsewhere on the desktop and start again.

2 A blank Notepad window is displayed, waiting for you to enter some text – see Figure 2.2.

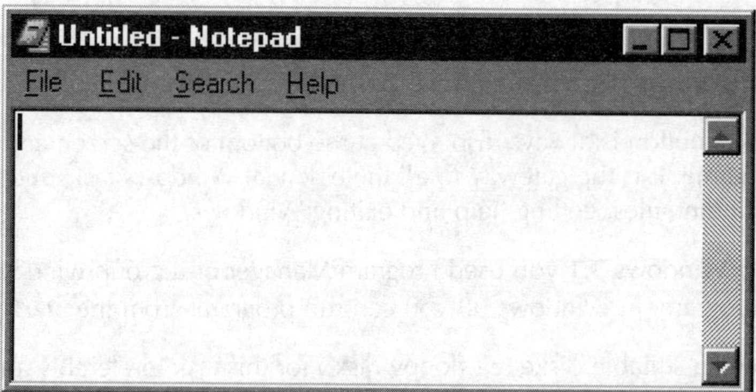

Figure 2.2

Notice that it contains many standard Windows features that you have already used, e.g. title, menu and scroll bars as well as **Maximize** and **Minimize** buttons. The flashing bar indicates the insertion point for the text.

3 For your future activities in Windows 98 you will need a set of files to work with. These can be 'dummy' files, meaning that it doesn't really matter what they contain. However *you must use the file names suggested* as we will be using them in later tasks such as listing, copying, renaming and sorting. So if your typing skills are minimal merely fill them with a jumble of characters. (Lecturers using these units as a course text can obtain these files on disk from the publishers – see 'About this book'.)

First click the **Edit** menu and make sure that the **Word Wrap** option is selected. This ensures that when the text that you type reaches the end of the line it 'wraps round' to the next line.

Simply type in a few lines of text now.

---

4 At the moment the text that you have created is only saved in the computer's main memory. The Notepad file has the temporary name 'Untitled' and will be lost as soon as you exit the Notebook application unless you save it as a named file.

Open the **File** menu and choose the **Save As** option. The **Save As** dialog box appears next – see Figure 2.3.

Figure 2.3

The **File Name** box is selected at the moment (i.e. highlighted) with the temporary name 'untitled' displayed.

Simply type the file name ***Sales - Memo 1*** over the top of this name (upper or lower case).

Now click the **Down Arrow** on the **Save In:** box. A list of available drives appears – see Figure 2.4.

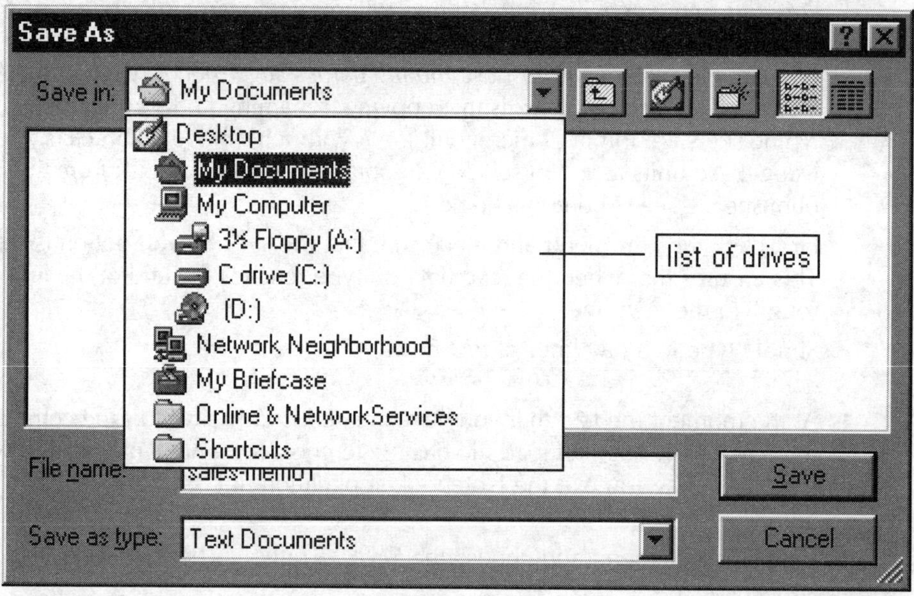

Figure 2.4

In these units we shall be using a diskette to save work. A: is your diskette drive; make sure that you have a suitably formatted diskette in A drive. If you are using a brand new diskette it may need formatting – see Unit 3, Task 1.

Now select the **3 $\frac{1}{2}$ Floppy (A:)** option.

Make sure that the **Save as type** box reads **Text Documents**.

Finally click the **Save** button. The command is executed and the file **Sales - Memo 1** is saved to diskette, the drive light comes on to show that the Notepad data is being written (saved) to disk.

If you make a mistake then click the **Cancel** button and start again.

A note on drives On your PC a hard disk is used to store Windows and usually other applications too, e.g. word processor, spreadsheet or database. If you have enough disk space you can also use the hard disk to save work that you create. It is common to save work on a diskette (also known as a floppy disk), however, especially if space on the hard disk is limited or you want to work on more than one computer.

5 The dialog box disappears and you are returned to the Notepad window which now displays the file name of the newly saved file Sales-Memo 1 (see 'Notes on File Names' at the end of this task)

6 Add a few more lines of text to this file. These changes will need saving permanently to disk too.
Open the **File** menu; choose the **Save** option (not **Save as**).
The drive light comes on again indicating that the changes are being permanently saved to the file **Sales-Memo 1** on disk.

7 The file can be saved under a new name. Add a few more lines of text to the file; open the **File** menu again, but this time choose the **Save As** option.

The **Save As** dialog box appears; amend the file name to **Sales-Memo 2**

Make sure that the **Save in:** box still shows **3 $\frac{1}{2}$ Floppy (A:)**

Click the **Save** button.

The drive light comes on as before to show that the new file **Sales-Memo 2** is being written (saved) to disk.

8 The Notepad window now displays the file name **Sales-Memo 2.** The original file **Sales-Memo 1** is saved and closed and the new copy opened.

Now we will use this method again to create six more files; first add a few more lines of text (this means that all files will vary slightly in size), then choose **Save As** from the **File** menu as before.

Name the files that you create as follows.

Sales - Memo 3

Sales - Memo 4

Accounts - Memo 1

Accounts - Memo 2

Accounts - Memo 3

Accounts - Memo 4

When you have created these files open the **File** menu and select the **Open** option; your display should resemble Figure 2.5 (on the following page) i.e. eight text files have been created using the Notepad application.

Click the **Cancel** button on the **Open** dialog box.

Note on naming conventions

The file name starts with the department name – Accounts or Sales – followed by the type of document – memo. The final number on the file name is the order of creation and ensures that each file name is unique. When you are creating files make sure that you use a meaningful, memorable naming convention and stick to it.

9 Add another line to the final file that you have created. Now try to exit the Notepad application as follows; open the **File** menu and select **Exit**. A dialog box appears, reminding you that you have not saved the changes made to the document. All Windows applications have this feature reminding you to save your work. Normally you would click the **Yes** button which saves and exits the document.

Click the **Cancel** button which returns you to the document.

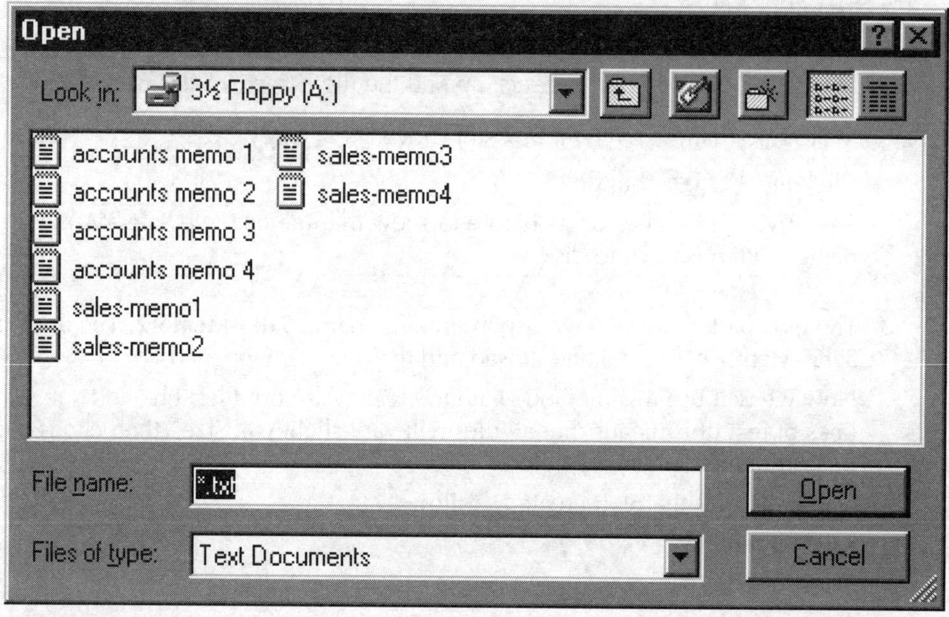

Figure 2.5

A situation where you *would* find it useful to click the **No** button and exit a document without saving is if you have made some major unwanted change to a document e.g. an accidental deletion. Exiting without saving would leave the document as it was the last time it was saved, before you made the unwanted alteration - although you would also lose any other changes that you had made.

10 Now exit the Notepad application again this time taking selecting the **Yes** option on the dialog box.

Notes on filenames

3.1 ⇨ 98 In Windows 3.1 a filename could only consist of up to eight characters, plus an optional extension of up to three characters, separated from the filename by a full stop or 'dot'. Windows 95 and 98 allow file names of up to 255 characters.

Although extensions are still used by Windows 98 to associate a type of file with a particular application the extension is normally hidden from the user.

When a long file name is displayed in Windows 3.1 the user only sees eight characters – which may not be very helpful.

Characters allowed in Windows 98 file names

The letters A - Z (upper and lower case)

Numbers 0 to 9

A space, a dash (-), a full stop, a comma, single quotes, a semicolon, brackets, and underscore (_)

Characters not allowed in Windows 98 file names

Slashes (\ and /), colon and double quotes, also ? * and |

File names are not case sensitive.

Files within the same folder cannot have the same name.

Task 2: Independent activities

You have now run an application, Notepad, and used it to create some simple text files. Let's experiment with running some other applications. We'll use Wordpad, the word processing application supplied with Windows, to create some more files.

3.1 ⇨ **98** Wordpad replaces Windows Write as the Windows 95 and 98 word processing package.

1 You have already created a number of Notepad documents (see the previous task); ensure that the diskette storing these files is still in the diskette (A) drive.

Use the **Start** button to open the **Programs** menu, then the **Accessories** as before.

Find the icon labelled **Wordpad** and double click it.

A blank Wordpad window is displayed, waiting for you to enter some text.

2 Create and save eight dummy files onto the diskette in the A drive in the same way as you did in the Notebook application in the previous task. From now on this diskette will be referred to as diskette 'a'.

Use the file names suggested below, not ones of your own.

Remember to select the **3 $\frac{1}{2}$ Floppy (A:)** option to save your work to diskette.

Make sure that the **Save as type** box reads **Word for Windows 6**. This will save it as a document compatible with the Word 6 word processing package.

Sales - Letter 1

Sales - Letter 2

Sales - Letter 3

Sales - Letter 4

Accounts - Letter 1

Accounts - Letter 2

Accounts - Letter 3

Accounts - Letter 4

3 When you have created all the above files quit the Wordpad application - this time do so by clicking the **Control** menu box at the top left corner of the Wordpad Window – see Figure 2.6.

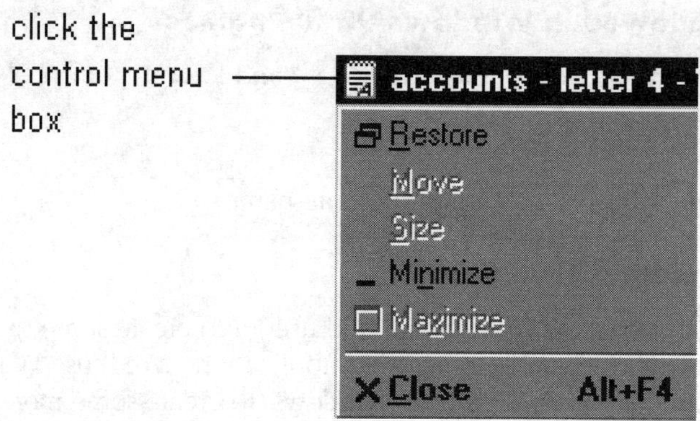

Figure 2.6

Select the **Close** option on the Control menu. The Wordpad application is closed and you are returned to the desktop.

Don't worry if a file name is incorrect; we will show you how to put this right later – see Unit 5. If the file is the wrong type or stored on the wrong drive it is best to delete it and create it again (see Unit 5).

Task 3: Other options on the Start menu

As mentioned in Unit 1, the **Start** menu is the gateway to all the essential Windows tasks such as starting programs, finding files, getting help and exiting Windows. We will briefly review some of the other options that it offers.

1 Click on the **Start** button and select the **Documents** option. Some of the most recently used files are shown. Select one and the file is retrieved (you may be prompted to insert a disk if the file is on diskette).
Exit from the file.

2 If you can't find a program using the **Programs** option on the **Start** menu (see Task 2 above) you can use the **Run** option instead. However, you will need to know the exact program name, and sometimes the drive and folder where it is stored. Select the **Run** option – a dialog box appears.

There is a small **Help** button in the top right hand corner, marked with a question mark – see Figure 2.7 opposite (this is a feature of many windows).

Click the **Help** button, then click on any feature of the dialog box that you want help with. In many cases, a panel of helpful information will appear.

3 Type ***CALC*** in the **Open:** box as shown above and click **OK**. The program CALC is run and the calculator appears. Leave the calculator window open – close the **Run** dialog box if you are returned to it.

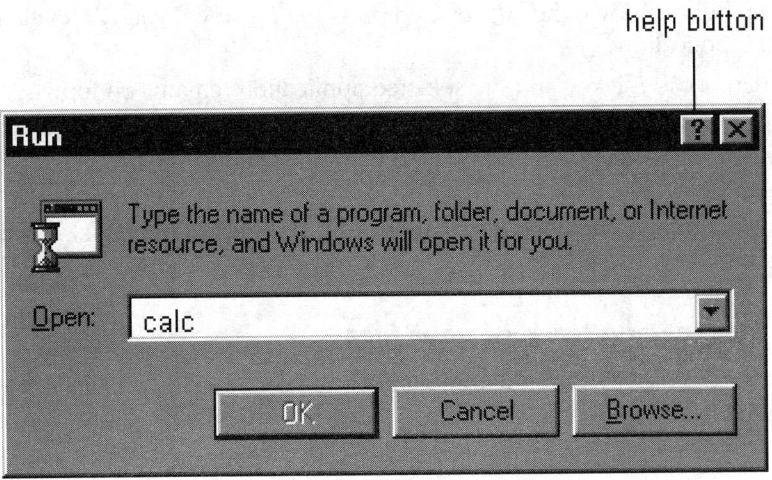

Figure2.7

4 Click the **Start** button and select **Settings** then **Control Panel**.

The Control Panel window displays icons which allow you to change various important settings such as screen display, keyboard, mouse etc.

Warning: Casual tinkering with these settings is irresponsible – particularly if you are sharing the PC with others. If in doubt – leave well alone!

5 Double click the **Date/Time** icon – a dialog box is displayed allowing you to alter the date and time.

6 Amend the day, month and year to find on what day your next birthday falls. Reinstate the correct date when you have finished and leave the Date/Time and the Control Panel windows open.

(!) Your system may have been set up so that you cannot amend the system date or time.

7 Now we move on to multitasking. At the moment you are running two applications at once – Calculator and Control panel. They are both minimised and shown as task icons in the taskbar

Click both icons and the windows are displayed.

Open both the Wordpad and the Paint applications.

Maximise an application. It should be clear that with multiple windows and multiple tasks displayed in the Taskbar it can be difficult to find the window you want and then bring it to the front in order to work on it.

8 To show which applications are running, press down the *Alt* key on your keyboard. Now press the *Esc* key. The first application that is running is shown 'on top'.

Keep holding down the *Alt* key and press the *Esc* key – you can cycle through all four applications.

Let go of the *Esc* key and the selected application remains on top.

Also try the *Alt* and *Tab* keys which produce a similar effect (the *Tab* key is on the left of the keyboard and marked with opposite facing arrows).

9 Finally close all the open applications (it is quickest to right click the buttons on the taskbar).

Task 4: Keeping track of your files

This task uses the My Computer application to keep track of your files. More advanced features are offered by the Windows Explorer application covered in Unit 4.

3.1 ➪ 98 File Manager is replaced by Windows Explorer and My Computer in Windows 98. The My Computer application offers a simpler interface than Explorer for basic operations confined to a single drive or folder. Both applications let you view files, they also allows you to copy, move and delete files, skills that we will be learning in Unit 5.

1 First make sure that all open windows are closed. The **My Computer** icon can be seen on the desktop. Double click it and the window shown in Figure 2.8 appears.

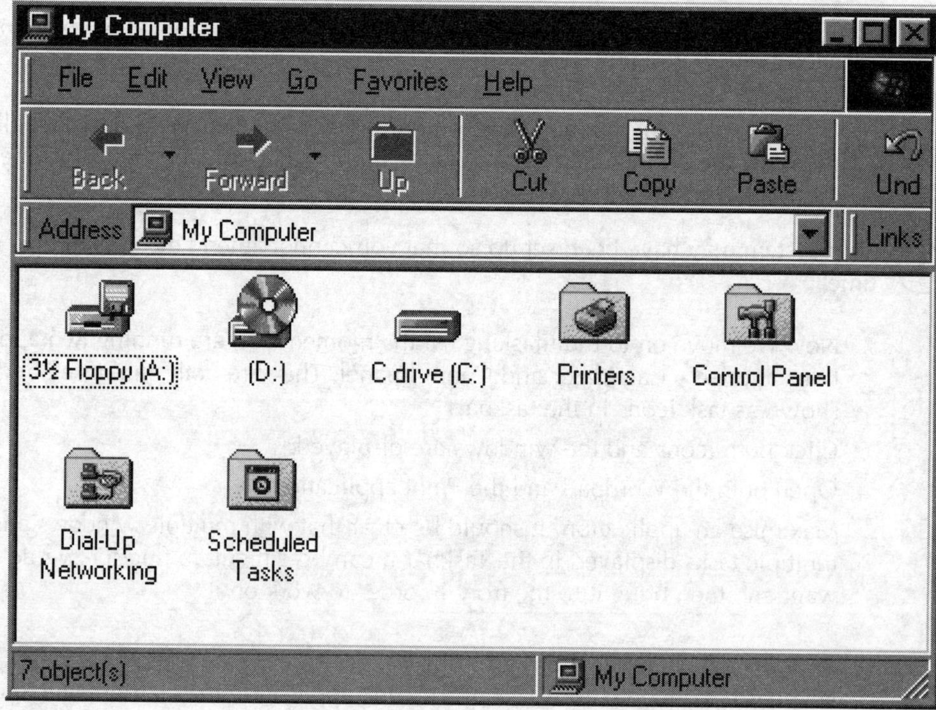

Figure 2.8

On the desktop are icons representing your computer's resources – printers and disk drives. Your window may be different to this.

2 Now you will select a disk drive. If necessary insert the diskette 'a' containing the files that we have created in the previous tasks.

Look at the disk icons displayed in the window. The icon for the diskette drive should be shown, marked **3 ½ Floppy (A:)**.

Double click this drive icon. The files that we have just created should be displayed in a window. If necessary enlarge the window so that all files are visible.

Check that all 16 files are present; if not return to tasks 1 and 2 and complete them.

Look at the title of the window – 3 ½ Floppy (A:). This tells you that the disk currently in use is A, the floppy or diskette drive.

3 Using the **View** menu at the top of the screen, we can view the files in a variety of ways.

Open the **View** menu, select the **Details** option and try these options in turn.

Large icons – the file names and icons are more readable; but fewer will fit in the window.

Small icons – more files can be seen.

List – this is normally the default display and the best for general use.

Details – fuller details of the files are displayed – size, type and the date and time of creation/modification. These are discussed more fully in Unit 4.

as Web Page – if this option is selected, i.e. ticked, then the window takes on the appearance of a Web page – try this, it is one of many Web integration features of Windows 98: windows are given the 'look and feel' of Internet documents. In this case there is less space to display the files but you can get further information on a file by clicking it – try this.

Forward *and* **Back** *buttons* are another 'web page' feature and allow you to review recent window displays – try them.

4 Try using the **Views** button as an alternative to the **View** menu – it is located on the right of the Standard Toolbar (if the toolbar is not visible then open the **View** menu and select **Toolbars-Standard Buttons** option).

5 Open the **View** menu and try these **Arrange Icons** options.

By Name is the default option: the files on disk are in alphabetic order of file name.

By Type the files are sorted into order of their type, for instance, the Notepad text files are grouped separately from the Wordpad files. Notice also that they use different identifying icons.

By Size Size is shown to nearest kilobyte i.e. approximately 1000 characters. The Wordpad files tend to be larger than the Notepad files as they have invisible formatting characters added to control the document layout.

Click any file name to select it, then open the **File** menu and select **Properties**, then **General**.

The exact file size to the nearest byte is shown. Click the **Cancel** button.

By Date The files are displayed in their order of creation, latest first. Notice that the time of creation is also shown and also determines the order.

6 Identify the following files on your diskette.

- The largest file.
- The file created last – look at the time as well as the date.
  Sort the files by name.

Click on the column headings – Name, Size etc. The files will be sorted in the order of the heading that you click. Click the same heading again and they are sorted in reverse order. This is a quicker alternative to using the **View** menu.

Task 5: Customising windows

Windows 98 allows you to customise the appearance of folders and many windows to resemble Web pages; this is largely a matter of personal preference. We will experiment with a few settings.

1 Open My Computer and insert the practice diskette in the drive if necessary.

2 Use the **Views** button on the right of the Standard Toolbar to alter your view of the files on disk (if the toolbar is not visible then open the **By Name** menu and select the **Toolbars-Standard Toolbar** option).

3 Click the **Start** button and select the **Settings** option.

Click **Folder Options**.

The **Folder Options** dialog box opens. Select the **Web style** option (see Figure 2.9 opposite).

Click the **OK** button and you are returned to the desktop. This has the effect of setting all your windows (not just My Computer) to a Web style.

Click the **Back** button to display the main My Computer window if necessary.

4 Click the **C drive** icon to open it; the window display is in Web style.

Click the **Back** button to return to the My Computer display.

5 Open the **Start** menu again and select **Settings - Folder Options** again.

Select the **Custom** option and click the **Settings** button.

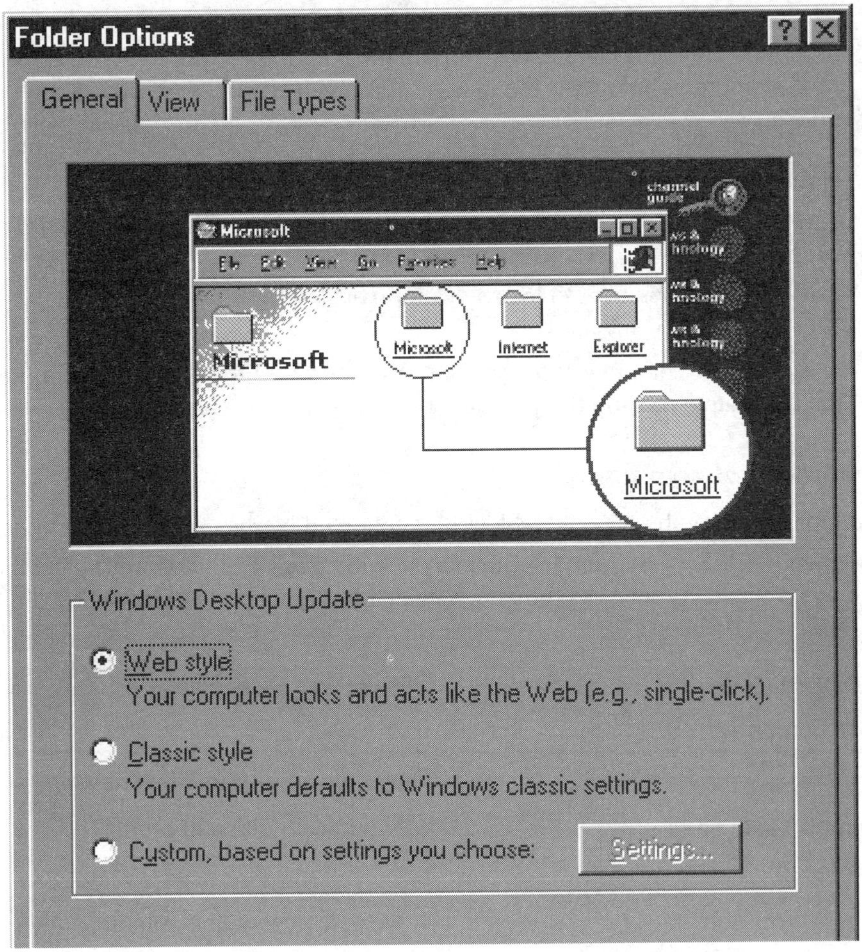

Figure 2.9

The **Custom Settings** dialog box is displayed. Use the **Help** button to discover what these settings control.

After you have finished reset the folder options to **Classic Style** using the **Folder Options** dialog box (see step 3 above).

Task 6: Using My Computer to start an application

As you have seen, the My Computer window provides a quick and easy way of finding files on disk; once you have located a file you can open it directly from My Computer.

1 Find the file **Sales-Memo 1** that you created in the Notepad application and double click the icon.

The file will be opened, overlying the My Computer Window. There was no need to open the Notepad application and then the file as My Computer performs these two operations for you.

2 To close the **Sales-Memo 1** file, open the **File** menu and choose the **Exit** option.

Both the application (Notepad) and the file are closed. You are returned to the My Computer window. As the file was not changed you were not prompted to save it.

3 Now repeat these operations for the file **Sales-Letter 1**.

The file is a Wordpad document so this time either the Wordpad or Word application opens.

Exit from the document to the My Computer desktop.

4 Exit from My Computer too. Don't use the **Control menu** icon this time; use the alternative method of opening the **File** menu and selecting **Close**.

Summary of commands

Commands show the object to select first, followed by the command to choose from the menu, e.g. Start Button-Help means click the **Start** button and select the **Help** command. Where a command is available from a particular window this is indicated in brackets.

Alt-Esc/Alt-Tab	Display and change tasks
(My Computer)	
View	View files on disk in different ways
View-Arrange Icons	View icons in different orders
(Notepad)	
Edit-Word Wrap	Move text to new line automatically
(Notepad and Wordpad)	
File-Exit	Quit application and close file
File-Open	Open existing file
File-Save As	Save new file
File-Save	Save changes to existing file
(Start Button)	
Start-Documents	Open recent documents
Start Run	Run an application
Start-Programs-Accessories-Notepad	Run Notepad
Start-Programs-Accessories-Wordpad	Run Wordpad
Start-Settings-Control Panel	Change various system settings
Start-Settings-Folder Options	Display folders in different ways

unit 3

Formatting, copying and printing

Introduction

In this unit you will learn how to format and copy a diskette, how to print and how to exit Windows.

What you should know already

How to use the standard Windows components – see Unit 1.

What you need

The diskette with the practice files created in Unit 2.

A new, unformatted disk.

What you will learn in this unit

By the end of this unit you will be able to:

- format a diskette
- copy a disk
- open a file from within an application
- check printer and page settings
- print a document
- exit Windows correctly.

The need to format

A new diskette it is normally sold unformatted; it cannot be used until it has been formatted. To practise this task you will need another diskette, preferably new and unused. I am assuming that your PC takes the standard three and a half inch, high density 1.44 Mb diskettes.

Formatting divides the diskette into electro-magnetic tracks so that information can be stored on it. If you format a used disk then any information already stored on it will be erased. It cannot be recovered using Windows.

Recognising high density disks All new PC's use the standard three and a half inch, high density 1.44 Mb diskettes. You are very unlikely to come across the older double density 720Kb disks, which can in any case be read by high density drives. How many square holes does your disk have? All disks have one: the 'write protect' notch which can be opened to protect the files from being changed.
Only high density disks have a second hole; this is your best guide, though most manufacturers stamp 'HD' on their disks.

Task 1: Formatting a diskette

1 Make sure that the My Computer window is open.

Insert a new, *unused* diskette, not the practice diskette, in A drive.

The files from the previous diskette used may still be displayed.

Double click the **A drive** icon. My Computer will now display the A drive window and any files it may contain.

(!) Check that you no longer need any of the files on your diskette.

If you have inserted a new, unformatted disk it will be unreadable and you will receive the message: 'The disk in drive A is not formatted. Do you want to format it now?'

Click the **No** button.

2 Now click the **Back** button on the A drive window. A disk cannot be formatted when its window is open or if there are files on that disk that are currently open or in use.

3 You are returned to the My Computer window; make sure that the **A drive** icon is still selected.

Open the **File** menu and select **Format** (or right click the **A drive** icon).

A dialog box **Format - 3 $\frac{1}{2}$ Floppy (A:)** is displayed – see Figure 3.1 opposite. The first option is already selected.

Capacity — All modern PC's use 1.44Mb disks – see introduction. If you are using a double density disk then click the down arrow box and select 720K.

Complete the other options as follows.

Label — Allows you to give the disk a name, displayed whenever the drive icon is selected. It is a useful identifier and can have up to 11 characters. Click this box and enter a suitable label, e.g. ***bakupfiles***.

Format Type — If you are using a used disk that has already been formatted you can use the **Quick** (erase) button. A 'blob' appears in it when it is selected.

If you are using a brand new unformatted disk click the **Full** button.

Other options — Make sure that the **Display Summary When Finished** option box is checked, i.e. ticked. A report on the format will be displayed.

Copy system files — We will be finding out more about system files in a later task. Leave this option unselected.

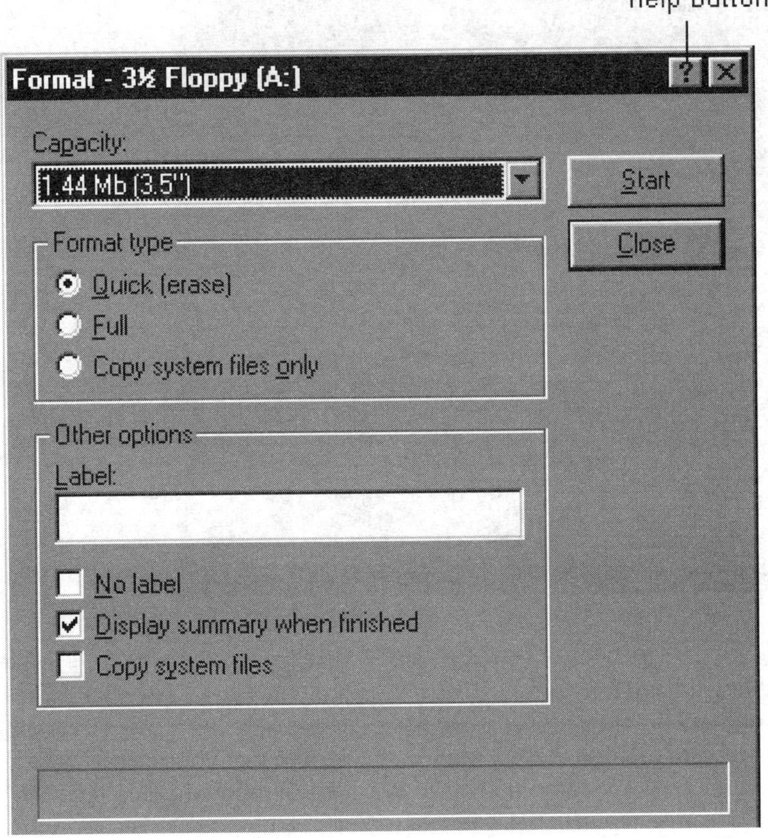

Figure 3.1

The Help button

The **Format** dialog box offers a special **Help (?)** button at the top right of the window – see Figure 3.1. To find out more about an option click the **Help** button then the option.

Finally click the **Start** button.

A formatting bar appears while the formatting takes place – if you are not using Quick Format then this is a fairly slow process.

4 Eventually this is replaced by the results box shown in Figure 3.2 on the following page.

It reports on the formatting; note that your diskette should now have a storage capacity of 1.44 megabytes which means it will hold approximately 1.44 million characters or bytes.

Click the **Close** button and return to the **Format** dialog box.

Unless you wish to format another disk click the **Close** buttons on the dialog boxes.

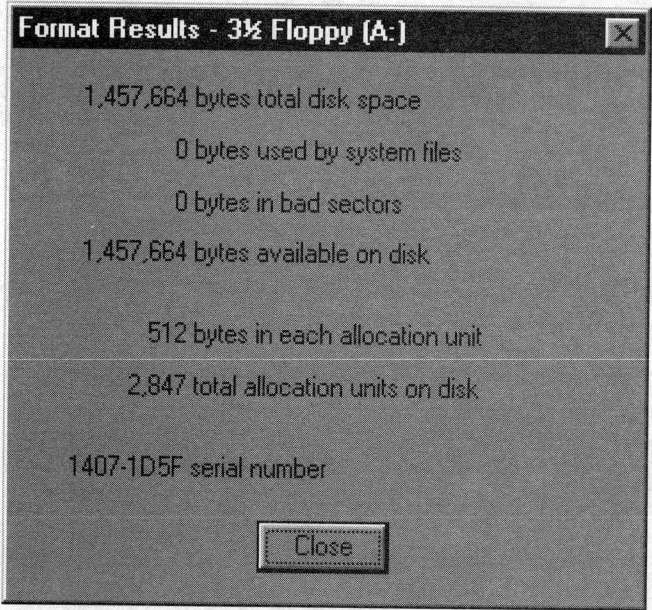

Figure 3.2

Now that we have formatted a diskette we are going to use it to take a backup copy of the dummy practice files that we have created. Although modern computer media are very reliable there is always the danger that your diskette may be lost, stolen or damaged. It is foolhardy not to back up important data regularly. Diskettes may be cheap to replace, but the data they contain certainly is not!

Task 2: Copying a disk

1 Remove the diskette that you have just formatted from the drive and make sure that it has a label. Write on it the following:

- your name and point of contact, e.g. 'J SMITH B Sc 1 Computing';
- the disk contents, e.g. 'Backup Windows Dummy Files'.

Make sure that this label is updated when required.

2 Suitably label the *original* diskette containing the 16 dummy files and insert it in the diskette (A) drive (if you have two diskette drives then put the newly formatted disk in the second drive).

Open the My Computer window if necessary.

Double click on the icon for the diskette drive.

Check that the 16 dummy files are displayed in the disk window.

Close the disk window or press the **Up** button on the menu bar to return to the My Computer display.

3 Open the **File** menu and select **Copy Disk**. (If this option is not displayed click

the disk icon once to select it, then repeat the command)

4 A dialog box appears as in Figure 3.3.

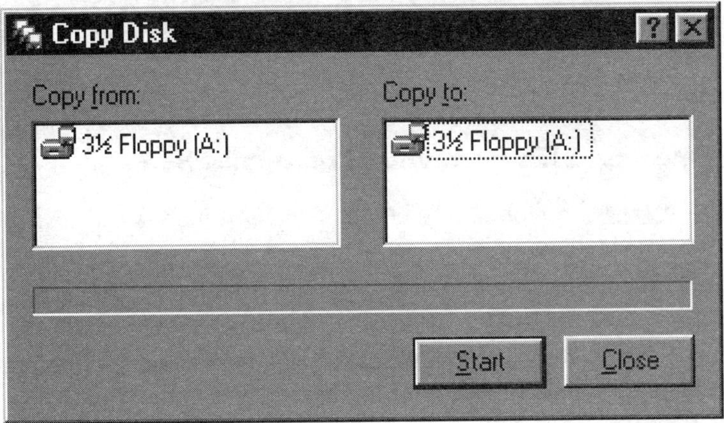

Figure 3.3

Make sure that **3 $\frac{1}{2}$ Floppy (A:)** is selected in the **Copy from:** box (if you have two diskette drives then select **3 $\frac{1}{2}$ Floppy (B:)** in the **Copy to:** box).

Click the **Start** button.

A 'Reading source Disk' message appears next. The files are being copied from *source* disk into main memory. This is a fairly slow process which records the progress of the copying.

5 If you are using one disk drive a dialog box asks you to 'Insert the disk you want to copy to (destination disk)'.

Do this and click the **OK** button.

6 When copying is complete a 'Copy completed successfully' message appears.

Click the **Close** button.

Double click the **A drive** icon to check that all 16 files have been copied. With disks containing more data you may need to swap the source and destination disks over more than once.

7 Remove the backup disk from the A drive. As an additional safeguard open the write-protect hole on the disk. This will prevent the files being amended or deleted. You will need to close it again whenever you wish to modify the contents of the disk.

8 Insert the original source diskette in the A drive. Close the My Computer window.

We've just seen that the My Computer application allows you to keep track of the files on your disks. However, if you are already using an application such as Notepad or Wordpad you don't need to exit to My Computer. It's just as easy to find and retrieve a file when you are working in an application.

In the next task we'll be using Wordpad as an example but the steps are essentially the same for all Windows applications – spreadsheets, databases, word processors or whatever.

Task 3: Opening a file from within an application

1 Click the **Start** button and select the **Programs** then the **Accessories** option. Open the **Wordpad** application.

A blank Wordpad document appears with the default title 'Document - Wordpad'

You have already created a number of Wordpad documents in the previous unit; ensure that the original diskette storing these files is in the drive.

2 Open the **File** menu. Notice that the four most recently used Wordpad documents are listed and could be opened.

Select the **Open** option - the **Open** dialog box appears.

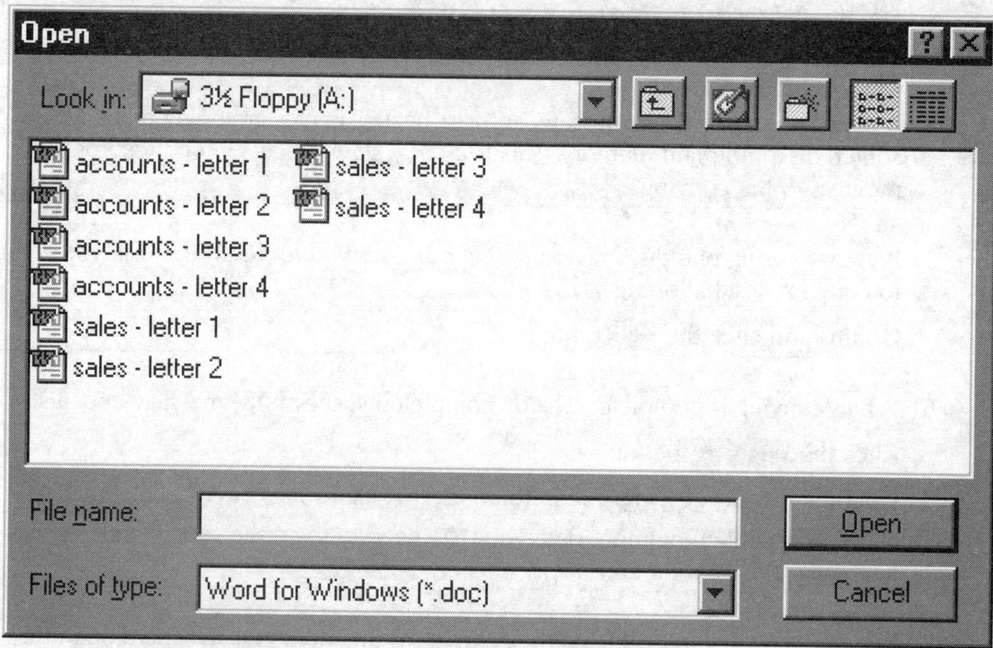

Figure 3.4

Look at the **Look in** box. Is A currently the active drive? If not, click the **Down arrow** button attached to the **Look in** box. A list box opens.

Click the **A drive** icon to select it.

The window shows the eight Wordpad files as in Figure 3.4; as you are opening a file from within the Wordpad application the other eight Notepad files will not be listed.

3 Double click on the file name **Accounts - Letter 1**. Windows looks for this file on your diskette (notice that the drive light on the front of the PC lights up).

The Wordpad window now shows the text of the **Accounts - Letter 1** file.

You now know how to retrieve a file from within an application.

4 Let's try this once more, this time for the document **Accounts - Letter 3**.

Repeat the above steps. The previous document **Accounts - Letter 1** is closed and the document **Accounts - Letter 3** replaces it in the Wordpad window.

5 A file can also be retrieved by typing the name in the **File Name** box.

To retrieve the document **Sales - Letter 1** open the **File** menu and select the **Open** option as before.

Now when the **Open** dialog box appears – see Figure 3.4 above – simply type the filename **Sales - Letter 1** in the **File Name** box and click **Open**.

This method of opening a file can be used if you are sure of the file name – it avoids looking through a long list. An error message usually means that you have misspelt the name or are looking on the wrong disk.

6 Go on to the next task now, leaving this document open.

Task 4: Printing a document

Once you have created something in a Windows application all that you normally need to do is to open the **File** menu and select the **Print** option. You can then specify the number of copies and other details. In the background controlling printing is the *Windows Printers Folder* which the user is normally unaware of. The main uses of Printers Folder are to set up the printer, change the printer settings, or to check on the status of a print job.

3.1 ⇨ **98** The Printers Folder in the My Computer Window replaces Print Manager.

1 In this task we will be printing off the Wordpad document **Sales - Letter 1**.

If this document is not open then repeat the previous task.

2 Check that the printer is:

- switched on
- set online – check switch and warning light
- connected via cable to your computer
- has paper in it.

(!) If you have no functioning printer you can still carry out the following steps, but an error message will appear if you attempt to print.

3 Open the **File** menu in the Wordpad document and select **Print Preview**. A window appears showing the layout of your document on the page.

Zoom in and **Zoom out** will show you this in more or less magnification – try this.

One Page will let you print the page currently displayed in the preview window.

Click the **Close** button.

---

4 Open the **File** menu and select **Page Setup**.

Experimenting with any of the following settings may mean that they are wrongly set for the next document – always check them if your document prints incorrectly.

A dialog box appears allowing you to alter various settings.

Portrait orientation prints down the page in the usual way.

Landscape orientation prints widthways across the page – useful for wide documents.

The *Paper size* and *Margins* can also be changed.

Click the **Printer** button – a further window appears showing the type of installed printer. If you are on a network you may have a choice of printers.

The **Properties** button in the printer window allows you to choose paper size, print quality etc.

Click the **Cancel** button and return to the **Page Setup** dialog box.

Click **Cancel** again.

---

5 Open the **File** menu and select **Print**.

The **Print** dialog box appears next, where you can select the pages and number of copies that you want to print.

If you are connected to a printer then click the **OK** button.

A ' Printing' message appears on screen and the document starts to print.

If you are not connected to a printer press the **Cancel** button.

---

6 Finally use the **File** menu to exit from Wordpad; you are returned to the My Computer desktop.

---

7 To explore other printer settings, open the My Computer window if necessary.

Double click the **Printers** icon: a window displays the icons for the available printer(s).

Click once to select the printer you are going to use.

Open the **File** menu: notice the options to pause and purge (cancel) printing jobs.

Select the **Properties** option from the **File** menu: a dialog box appears.

There are various tabs (options) along the top depending on your printer; many offer settings that that rarely, if ever need adjusting.

Find out which options allow you:

- to select different paper sizes.
- to alter the print quality.
- to test the printer and adjust the printer cartridge.

Help: Remember that you can get information on a particular feature – click the **Help** button (top right marked with a '?' sign) then the feature.

8 Close the dialog box and the My Computer window.

Unit 7 task 6 shows you how to create print queues and print more easily.

The **Start** menu is used to end your Windows session. Do not simply turn off the computer without exiting from Windows first as:

- you may have applications still running with work you have not saved – this will be lost and your files could be damaged
- if you are on a network and log on and off with a password this could cause problems next time you log on
- any windows left open will be automatically re-opened the next time that you start Windows – this adds to the start up time.

Task 5: Exiting Windows

1 Close down any applications or files that are running – right click the button on the taskbar then select the **Close** option.

2 Click the **Start** button. A menu appears.

Select the **Shut down** option. A dialog box appears offering three options or the chance to change your mind – see Figure 3.5.

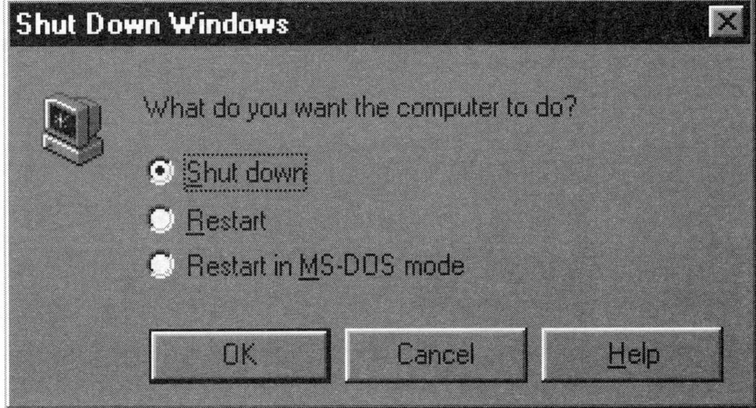

Figure 3.5

(If you have omitted step 1 you will be reminded to save any changes.)

3 Use the **Help** button to get information about the options – they may vary, depending on whether your PC is connected to a network.

If you wish to finish then make sure the first option, **Shut Down** is selected.

If you wish to re-start the computer (perhaps you are experiencing system problems) then select the second option.

If you wish to re-start the computer and use an older MS-DOS type application then select the third option.

---

4 Click the **OK** or the **Cancel** button as appropriate.

If you have been using an application and have omitted to save some work then another dialog box will prompt you to save it. Remember to remove your diskette.

Summary of Commands

Commands show the object to select first, followed by the command to choose from the menu, e.g. Start Button-Help means click the **Start** button and select the **Help** command. Where a command is available from a particular window this is indicated in brackets.

(My Computer)

File-Copy Disk	Copy diskette
File-Format	Format diskette
Printer icon-File-Properties	Amend printer settings

(From within an application)

File-Open	Open an existing file
File-Page Setup	Amend layout of printed page
File-Print	Print file currently open
File-Print Preview	Preview layout of printed page

(Start button)

Start-Programs-Accessories-Wordpad	Run Wordpad
Shut Down	Exit Windows

unit 4

Explorer – Viewing and locating files

Introduction

In this unit you will be looking at how files are stored and using Windows Explorer to locate and sort files in different drives and folders.

When you use My Computer (see Unit 1) you need to have several windows open in order to view the contents of two folders. In Windows Explorer you can review all your drives and folders using one window.

What you should know already

How to use the standard Windows components – see Unit 1.

What you need

The original diskette 'a' with the practice files created in Unit 2.

What you will learn in this unit

By the end of this unit you will be able to:

- use Explorer to change drives and folders
- use Explorer to view the contents of drives and folders
- sort files by type
- use the Find utility to search for files
- create, delete and rename folders.

3.1 ⇨ 98 In Windows 95 and 98 a directory is called a *folder*.
Windows Explorer and My Computer replace File Manager.

What does Explorer do?

Explorer performs the basic 'housekeeping' tasks associated with organising and maintaining the files on your computer system. With it you can :

- change from one disk drive to another
- change from one folder to another
- create a structure of folders
- view the files that you have in a variety of ways – by size, date, type etc.
- copy, rename, move and delete files
- format and copy disks
- start up an application.

Do I need Explorer to perform these tasks?

It is possible to carry out at least some of the above tasks while you are using an application, e.g. a word processor or database. However there will be situations when you are in Windows and want to review and tidy up your files, which may be located in several folders or diskettes. In this situation Explorer is the quickest and easiest option to use.

Task 1: Fundamental ideas – files, folders and drives

This extended task introduces you to the various parts of the Explorer window. Along the way it explains the key concepts of file, folder and drive.

1 Insert the diskette 'a' containing the practice files that you created in Unit 2 into the diskette drive. We will be using them in the tasks that follow.

2 To start up Explorer from the **Start** menu, right click the **Start** button and select **Explore** from the pop-up menu. The Explorer window opens.

Maximise the window.

The window shown in Figure 4.1 appears.

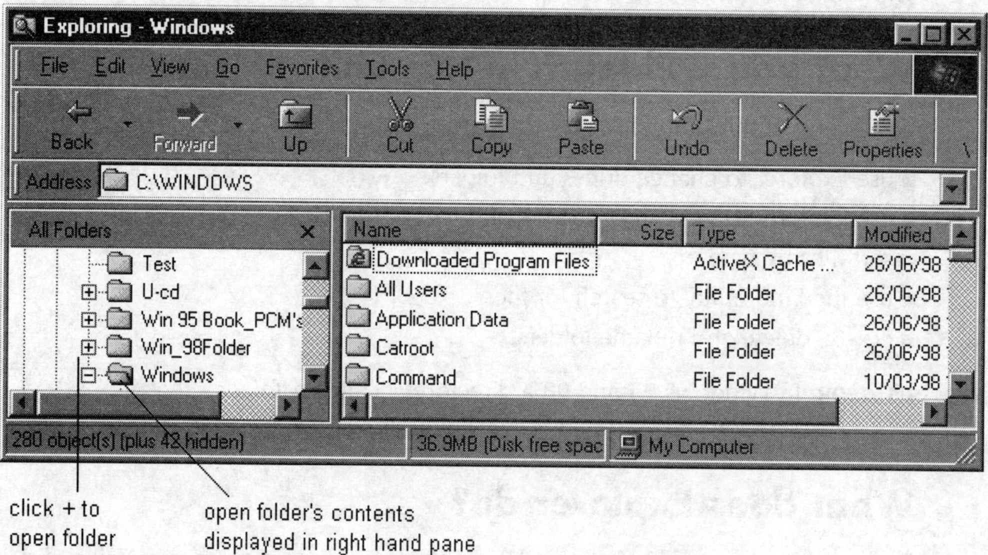

Figure 4.1

It contains the now familiar Windows features: title, menu and tool bars, plus **Maximize**, **Close** and **Minimize** buttons.

In the window are icons representing files, folders and disk drives. Don't worry if yours differ from those illustrated; we'll be working on ones that are common to all Windows systems.

3 If the right hand side of your display does not conform to this overall layout open the **View** menu and check:

- that the **Details** option is selected (marked with a blob)
- that the **as Web Page** option is deselected (not ticked).

4 At the top is the address box showing the disk and folder currently selected, normally the C drive and the Windows folder. The Explorer window is split into two halves or panes.

- The left pane shows the various drive icons – A, C, D etc., plus the various folders they contain. Your drive may also have a name or volume label (see Unit 3, Task 1). If you cannot see them then use the left hand scroll bar.

  If no drives are shown click the button next to the **My Computer** icon in the left hand pane, marked with a **+**.
- The right side shows the various files and folders on the drive selected in the left hand pane.

Drives, folders and files are your three basic units of organisation and we are going to take some time to explore them.

Now we must consider some basic concepts and terms.

- *Disk drives* Your computer probably has at least two drives, the diskette drive, known as the A drive, and the hard disk, known as the C drive. You may well have other drives, e.g. you may be connected to a network and have a CD-ROM drive (usually drive D). Whenever you refer to a drive you do so using the letter followed by a colon symbol, e.g. a: or c: (upper or lower case)

  The diskette drive is used to store data in a portable form (i.e. on diskettes or floppy disks which can be removed). The hard disk and its drive unit are permanently fixed in the machine and hold Windows and other applications, e.g. spreadsheet, word processor or Web browser It can also be used to store data. As the hard disk and its drive are one non-removable unit, the terms 'disk' and 'drive' are used interchangeably.

- *Files* Whatever you create on a computer has to be saved as a file. A file can contain a word processed letter, a spreadsheet, digitised sound or images etc. When you save a file you are copying information from the computer's main memory (RAM), which is temporary, to a permanent site on disk. If you did not save your work in this way it would be lost when the computer was turned off. A file on a computer is similar to a paper file in a filing cabinet. Both need a file name in order to file them away and retrieve them.

- *Rules for file names* See Unit 2, Task 1. The different types of file are dealt with more fully in Task 2 below.

- *Folders* A diskette can store dozens of files, a hard disk can store thousands. To make files easier to locate they are grouped into separate folders. These can be divided into further subfolders – like drawers in a filing cabinet. A typical structure is shown in Figure 4.2.

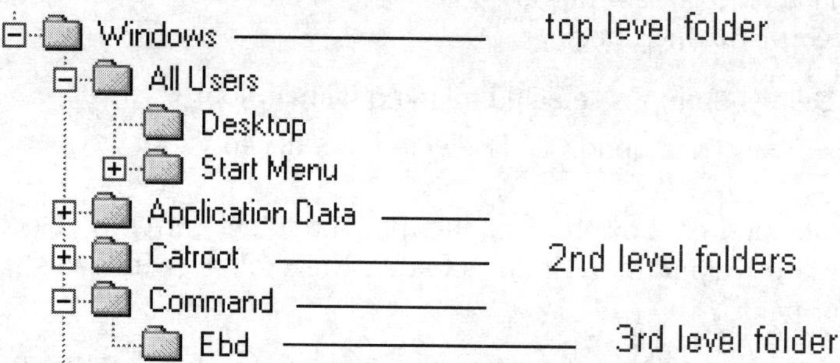

Figure 4.2

This illustrates the hierarchic tree structure adopted by Windows. The drive is divided into many folders, each of which in their turn can contain further files and subfolders, like branches on a tree.

In Figure 4.2 The Windows folder is the 'top level' folder; at the root level of the disk drive. It holds a collection of further subfolders : All Users, Application Data, CatRoot, and Command. These are the 'second level' folders.

The Command folder holds a further subfolder called Ebd. This could be regarded as 'level 3'; it could hold further 'level 4' folders and so on.

Let's see how files and folders are stored. (Remember that yours will be different to the ones on my PC)

3.1 ⇨ 98 If you create files in Windows 98 with names longer than eight characters and then view them in Windows 3.1, the user will only see the first eight characters, which may not be unique. To avoid duplicate file names a number is added to them, e.g.,

Sales.Report.Muir.August 97 is shown as **Salesr~1.Aug**

Sales.Report.Muir.August 98 is shown as **Salesr~2.Aug**

5 To change drives, scroll to the top of the left hand pane and look at the drives displayed. The drive icon itself is shown, plus an **Open/Close** button marked with a **+** sign for closed or a **–** sign for open.

If no drives are shown click the **Open/Close** button next to the **My Computer** icon.

Click on the icon for **C drive**. It is now highlighted indicating that it is the 'active' drive. Only one drive can be active at one time.

Click the **A drive** icon. A is now the active drive. The address box at the top of the window changes to show this.

Now change back to C drive.

---

6 To display folders, go through the list of drives on the left hand side of the window and click the **Open/Close** buttons so that they are all closed i.e. showing a **+** sign.

Don't worry about the right hand pane yet.

If no drives are shown make sure that the button next to the **My Computer** icon is open. When the **My Computer** icon is closed no drive icons are visible. This is because Windows treats My Computer as a sort of master folder holding all the drives.

7 Now click the **Open/Close** button next to the **C drive** icon – it should then display a – sign.

The drive is expanded showing the folders on this drive – see Figure 4.3.

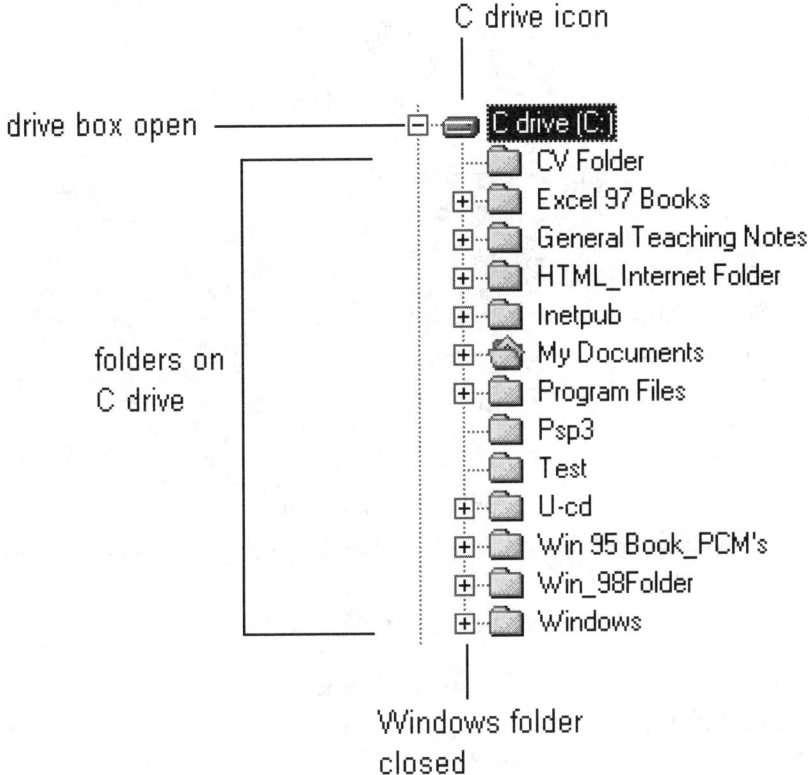

Figure 4.3

Click the **Open/Close** button again and the C drive folders are no longer displayed.

Now open C drive again and the other drives too – the list becomes quite long and you may need to use the scroll bar. C remains the active drive: you would need to click the drive icon, not the **Open/Close** button, to change drives.

8 To display subfolders, find the Windows folder (it is usually located on the C drive) and open the it: it should display a **–** sign. It opens to display further subfolders (see Figure 4.4).

The Windows folder contains files necessary to run Windows 98. It is divided into various levels of subfolders as a tree or hierarchy.

(A folder containing other closed subfolders is marked with a **+** sign).

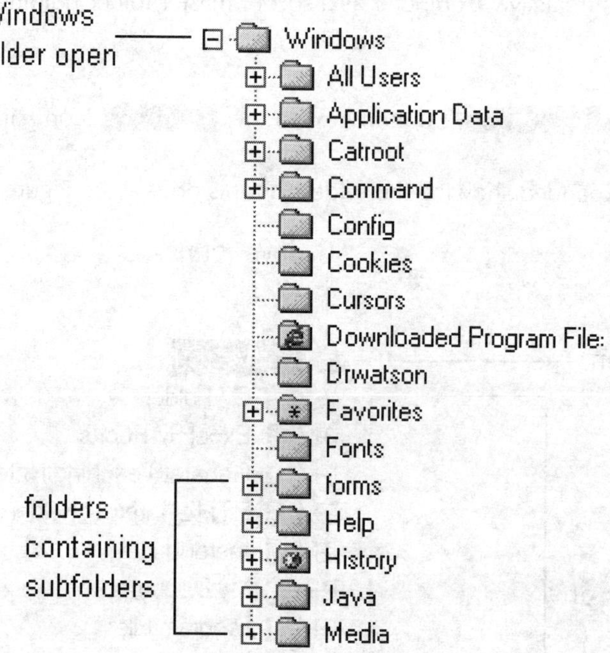

Figure 4.4

Open the System folder and further subfolders are shown. At least one of these has an **Open/Close** button; the ones that do not contain no further folders, only files.

Close the System Folder using the **Open/Close** button.

9 To display individual files click on the **Folder** or **Drive** icon (as opposed to the **Open/Close** button). The right hand window shows you the files and other folders that it contains. Try this as follows.

Make sure that the drive containing the Windows folder is still selected (probably C).

Close the drive using the **Open/Close** button – in the right hand window the files and folders on this drive are still shown.

Open the drive using the **Open/Close** button – the right hand display doesn't change.

Now click the Windows **Folder** icon to select it (not the **Open/Close** button). Windows is selected as the 'current' folder and the icon changes to show the folder as open.

The title bar and the files listed in the right hand window also change and the address box should read 'C:\WINDOWS'.

10 Use the scroll bars on the *right hand* window to review the contents of the Windows folder: after the folders, a number of the files necessary to run Windows are displayed – see Figure 4.5.

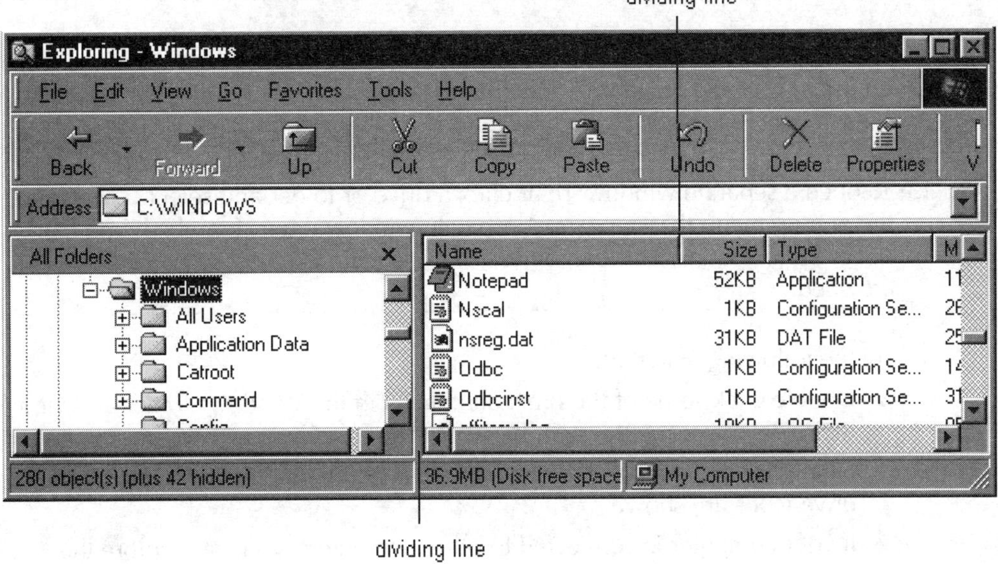

Figure 4.5

Scroll through the list. Some of them you may recognise, e.g. Notepad and Wordpad.

You will find that you can display more files at a time if you open the **View** menu and select **List**.

You can also see more files if you use the mouse to drag the dividing line between the two halves of the folder screen to the left (marked on Figure 4.5) – don't overdo this.

Keep the Windows folder open.

11 The **View** menu at the top of the Explorer screen offers various ways of viewing the folders for your disk.

Open the **View** menu and select these options in turn.

Large Icons – only useful when viewing a small number of icons.

Small Icons/List – display the maximum number of files/folders.

Details – shows details of file size, type and date. The dividing lines between the column headings (marked on Figure 4.5) can be dragged to narrow or widen them. Try this.

Click the column heading over each column (it sorts the listing on that column) by name, size, type etc.

Click the heading again and the order is reversed. Notice that folders are always grouped separately to files.

3.1 ⇨ 98 **as Web Page** – if this option is selected, i.e. ticked, then the window takes on the appearance of a Web page – try this, it is one of many 'Web integration' features of Windows 98. In Explorer it offers no particular advantage so deselect this option.

12 Try toggling the **Views** button as an alternative to the **View** menu – it is located on the right of the Standard Toolbar (if this toolbar is not visible then open the **View** menu and select **Toolbars-Standard Toolbar** options).

13 To open a separate window, right click a drive or folder and select **Open** from the pop-up menu that appears. A separate window opens for which you can select **View** options. This can be useful if the main Explorer window gets overcrowded.

14 Try the following activities.

- Double click some of the other subfolders in the Windows folder and view their contents using the right hand window.

  Finally use the left hand window to close all the open folders so that only drive icons are shown.
- If your computer is connected to other computers, you can explore the network using *Network Neighbourhood,* displayed as a folder on your desktop.

  In Explorer use the **Up** button on the Standard Toolbar. Click it to go up a directory level until 'Desktop' is displayed in the address box.

  Open the Network Neighbourhood folder to display shared resources, e.g. printers, files and CD-ROM drives. Sometimes you may need to provide a password to access them.

In the last task we explored three key concepts.

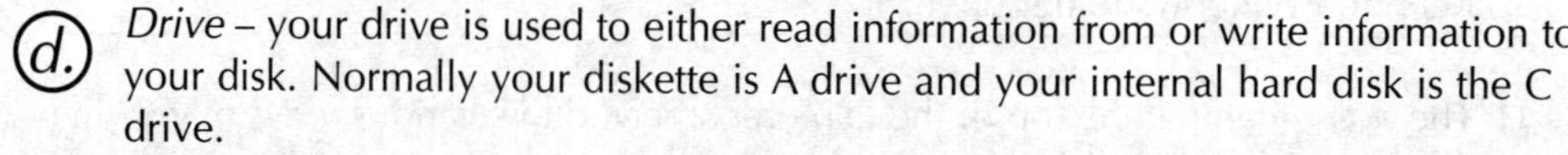

Drive – your drive is used to either read information from or write information to your disk. Normally your diskette is A drive and your internal hard disk is the C drive.

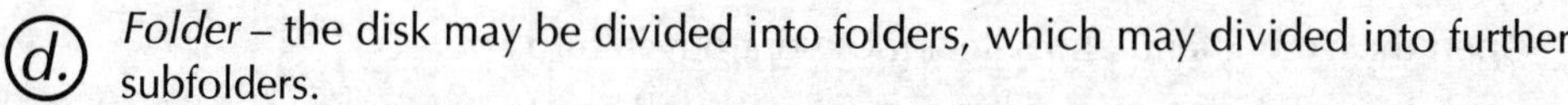

Folder – the disk may be divided into folders, which may divided into further subfolders.

File – Everything stored on disk is saved using a file name. Groups of related files are stored in folders.

In the next task we'll be finding out more about the different type of files.

Task 2: Viewing different file types

1 Make sure that the Explorer window is open and the contents of the Windows folder are displayed in the right hand window. Scroll down until some files are displayed.

If necessary maximise the Explorer window so that a reasonable number of files can be viewed.

2 To see file details, open the **View** menu and select the **Details** option.

A display resembling Figure 4.6 appears. They have been labelled a – e for reference.

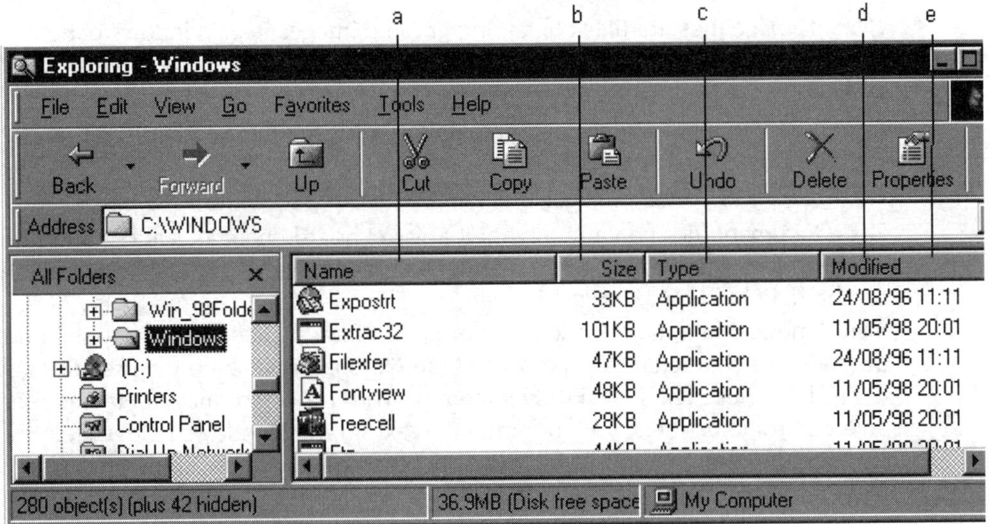

Figure 4.6

a The file *name*. Notice that the icon design helps to indicate the type of file.

b The file *size* in kilobytes. One byte holds the equivalent of a character, e.g. a keyboard character such as), 0, c, or special characters normally invisible to the user. In an executable program file, a byte holds one machine instruction. A kilobyte or 1Kb is roughly 1,000 bytes (actually 1024 bytes), a megabyte or Mb equals about a million bytes and a gigabyte a billion bytes.

Click (do not double click) a few file names: along the bottom of the window is shown the exact size of the file currently selected.

Click elsewhere on the window to deselect the file. When no file is selected then the total size of the current disk, the total number of files in the current folder and the free disk space are shown along the bottom of the window.

c The file *type* – see below.

d and e The *date* and *time* that the file was created or last modified. Many files will share the same date and time i.e. when they were first installed on disk.

3.1 ➪ 98 If you wish to see the file extensions open the **View** menu and select **Folder Options**. Then click the **View** tab and click the **Hide file extensions for known file types** box to deselect it and click **OK**.

3 Click on the **Type** heading to sort the files into type.

Folders are always listed first in alphabetical order, then a number of different file types are listed – this is a good time to review them. Scroll through the list of files and identify the following types of files.

Application files are program files; they contain computer-readable code written by programmers. Double clicking them executes or runs them. Normally it is easier to run them from the **Start** menu.

Bitmap Image files are files containing graphic images, e.g. Windows patterns and backgrounds or images that have been scanned or downloaded from the Web.

Configuration Settings files contain text that holds the information to set up Windows to run in a particular way.

GIF Image files contain images that can be incorporated into Web pages.

Text Document files contain only the basic keyboard characters a to z and 0 to 9, plus punctuation marks and other keyboard characters that can be typed. They can be read by a wide range of programs. They are often referred to as ASCII files (American Standard Code for Information Interchange), as they contain only the standard characters. We have used the Notepad application in previous tasks to produce these text files. Files created by word processor may contain unreadable control characters, e.g. to format the text. In the Windows Folder they contain information about Windows which can be called up, sometimes from within an application.

---

4 You can use Explorer to open any document or run a program application. Make sure that the Windows folder is open.

- Sort the files into Name order.
- Double click the following icons – *you will need to close the document or application before opening the next one.*

MsHearts – a game window opens.

Notepad – the Notepad application is run.

Bubbles – the bubbles bitmap image is shown in the Paint application window.

Win – the settings for Windows are displayed.

Winlogo – a .gif image is displayed.

Open the **Fonts** subfolder and double click **Arial** – the font is displayed.

Searching for a file or folder

With so many files and folders on your computer it can be difficult to find the ones you want. Windows provides a Find utility which helps you to locate files or folders anywhere on your PC, providing you can remember at least part of the name (you can also search by file date and type). Files with similar names, date etc. are listed in the Find window from where you can open them or select them for moving, copying or deletion. If you are not familiar with the syntax for referring to drives, folders and files then read this next part.

- *The Path* It is important to give the exact location or *path* where the file is stored, i.e. in which *drive* and *folder* (if any). The drive is always referred to by its drive letter followed by a colon, e.g. A: and B: are diskette drives, C: and D: hard disks.

  The folder and/or file names follow the drive letter, separated by a backslash (\ ).

  For example, if the file **Jim.Memo 1** is on a diskette in A drive you must give its full path:

  A:\Jim.Memo 1

  If the file **Sales_Figures_August** is in the **Sales** folder on C drive then the full path is **C:\Sales\Sales_Figures_August**

  Note that there are no spaces between the colon, slash, drive, folder and file names.

- *Wild Card Searching* If you cannot recall the exact file name or wish to find files with similar names then you can use the 'wild card' characters * and ?:

  The * or 'star' can stand for any number of characters.

  For example, *.AUGUST means any file name ending in the letters .AUGUST

  LET*.* means a file name starting with the three characters LET and ending in anything

  . signifies all files (any name, any extension).

  The ? symbol substitutes for individual characters; suppose that you want to find all file names containing the three characters ACC in positions 5 to 7 of the file name, e.g. MEM-ACCOUNTS 1 or LET-ACCOUNTS 2

  The file name ????ACC* means 'starting with any four characters, then the characters ACC, then any other characters at the end (*)'

  In practice the wild card characters are often unnecessary, as we will see in the tasks that follow.

Task 3: Searching for a file or folder

1 Make sure that the Explorer window is open. If necessary, enlarge the Explorer window so that a reasonable number of files can be viewed.

2 Insert the diskette containing the practice files that you created in Unit 2.

3 Select the icon for the diskette drive – the 16 practice files are displayed.

4 Open the **Tools** menu and select the **Find: All Files** then the **Files or Folders** option. The Find window is displayed.

5 Check that the **Look in:** box is set to read the diskette drive; if not click the <u>Down</u> <u>Arrow</u> key and select **3 $\frac{1}{2}$ Floppy (A:)** from the list.

6 Make sure that the **Named:** box is blank and click the **Find Now** button. All 16 files are displayed.

7 Now enter ***memo*** in the **Named:** box and click the **Find Now** button. The eight files containing the letters 'memo' in their name are listed.

8 Now click the **Named:** box to highlight the search term ***memo***. Amend it to ***sales*** and click the **Find Now** button. Eight files are listed containing these letters.

9 Now try out the following search terms and note the results:

cc

1

let

10 Once you've located a group of files you may want to quickly review their contents. Quick View allows you to do this without waiting for a large application such as a word processor to load.

Right click one of the Wordpad files that you created and select **Quick View**. The document opens. Try this with several documents; it's quicker than opening them in Wordpad.

If this option is not available then Quick View has not been installed.

11 Use the Find facilities to do the following searches on your hard drive.

- *Searching by date* Use the **Look in:** box to change to your hard drive (see previous task)

  Click the **Date** tab at the top of the **Find** dialog box.

  Find all files modified in the last two months.

- *Searching by file type* Click the **Advanced** tab at the top of the Find window.

  Click the down arrow on the **Of type:** box.
  Find all text document files.

- *Searching by file content* Click the **Name and Location** tab.

  Use the **Containing text:** box to locate files that contain the word 'network'. What difference does it make if the **Include subfolders** box is deselected?

12 Close the **Find** dialog box.

As you have seen, the **Find** command provides a quick and easy way of finding files on disk; once you have located a file you can then open it directly from the **Find** dialog box or from Explorer. You can often use the **Find** command to list certain files as a preliminary to moving, copying or deleting them, activities that we will be practising in future tasks.

In previous units we created 16 dummy files, eight using the Notepad text editor application and eight using the Wordpad word processor application.

These are:

Sales - Memo 1
Sales - Memo 2
Sales - Memo 3
Sales - Memo 4
Sales - Letter 1
Sales - Letter 2
Sales - Letter 3
Sales - Letter 4
Accounts - Memo 1
Accounts - Memo 2
Accounts - Memo 3
Accounts - Memo 4
Accounts - Letter 1
Accounts - Letter 2
Accounts - Letter 3
Accounts - Letter 4

We are going to organise these files into folders and subfolders; all the files concerned with the Sales Department will be placed in a folder **Sales** and those concerned with the Accounts Department in a folder **Accounts**. The folder tree will look like Figure 4.7.

Figure 4.7

Note on folder names

Folder Names follow the same rules as file names – See Unit 2, Task 1.

Task 4: Making and renaming folders

1 Make sure that the diskette containing the above files is inserted in the diskette drive.

Open Explorer and ensure that the diskette drive is selected.

Click the drive icon to display the files. If the files are not displayed, check that the correct diskette is in the drive and that no Find conditions are still in force from the previous task.

2 To create a new folder open the **File** menu and select **New** then the **Folder** option.

The new folder appears in the right hand window labelled 'New Folder' - see Figure 4.8.

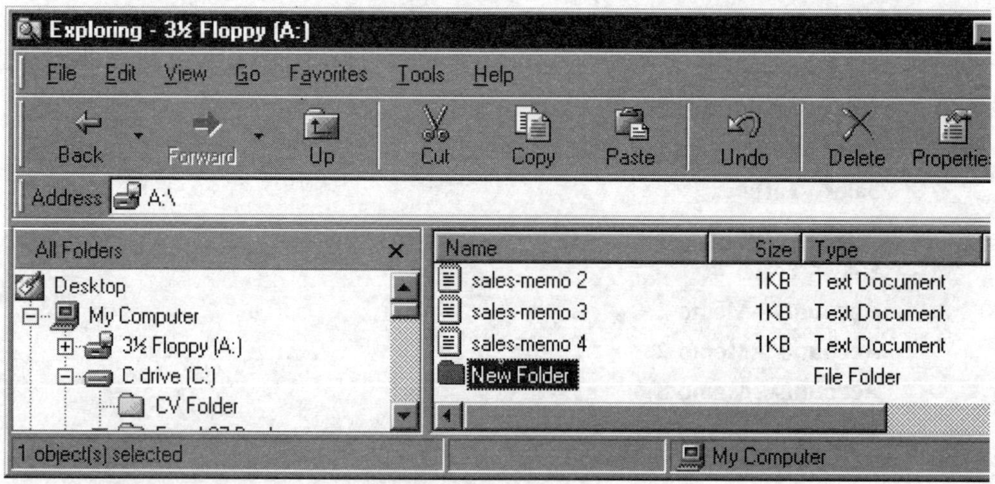

Figure 4.8

3 To rename a folder, make sure that the new folder is selected (if not click it once).

Open the **File** menu and select **Rename**.

Type the name ***Sales Folder*** and the folder is re-named.

Click elsewhere on the window to deselect the folder.

4 To remove a folder, click the **Sales Folder** once to select it.

Open the **File** menu and select **Delete**. A dialog box appears, asking you to confirm the deletion.

Click **Yes**.

The folder is deleted.

5 Click the diskette drive to select it.

Re-create the **Sales Folder** and a second folder called **Accounts Folder**.

The window should now resemble Figure 4.9 opposite.

6 Double click each new subfolder in turn. No files or folders are displayed on the right hand side of the screen; as yet there are no files in these subfolders. Select the diskette drive icon again.

Figure 4.9

Summary of commands

Menu commands show the menu name first, followed by the command to choose from the menu, e.g. Edit-Clear means open the **Edit** menu and select the **Clear** command. Where a command is available from a particular window this is indicated in brackets.

Start-Programs-Windows Explorer	Start Windows Explorer
(Windows Explorer)	
File-Delete	Delete file or folder
File-Rename	Rename folder or file
File-New-Folder	Create new folder
Tools-Find-Files or Folders	Search for named file or folder
View-as Web Page	Web page display
View-Details	View all details of files
View-Options	Show/Hide various files/file details
View-Large Icons	View files as large icons
View-List/Small Icons	View files as small icons

unit 5

Copying, renaming and deleting files

Introduction

In this unit you will be learning how to move and copy files between different folders and disk drives. You will be renaming files and finding out how to delete files and how to recover them from the Recycle Bin.

What you should know already

How to use the standard Windows components – see Unit 1.

What you need

The diskette with the practice files created in Unit 2, plus a further blank diskette.

What you will learn in this unit

By the end of this unit you will be able to:

- move, copy and rename files and folders
- delete files and folders
- check the Recycle Bin for deleted files and folders
- restore deleted files and folders
- display multiple folders.

Moving and copying files

Typical situations when you would want to move or copy files include the following.

- Making a copy of a diskette. You have already done this in Unit 3, Task 2.
- Copying files from one folder to another.
- Copying files from hard disk to diskette, e.g. to create backups, or to work on another PC.
- Copying files from diskette to hard disk, e.g. installing a new application. Because of the threat of viruses many organisations do not allow this and/or prevent it by technical means.

In the next task we will copy and move files from the main folder into the two new subfolders, **Sales** and **Accounts**, that we have created in Unit 4. *Moving* a file does just that – removes it to a new location; *copying* a file keeps the original where it is and places the copy in the new location. We will practice both operations.

You can either use the mouse to 'drag and drop' the file in its new location or use the **Cut** and **Paste** commands.

Moving or renaming files or folders associated with programs may prevent the program from working. If in doubt leave well alone.

Task 1: Moving and copying individual files

1 To copy files, make sure that the diskette containing the practice files is inserted in the diskette drive, then open Explorer (right click the **Start** button).

When the Explorer window opens ensure that the icon for the diskette drive is selected (click the icon for the a: drive, at the top left of the window). The window should now resemble Figure 5.1.

If necessary maximise the Explorer window so that all files and folders on your diskette can be seen. You will probably find the following tasks easier if you open the **View** menu and make sure that the **Details** option is selected and the **as Web Page** option is deselected.

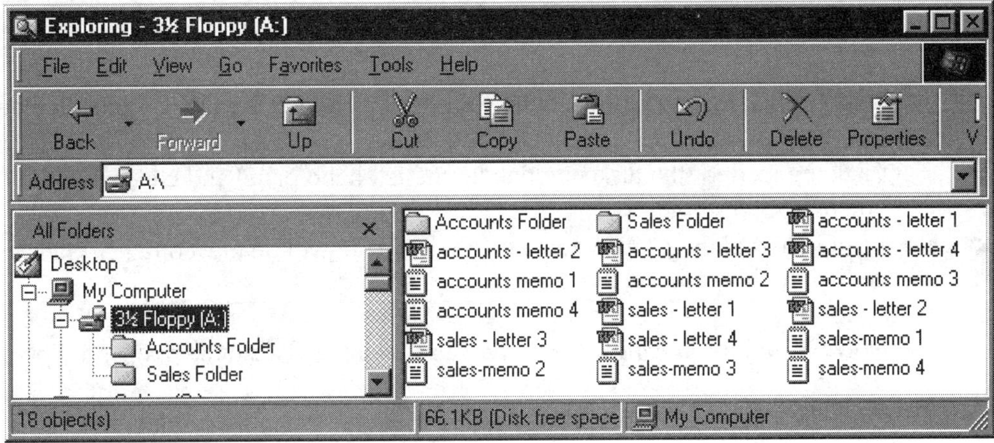

Figure 5.1

2 Hold down the *Ctrl* key on the keyboard.

Move the cursor onto the file **Sales - Memo 1**.

Hold down the mouse button and drag the file on top of the icon for the **Sales** folder – see Figure 5.2 on the following page.

The cursor changes to a file icon with a plus sign – this indicates that the file is being copied rather than moved.

First release the mouse button *then* the *Ctrl* key. The file 'drops' into the **Sales** folder.

A confirmation message appears; this should confirm the file name, the copying operation, and the destination – the **Sales** folder.

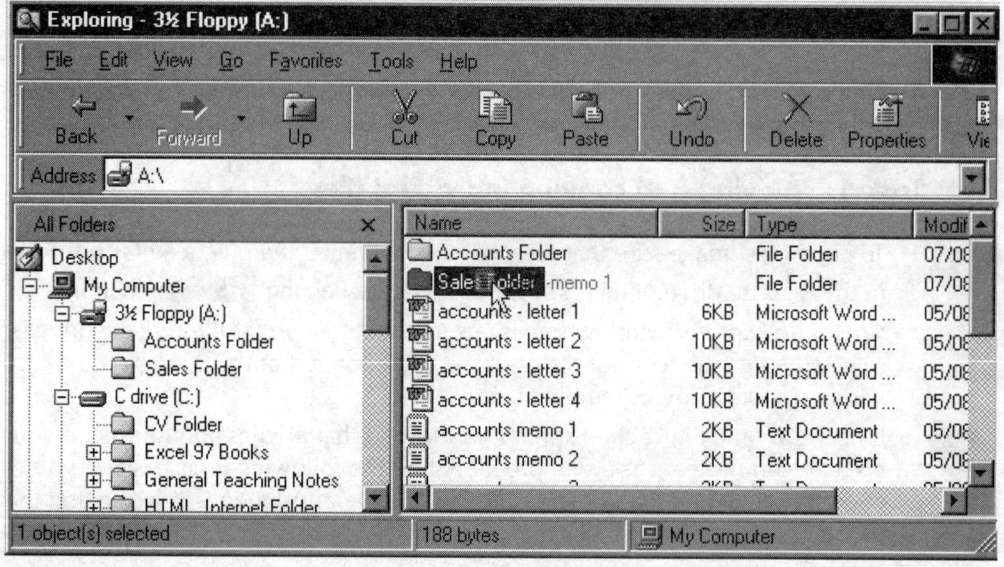

Figure 5.2

3 Double click the icon for the **Sales** folder to check that the file has actually been copied.

Click the icon for the diskette drive (in the left hand pane) and check that the original is still displayed.

If you released the *Ctrl* key too soon then the file will be moved rather than copied. In this case use the **Edit-Undo** command.

---

4 Now we will try *moving* a file to the **Sales** folder. It is a simple drag and drop operation; the *Ctrl* key is not used.

Click the diskette drive icon if necessary to return to the main folder

Now move the screen pointer onto the file **Sales - Memo 2**.

Hold down the mouse button and drag the file on top of the icon for the **Sales** folder.

Release the mouse button and the file drops into the **Sales** folder.

Check that the original is no longer there, then open the **Sales** folder to check that the file has actually been moved to this new location.

There should now be two files in the **Sales** folder. **Sales - Memo 1** and **Sales - Memo 2**. Make sure that your window resembles Figure 5.3.

If you move or copy files incorrectly open the **Edit** menu at the top of the Explorer window and select the **Undo** option.

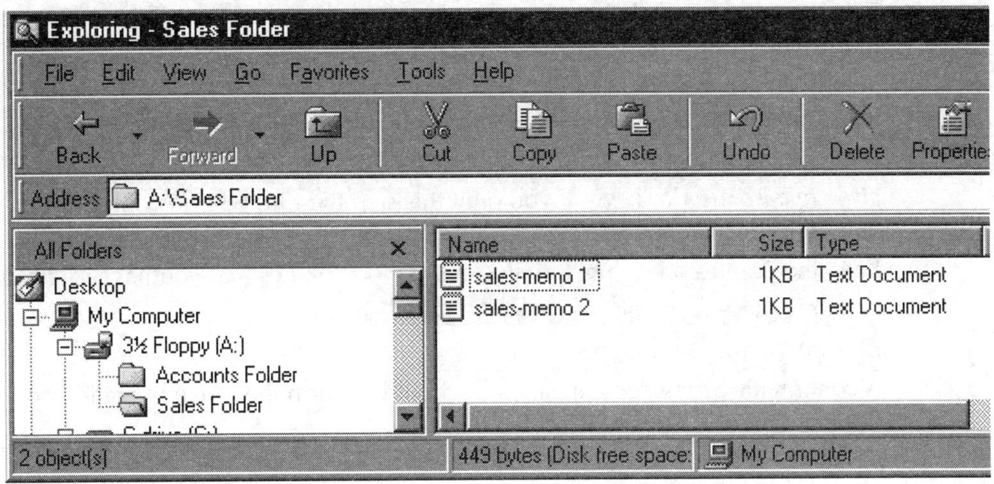

Figure 5.3

Task 2: Moving and copying groups of files – mouse method

1 Now we will copy and move several files at once.

If necessary make sure that the original diskette containing the practice files is inserted in the A drive, open Explorer and check that the diskette drive window is selected, not a subfolder.

Maximise the window.

2 To copy groups of files we will start by copying some of the file names starting with the characters **Sales** from the main folder to the **Sales** folder.

Hold down the Ctrl key and click the following three file names: **Sales - Letter 1**, **Sales - Letter 2** and **Sales - Letter 3**.

If you select the wrong file name simply click it to de-select it.

All three file names should now be highlighted.

Next, *keeping the Ctrl key pressed down*, keep the pointer on the block of files that you have selected and drag these files onto the **Sales folder** icon and release the mouse button *then* the Ctrl key.

A confirmation message appears; this should confirm the copying operation and the destination – the **Sales** folder.

3 Click the **Sales folder** icon to check that three files have actually been copied and return to the drive window to check that the originals are still there.

Click on the window to remove the highlight from the copied files.

If the originals are missing from the root folder then you have moved the files rather than copied them; a common reason is releasing the *Ctrl* button before releasing the mouse button. If this has happened then copy the files back from the Sales to the drive window using the dragging procedure described in step 2. Another method is to open the **Edit** menu at the top of the Explorer window and select the **Undo** option.

4 To move a group of files starting with the characters SALES from the main folder to the **Sales** folder, hold down the <u>*Ctrl*</u> key and click the following three file names: **Sales - Memo 3**, **Sales - Memo 4** and **Sales - Letter 4**.

If you select the wrong file name simply click it to de-select it.

All three file names should be highlighted now.

Now *release* the <u>*Ctrl*</u> key – if you omit this step the files will be copied rather than moved.

Keep the pointer on one of the files in the block of files that you have selected and drag these files onto the **Sales folder** icon.

Release the mouse button.

A confirmation message appears; this should confirm the move operation and the destination – the **Sales** folder.

---

5 Click the **Sales folder** icon to check that the three files are now in this folder and click the drive window to check that they have been moved.

All eight files with SALES in their file names should now be in the **Sales** folder – see Figure 5.4; they have been moved or copied there from the drive window. Check this and move or copy them if they are not there.

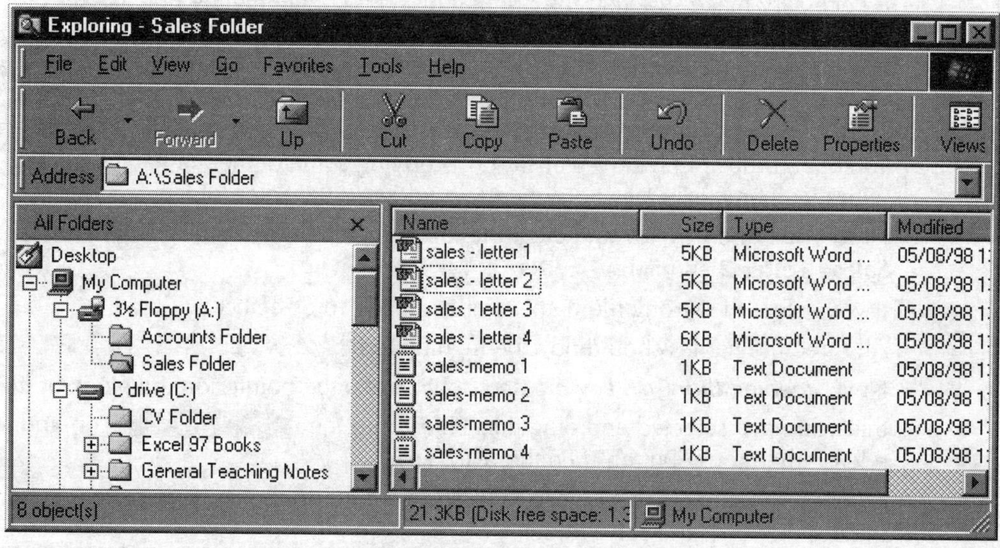

Figure 5.4

Look in the **Accounts** folder as well as the main folder; it should be empty; if it contains files with SALES in their file names then move them into the **Sales** subfolder.

---

6 Close the Explorer window.

In the next task you will learn how to open more than one folder window at the same time using the My Computer application. This is useful if you want to check and compare the contents of two folders 'side by side' before moving or copying.

Task 3: Displaying two folders

1 If necessary, make sure that the original diskette 'a' containing the practice files is inserted in the A drive and click the **My Computer** icon on the desktop (see Unit 1 tasks 1– 3).

Double click on the icon for the diskette drive. The diskette window opens.

2 Open the **View** menu and make sure that the **Details** option is selected and the **as Web Page** option is deselected.

3 Double click the icon for the **Sales** folder – a further window opens displaying the files.

Now double click the icon for the **Accounts** folder – it should open too.

Repeat step 2 for each of these windows.

4 Check the taskbar – four tasks should be running (see Figure 5.5).

Figure 5.5

5 You may recall from Unit 1 that windows can be arranged in various ways. Right click a blank area on the taskbar (i.e. not one of the buttons) and experiment with the **Cascade** and **Tile** options.

If one of the folders is not visible click the appropriate button in the taskbar.

The windows can be made smaller if necessary so that all files are still visible (see Figure 5.6).

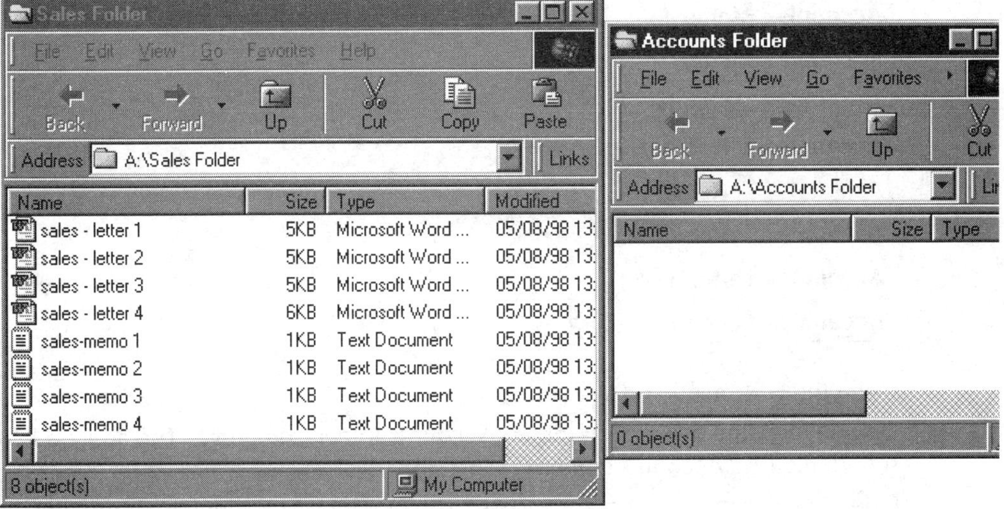

Figure 5.6

This display allows you compare their contents and to copy or move files.

3.1 ⇨ 98 If you are used to File Manager then you may prefer the My Computer display to Windows Explorer for simple folder structures. Explorer is easier for browsing multiple drives and levels of folder, but My Computer makes it easier to view the contents of two folders simultaneously.

6 Hold down the *Ctrl* key and drag the file **Sales - Letter 1** from the **Sales** to the **Accounts** folder. Check that the original is still in the **Sales** folder.

7 Close all the My Computer windows.

To copy and move files successfully using drag and drop techniques requires both the source files and the destination folder or drive to be visible in the window. If there is a long list of files or folders it may be difficult to locate the destination that you want to copy to. In this case you may find it easier to use the **Move** or **Copy** commands provided both as buttons and on the **Edit** menu.

Task 4: Copying and moving groups of files – menu method

1 To copy groups of files, make sure that the original diskette 'a' containing the practice files is inserted in the diskette drive, open Explorer and check that the diskette drive window is selected, not a subfolder.

Maximise the window.

Open the **View** menu and make sure that the **Details** option is selected and the **as Web Page** option is deselected.

2 We are going to copy all the files concerned with accounts into the **Accounts** folder.

Hold down the *Ctrl* Key and click the following eight files to select them (the *Shift* key can also be used in a similar way to select a single block of files).

Accounts - Memo 1

Accounts - Memo 2

Accounts - Memo 3

Accounts - Memo 4

Accounts - Letter 1

Accounts - Letter 2

Accounts - Letter 3

Accounts - Letter 4

3 Open the **Edit** menu and select **Copy**.

Double click the destination folder (**Accounts** folder) to open it. The address box should read A:\Accounts Folder.

Open the **Edit** menu again and select **Paste**. A dialog box should confirm that copying is taking place.

Check that the eight files have been copied (see Figure 5.7).

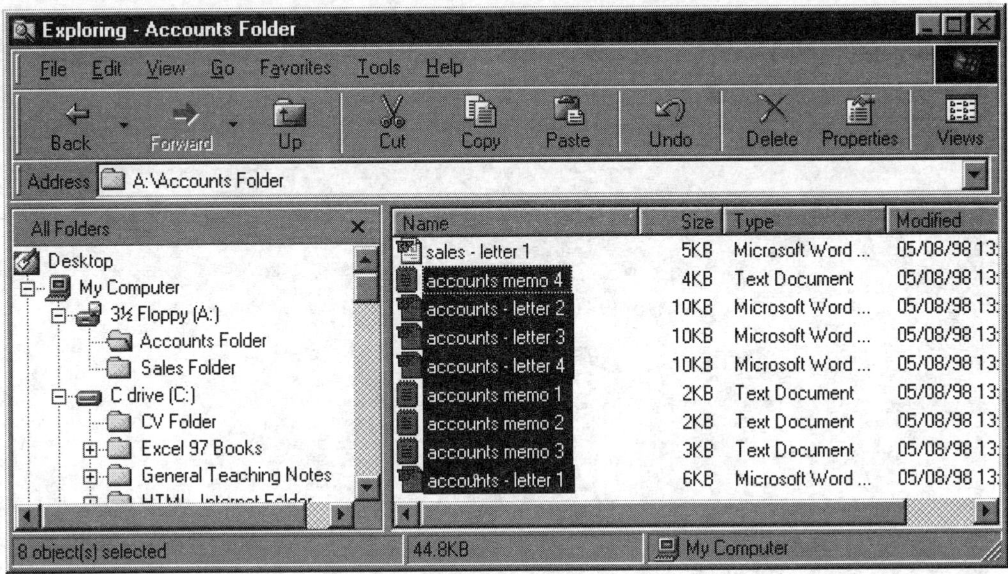

Figure 5.7

You may wonder what would happen if we copied the same files again; would we create files with identical names in the same folder? The answer is no! Windows only permits identical file names in different folders. (We have this situation with the files that we just copied, the original eight files are still in the root folder of A: drive and the copies in the **Accounts** Folder.)

If you copy the same files twice the originals are overwritten by the copies. This is useful when you want to replace an original with a new version of a file – there is no need to delete the original, just copy over it. However, if you have created two completely different files with the same name you would need to rename one of them.

4 To make this point repeat the copy command above.

This time use the **Copy** and **Paste** button provided on the toolbar at the top of the window (if they are not visible open the **View** menu and select **Toolbars-Standard Buttons**).

You are warned that the original files in the **Accounts** folder will be overwritten (see Figure 5.8 on the following page).

5 You can tell by the size and creation date that the two files are identical. Click **Yes**.

The next file to be copied is confirmed; if you are satisfied click **Yes** again. This process will continue until all the original copies are replaced.

Click **No** if for any reason you do not want the original overwritten.

Click **Yes to All** if you want all the originals overwritten without further confirmation messages.

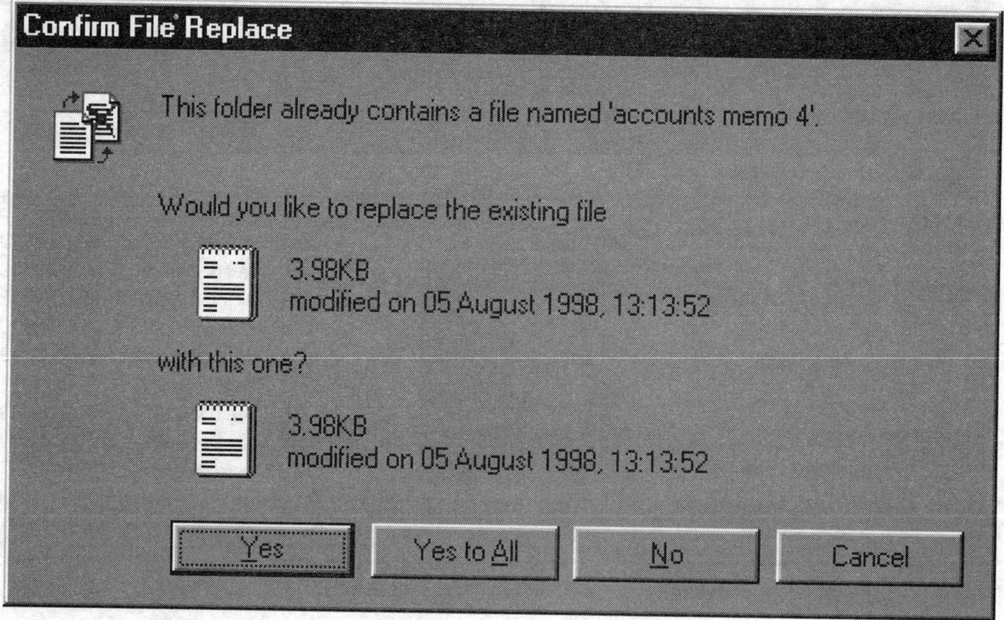

Figure 5.8

6 You may move files using the **Edit-Cut** command. This command is equivalent to the **Move** command. We will not practise it specifically as it works in the same way as the **Copy** command that we have just carried out.

Copying folders Folders can be copied or moved in exactly the same way as files, using either the **Copy** and **Paste** commands or the 'Drag and Drop' technique.

7 Windows provides a My Documents folder on the desktop to hold your personal files and folders. Using either Explorer or My Computer copy the **Accounts** and the **Sales** folders from your practice diskette to the My Documents folder.

If you only have one diskette drive (the usual situation) then you may wonder how you can copy files from one diskette to another. An easy way is to use the main desktop as a temporary holding area while you swap over the diskettes. We will try this with our two practice disks.

Task 5: Copying files between diskettes

1 Insert the practice disk that contains the copies of the practice files (see Unit 3, Task 2). We will call it practice disk 'b' from now on.

Open Explorer if necessary and check that the diskette drive window is selected, not a subfolder.

Adjust the size of the window so that the main desktop is in view.

Open the **View** menu and select make sure that the **Details** option is selected and the **as Web Page** option is deselected.

2 Select one of the practice files in the right hand window and use the mouse to drag it onto the desktop – see Figure 5.9.

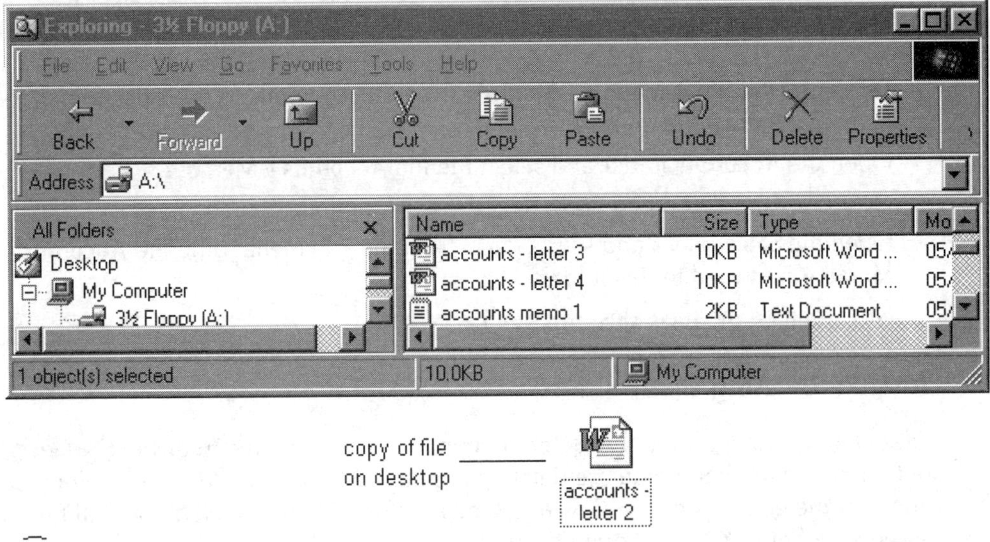

Figure 5.9

3 Now eject diskette 'b' and insert practice diskette 'a'.

Open the **View** menu and select **Refresh** to display the files and folders on this diskette.

4 Drag the file from the desktop to the right hand window of Explorer (not into one of the folders)

It is copied to the second diskette. If you get a 'Confirm File Replace' message (see Figure 5.8 above) then click the **Yes** button.

5 Finally, delete the file from the *desktop* by dragging it into the Recycle Bin.

Task 6: Renaming Files

Often, we need to need to change the name of a file, perhaps because it is incorrect or to distinguish it from an earlier or later version. We can simply rename the existing file or make a copy of it under another name. We will try both of these.

1 To rename a file without copying, first make sure that practice diskette 'a' is inserted in the diskette drive, start Explorer, open the **Sales** folder and select the file **Sales - Letter 1** (click it once).

We will give it the extension .JM to identify the author, i.e. **Sales - Letter 1.JM**

2 Open the **File** menu and select the **Rename** option. The file name can now be altered.

Move the screen pointer to the end of the file name and click once. A text insertion cursor is placed there.

Add the characters **.JM** then click elsewhere on the window to deselect it.

Use the **Edit-Undo Rename** command to undo the renaming.

3 Let's copy the file **Accounts - Memo 4** from the **Accounts** to the **Sales** folder, renaming it **Sales - Memo 5**.

Open the **Accounts** folder and select the file **Accounts - Memo 4**.

Next open the **Edit** menu and select the **Copy** option.

Open the **Sales** folder and select **Paste** from the **File** menu – the file **Accounts - Memo 4** is copied to this folder.

Now rename the file **Sales - Memo 5**.

Task 7: Deleting files

Files can be deleted using the **Delete** command on the **File** menu or the **Delete** button on the toolbar. If you are deleting a group of files or a folder be careful that it does not include files that you want to keep. Before a file is deleted you will be asked to confirm it. Even though deleted files on a hard disk can be recovered for a limited period of time it is unwise to rely on this.

1 First, let's create a folder with some files in it for us to practise deletion. It will be named **Test**.

If you are using a PC on a network you may need to check whether you can create a folder on a hard drive.

Make sure that diskette 'a' containing the practice files is inserted in the diskette drive, open Explorer and make sure that the main hard drive window (e.g. C:) is selected, not a subfolder.

Maximise the window.

Open the **View** menu and select make sure that the **Details** option is selected and the **as Web Page** option is deselected.

2 Open the **File** menu and select **New** then **Folder**.

The new folder is listed in the window.

Amend the name to ***Test Folder*** – simply overtype the default name, there is no need to use the **File - Rename** option for a newly created folder.

3 Now, using the operations that you learnt in Task 4, copy all the files from the **Sales** folder on the practice diskette to the **Test** subfolder on the hard drive.

You can use the **Edit - Select All** command to select all the files in the folder before copying them.

4 Open the **Test** folder on the C drive; check that you have the files listed in Figure 5.10 opposite.

If not you will need to copy them over again.

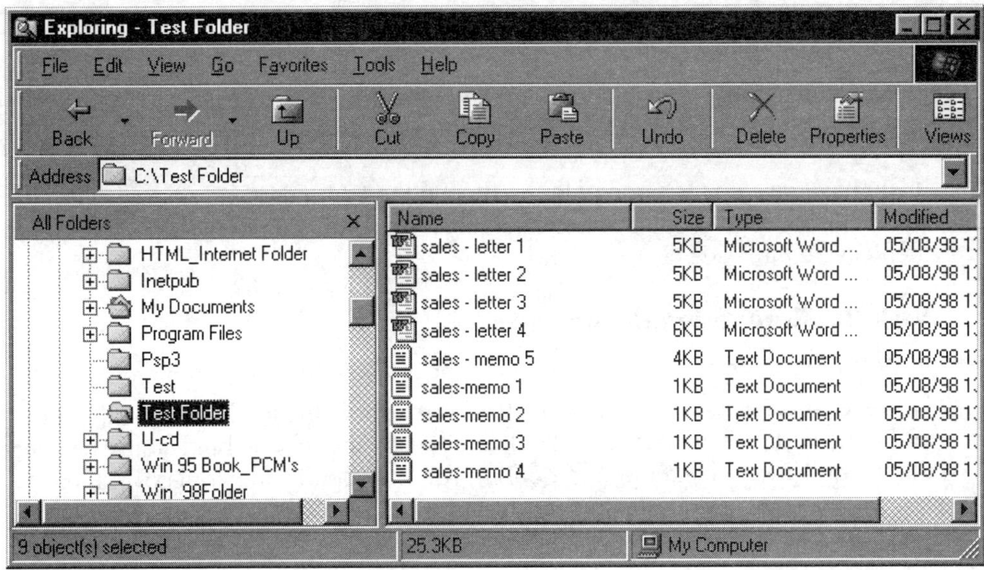

Figure 5.10

5 To delete individual files, select the file **Sales - Letter 2**.

Open the **File** menu and select **Delete**.

The dialog box shown in Figure 5.11 appears, confirming the file that you have specified for deletion.

Figure 5.11

You are offered the chance to change your mind. Check you have chosen the correct file.

Click the **Yes** button and the file **Sales - Letter 2** is deleted – check this in the file listing.

The Delete command is also available if you right click the file (or folder).

6 To delete several files, hold down the *Ctrl* key and select files **Sales - Memo 1**, **Sales - Memo 2** and **Sales - Memo 3**.

This time use the **Delete** button on the toolbar.

A dialog box appears. Notice that the three file names are not specified so you must be absolutely sure you have selected the right files.

Select the **Yes** option and the three files **Sales - Memo 1**, **Sales - Memo 2** and **Sales - Memo 3** are deleted – check this in the folder listing.

If you have deleted the wrong files then open the **Edit** menu and select **Undo Delete**. If you don't do this immediately then you will need to recover them from the Recycle Bin – see next task.

Task 8: Recovering deleted files

In Windows 98 deleted files are stored in the Recycle Bin and can be recovered. However space is limited – normally to about 10% of the total space on the drive – and the oldest files are permanently deleted when the recycle bin is full. This means that if you leave deleted files for too long you may not be able to recover them.

It is therefore good practice to open the recycle bin periodically and clear out files you are certain you no longer need – it also saves on disk space.

1 Minimise the Explorer window if necessary. Find the **Recycle Bin** icon on the main desktop and double click to open it. The window is similar to the Explorer display and shows the files deleted in the last task (see Figure 5.12).

Open the **View** menu and make sure that the **Details** option is selected and the **as Web Page** option is deselected.

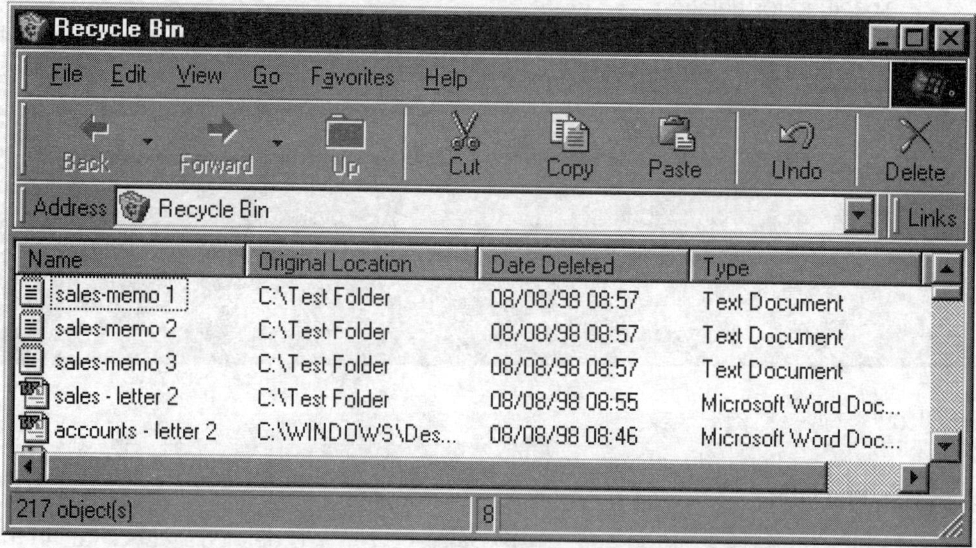

Fig 5.12

2 To check the size of the Recycle Bin, right click a blank part of the Recycle Bin and select **Properties** from the menu. A dialog box appears.

Check that the **Global** tab is selected which determines the settings for all drives.

The default size of the recycle bin is 10% of total drive space.

Notice that there is also the option to delete files immediately, without moving them to the Recycle Bin.

Click the tabs for any other drives; they are set to 10% too.

There are no tabs for diskette drives, deleted files on diskette are deleted permanently.

Close the **Properties** dialog box.

3 To delete a file permanently, open the Recycle Bin window again and find one of the files that you have deleted in Task 7.

Choose **Delete** from the **File** menu. Confirm the deletion and the file is permanently deleted.

4 To restore a deleted file, select the file from the Recycle Bin.

Choose **Restore** from the **File** menu. The file is restored to its original location in the Test folder.

5 Now let's clear out the recycle bin; there should be at least two files left in it. *Check that there are no other files that you may wish to restore at a later date.*

Open the **File** menu and select **Empty Recycle Bin**.

Confirm the deletion and the bin is emptied.

6 Close the Recycle Bin.

Carry straight on with the next task.

Task 9: Deleting folders

Folders can be deleted in the same ways as files, so all the operations learnt in the previous task apply equally to folders. Folders deleted from a hard disk, like files, can be undeleted. However you must take even more care as deleting a folder will delete any files and further subfolders it contains. You must check the confirmation messages very carefully!

We will delete the **Test Folder** and the remaining files it contains.

1 Open the Explorer Window if necessary and click the folder icon for the **Test Folder** once so that it is selected (highlighted).

Open the **File** menu and select **Delete**.

When the **Confirm Folder Delete** dialog box appears check that the folder name **Test Folder** is shown – see Figure 5.13 on the following page. If so click the **Yes** button.

If any other name is shown then take the **No** option, select the correct file and try again.

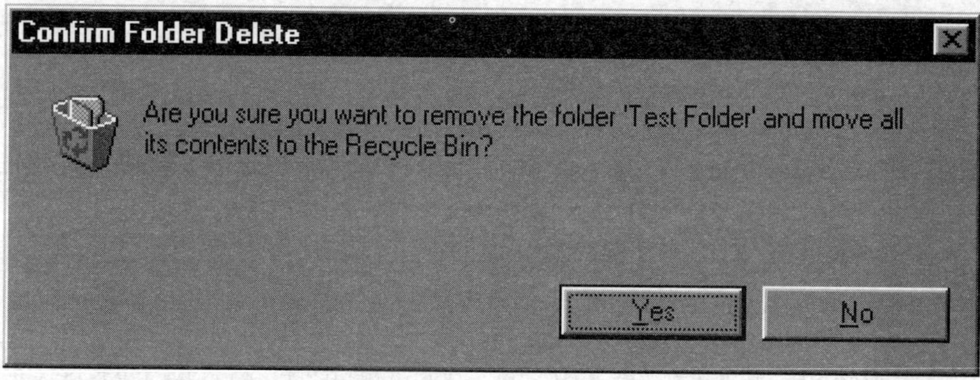

Figure 5.13

2 To restore a folder, open the Recycle Bin and check the deleted files have been placed there. Notice that the files are listed separately from the **Test** folder.

Restore one of the files and then check the hard drive using Explorer. You will find that the **Test Folder** has been restored and that it contains the restored file (use the **View-Refresh** option to locate the **Test Folder**).

3 Delete the **Test Folder** again and empty the Recycle Bin.

4 Make sure that diskette 'a' containing the practice files is in the diskette drive.

Open Explorer if necessary and check that the main diskette drive window is selected, not a subfolder.

Maximise the window.

All files with SALES in the file name are now located in the **Sales** folder, all files with ACCOUNTS in the file name are located in the **Accounts** folder. All files not in these folders, i.e. in the root folder of the diskette, are duplicates of these and can be deleted. Do this.

When you have done so check the Recycle Bin – none of the deleted files have been moved there.

Deleted files on diskette cannot be recovered.

Summary of Commands

Menu commands show the menu name first, followed by the command to choose from the menu, e.g. Edit-Clear means open the **Edit** menu and select the **Clear** command. Where a command is available from a particular window this is indicated in brackets.

(Explorer/My Computer)

Edit-Copy	Select a file or folder for copying
Edit-Cut	Select a file or folder for moving
Edit-Paste	Copy/Move selected file or folder
Edit-Undo	Undo a Copy, Delete or Move command
File-Delete	Delete file or folder
File-New-Folder	Create new folder
File-Rename	Rename a file or folder
View-Details	View all file details
View-Options-Folder	Display/Do not display multiple windows
View-Refresh	Update display of files/folders

(Recycle Bin)

File-Empty Recycle Bin	Permanently delete files or folders
File-Restore	Restore a deleted file or folder

unit 6

More on disks and files

Introduction

In this unit you will be learning how to create a system disk, how to display hidden files, and how to associate a file with an application. There is a final independent task which involves organising your practice files into folders and subfolders.

What you should know already

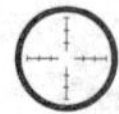

How to use the standard Windows components – see Unit 1.

What you need

The two practice diskettes created in Units 2 and 3.

What you will learn in this unit

By the end of this unit you will be able to:

- create a system disk
- display hidden files and check their properties
- display file extensions
- associate a file with an application.

A system disk

Windows 98 contains a number of key system files that are essential for your PC to start and to run. If they are accidentally removed or damaged by a virus you will need a system disk to start or 'boot up' your computer.

You can transfer the key system files to diskette using the My Computer application. These files will allow the system to re-start. You can either add the system files when formatting a disk (see Unit 3, Task 1) or at a later stage as we are doing now. We will use the backup diskette 'b' as this is already formatted but any disk will do. Make sure that the write protection notch is closed.

You only need one system disk; it is not necessary to copy system files onto diskettes only used to store files.

Task 1: Creating a system disk

1 Insert the backup diskette and open the My Computer window.

Single click the icon for the diskette drive to select it (do not double click it to open the window)

A disk cannot be formatted when its window is open.

2 Open the **File** menu and select **Format**. A dialog box **Format - 3 $\frac{1}{2}$ Floppy (A:)** is displayed. As the disk is already formatted we will not format it as this would erase the backup files.

3 Select the option **Copy system files only**.

Click the **Start** button. Backup disk 'b' is now a system disk and should be marked for future reference.

When complete click the **Close** button and continue with the next task.

Hidden files

Normally you can view all the files on disk using My Computer or Windows Explorer. However, some files are always hidden to protect them from interference, notably some of the key system files mentioned in the previous task. It is essential that these files are not deleted or renamed, otherwise the computer will not run properly. Hiding files that are not normally moved or deleted also reduces the size of the display.
Sometimes it is useful to check that these hidden files are on your system disk.

Task 2: Displaying hidden files

1 Insert the system disk that you created in the last task if necessary.

Call up My Computer if necessary and double click the diskette drive icon.

The file COMMAND is listed; this is the command processor program that executes the older MS-DOS commands.

Other files may also be displayed in the drive window, e.g. IO.SYS and MSDOS.SYS

The .SYS extension identifies them as system files.

If they are *not* displayed then proceed to step 2.

2 Open the **View** menu and select **Folder Options**. A dialog box appears.

Click the **View** tab at the top of the window and select the **Show all files** option.

Click **OK**. Various hidden files should now be displayed.

3 To find out more about the two system files IO.SYS and MSDOS.SYS, right click one of the file names and select **Properties** from the pop-up menu that appears.

A dialog box appears.

The final section of the dialog box lists the file attributes.

Read-only – the file is protected from amendment: it can be read but not written to. You can use this option to protect other files from accidental changes or deletion.

Hidden – the file is not normally listed in Explorer or My Computer, it is hidden by the Windows operating system. Again, you can use this option to protect your files.

System file – this is part of the computer's operating system.
Archive – when a file is first created, or if it is altered, its archive flag is set to 'On' (A) This is checked by backup programs to control whether it is backed up. Once it has been backed up (archived) its archive 'flag' is set to 'Off'; this is checked by a backup program and it is not included in the next back up. If the file is changed the archive flag is set 'On' again.

4 Now we will hide these files again.

Follow the instructions in step 2, to re-select the **Do not show hidden or system files** option.

Only the COMMAND file is now displayed in the drive window. IO.SYS and MSDOS.SYS etc. are hidden.

5 Close the My Computer and A: drive windows.

A Final Warning Do not list hidden files on a regular basis. They are hidden to prevent their being deleted, re-named or moved. It is all too easy to do this particularly if you are selecting blocks of files.

Similarly do not hide regular files – you may forget where you have hidden them!

Files and applications

In MS-DOS and earlier versions of Windows a file name could only consist of up to eight characters, plus an optional extension of up to three characters, separated from the filename by a full stop or 'dot'. Windows 98 allows file names of up to 255 characters.
Extensions are still used by Windows 98 to associate a type of file with a particular application but the extension is normally hidden from the user, e.g. Wordpad and Microsoft Word both use the .DOC extension. This association saves time when you want to retrieve a file; you have no need to start the application and then open the file – opening the file automatically starts the associated application. If data files are not given the standard default extension then Windows cannot automatically associate them with the software package (i.e. the program) that created them. This means that when you try to open the file by double clicking the icon, e.g. in Explorer, you will get an error message. In this case you must tell Windows which program is associated with the data file.

If you have a set of files which share a non-standard extension you can create your own association.

Task 3: Associating a file with an application

1 Make sure that diskette 'a' containing the practice files is inserted in the diskette drive, open Explorer and check that the diskette window is selected.

Maximise the window.

2 Open the **Sales** folder and double click the file **Sales - Letter 2**.

The Wordpad (or Word) application starts automatically. Windows will automatically associate the file with the Wordpad application program that was used to create it.

Exit from the document back to Explorer – the file and its associated program are closed.

3 Now open the **View** menu and select **Folder Options**.

A dialog box appears. Click the **View** tab.

Find the option: **Hide file extensions for known file types**.

This option is normally selected so that file types 'known' or registered with Windows 98 do not display their extensions.

Deselect this option and click the **OK** button.

4 The practice files are now shown with their extensions (see Figure 6.1). You may have to widen the Name column to see them (drag the column divider).

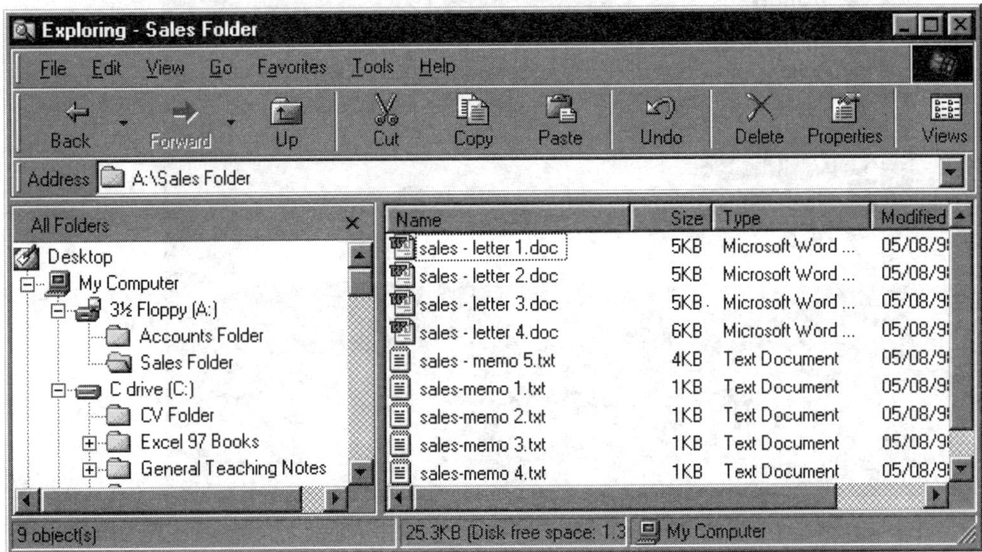

Figure 6.1

The files created in Notepad, the Windows text editor, have the extension .TXT automatically assigned to them; files with the extension .DOC were created in Wordpad, the Windows word processor.

5 Select the file **Sales - Memo 1.txt**. Do not open it.

Open the **File** menu and select **Rename**.

Change the extension .Txt to **.JMM** – the file is renamed **Sales - Memo1.JMM**

Click elsewhere on the window. A dialog box appears warning you that the file may become unusable. Click the **Yes** button.

The file is now renamed. Notice that the design of the icon has changed as Windows no longer associates it with any application.

6 Double click the renamed file to open it.

The **Open with** dialog box appears – see Figure 6.2. You are being asked to associate the file with a registered Windows application.

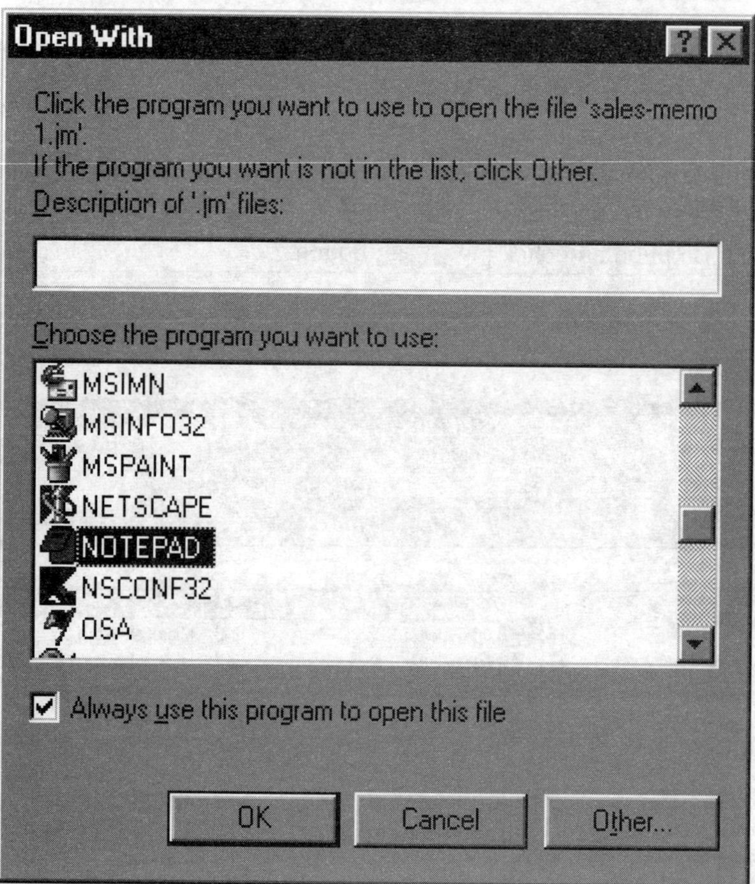

Figure 6.2

7 Scroll down the list of applications and select **Notepad**.

Make sure that the box **Always use this program to open this file** is selected. This creates a permanent association between Notepad and this type of file.

Click **OK**. The document is now opened in the Notepad window.

8 Exit from the document back to Explorer – the file and its associated program are closed.

Windows can now associate the file **Accounts - Memo 1.JMM** with the Notepad application. To make this point open and close it again.

9 Hide the file name extensions by repeating step 3 above and re-selecting the option: **Hide file extensions for known file types**.

Task 4: Independent activity

Your practice files are now stored in two folders – **Sales** and **Accounts**. They consist of two file types – see previous task.

Create two further subfolders within each folder called **Memos** and **Letters**.

Move all files with the word **letters** in their file name to subfolder **Letters**

Move all files with the word **memos** in their file name to the sub folder **Memos**.

The final structure will be as follows.

Sales folder

- Memos
  - **Sales - Memo 1**
  - **Sales - Memo 2**
  - **Sales - Memo 3**
  - **Sales - Memo 4**
- Letters
  - **Sales - Letter 1.JM**
  - **Sales - Letter 2**
  - **Sales - Letter 3**
  - **Sales - Letter 4**

Accounts folder -

- Memos
  - **Accounts - Memo 1**
  - **Accounts - Memo 2**
  - **Accounts - Memo 3**
  - **Accounts - Memo 4**
- Letters
  - **Accounts - Letter 1**
  - **Accounts - Letter 2**
  - **Accounts - Letter 3**
  - **Accounts - Letter 4**

To create a folder within another folder you will need to open the **Accounts** and the **Sales** folders before taking the **File - New - Folder** option.

Summary of Commands

Menu commands show the menu name first, followed by the command to choose from the menu, e.g. Edit-Clear means open the **Edit** menu and select the **Clear** command. Where a command is available from a particular window this is indicated in brackets.

(Explorer/My Computer)

File-Format	Format/Create system diskette
File-Rename	Rename a file or folder
View-Folder Options-View	Show/Hide various file types/file detail

unit 7

Customising your system

Introduction

In Windows 98 you can create shortcut icons on the desktop to start applications or open folders. You can also have applications start up as soon as you start Windows and send documents direct to the printer by 'dropping' them into a special print folder.

What you should know already

How to use the standard Windows components – see Unit 1.

What you need

The original diskette 'a' with the practice files created in Unit 2, Task 2.

What you will learn in this unit

By the end of this unit you will be able to:

- create shortcuts to programs, drives and folders
- create a startup application
- add quick launch buttons to the taskbar
- create shortcuts to printing
- manage print jobs.

Shortcuts

The standard way of starting a program is to open a series of menus and windows using the **Start** button, Explorer or My Computer. Windows 98 lets you bypass these steps by creating shortcut icons on the desktop. Let's try this for the Wordpad and Paint applications.

Task 1: Creating a shortcut to a program

1 Right click the **Start** button and take the **Explore** option.

Adjust the size of the window if necessary so that part of the desktop is visible.

Open the **View** menu and make sure that the **Details** option is selected and the **as Web Page** option is deselected.

2 If necessary, scroll the left hand side of the Window so that the various drive icons are displayed. If no drive icons are displayed then double click the

My Computer icon.

First we need to find the drive which holds the Wordpad application – usually drive C.

The C drive should have a number of folders listed; if not, double click the drive icon.

Check for the **Program Files** folder – see Figure 7.1. If you can't find it explore another disk drive or use the **Find** command – see Unit 4, Task 3.

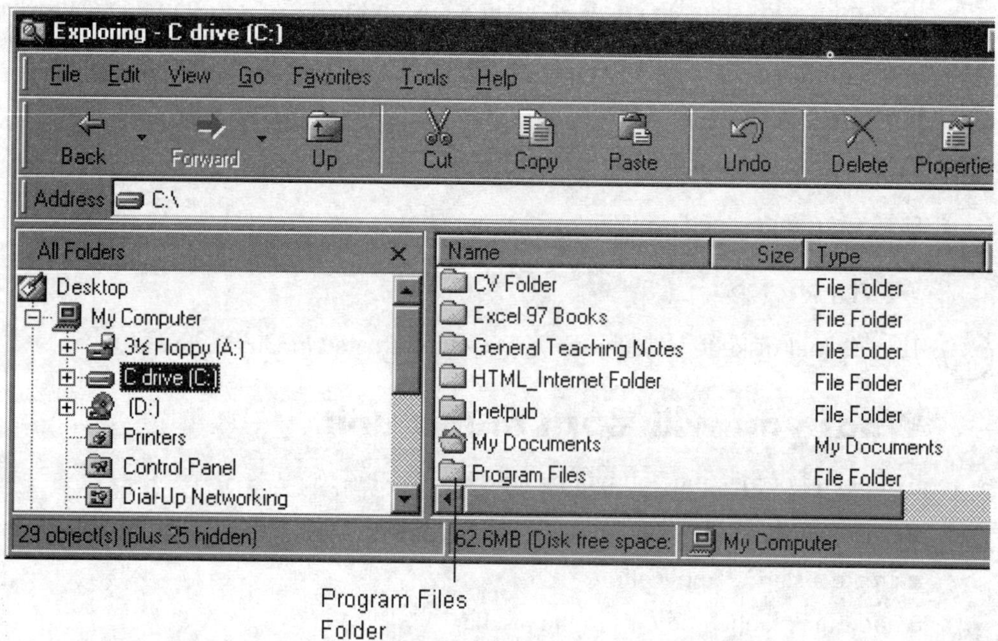

Figure 7.1

3 Double click the **Program Files** subfolder.

Within the **Program Files** subfolder are more subfolders – open the **Accessories** subfolder.

Various application icons are displayed, including Wordpad – see Figure 7.2 opposite.

4 Use the mouse to drag the Wordpad icon onto the desktop.

Release the mouse button.

5 A new icon appears on the desktop **Shortcut to Workpad** (if a menu appears select the option **Create Shortcut(s) here**).

Double click the icon and the Wordpad program starts. This is a much faster way of starting the application than using a series of windows and menus.

Close Wordpad

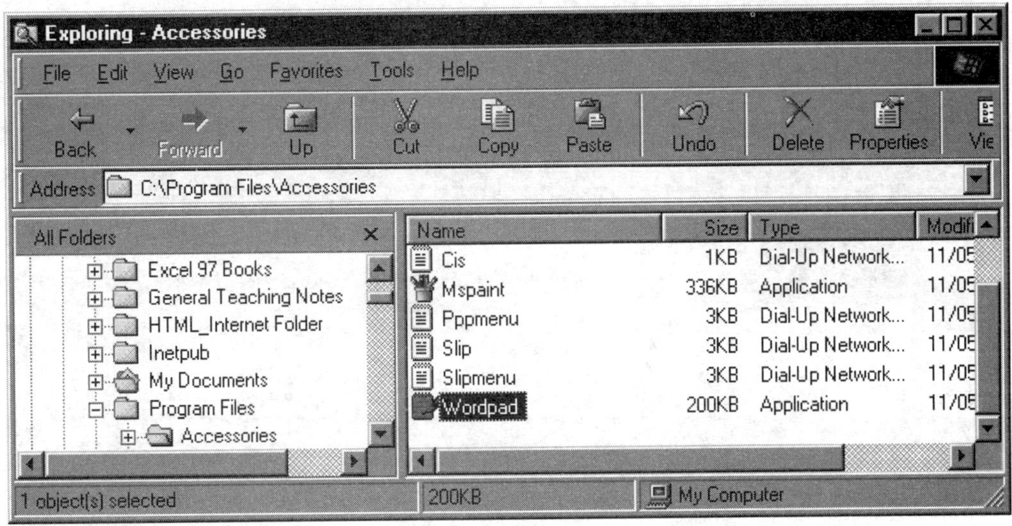

Figure 7.2

Right clicking the shortcut icon displays a menu allowing you to delete, rename and copy the shortcut. The **Properties** option also allows you to select another icon for the shortcut.

6 Create a desktop shortcut for the Notepad program. It is in the Windows folder. Rename it ***Start Notepad***.

7 Shortcut wizard makes creating a shortcut even easier.

(A *Wizard* is a series of dialog boxes guiding you the steps of a process and is used extensively in Microsoft applications.)

8 Insert practice disk 'a' in the diskette drive.

Right click anywhere on the desktop – a menu opens.

Select the **New** then the **Shortcut** option.

9 The **Create Shortcut** dialog box is displayed (see Figure 7.3 on the following page).

10 You can create a shortcut to a file or to a drive as well as a program. We'll do this for the diskette drive.

Enter the drive reference letter in the command line box, e.g. **a:** and click the **Next** button.

The next dialog box appears asking you to name the shortcut. Enter the name ***Select Drive A*** and click the **Finish** button.

The shortcut icon appears on the desktop. Now double click the icon to test it.

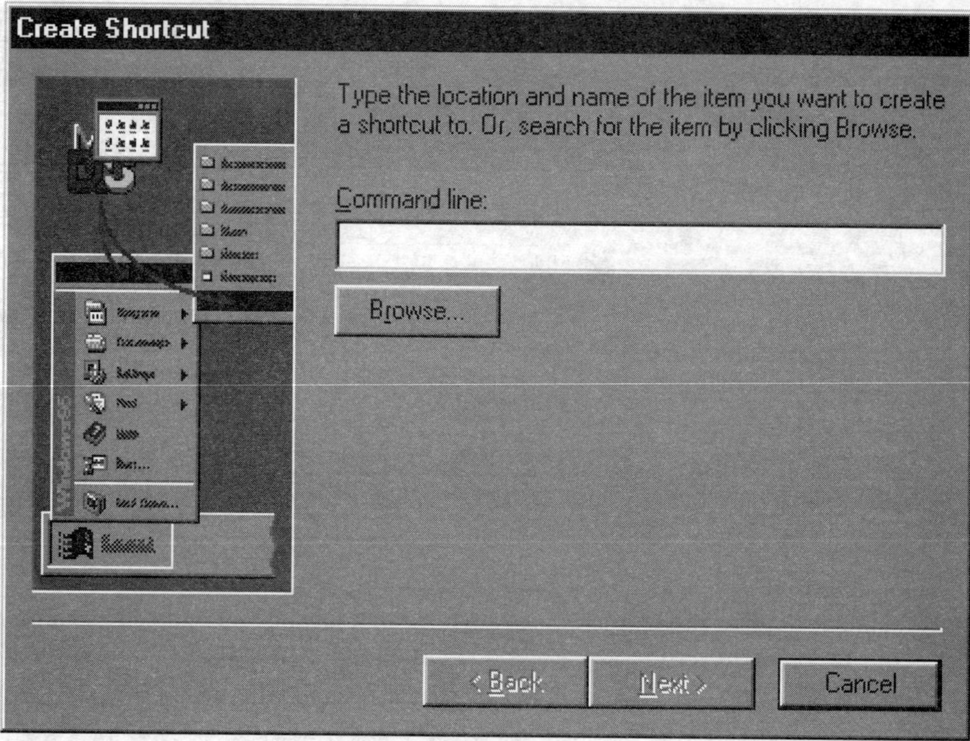

Figure 7.3

Task 2: Creating a shortcut to a folder

In the previous task we created a shortcut to a program and a drive. In this task we will create a shortcut to a folder on diskette (obviously, this will only work if the correct diskette is inserted in the drive).

1 If necessary insert practice disk 'a' in the diskette drive and start Explorer again (right click the **Start** button).

2 Double click the diskette drive icon and identify the **Sales** Folder.

Move the cursor onto the **Sales Folder** icon, hold the *right* hand mouse button down and drag the icon onto the desktop.

Release the mouse button and a menu appears. Select the option **Create Shortcut(s) here.**

3 A new icon appears on the desktop: **Shortcut to Sales Folder**. This can be deleted, renamed etc. as before, by right clicking the icon.

Double click on the icon and the Sales Folder window opens, displaying the files that it contains.

Close the folder window.

4 You also have an **Accounts** folder on your practice diskette. Create a shortcut to this folder too.

Task 3: Creating a shortcut folder

We now have five shortcut icons on the desktop (see Figure 7.4). To reduce clutter they can be placed in a folder.

Figure 7.4

1 Right click anywhere on the desktop – a menu opens.
Select the **New** then the **Folder** option.
Rename the folder **Shortcuts**.
Now use the left mouse button to drag the shortcuts into the folder.

2 Double click the folder – the window shows the shortcuts (see Figure 7.5).

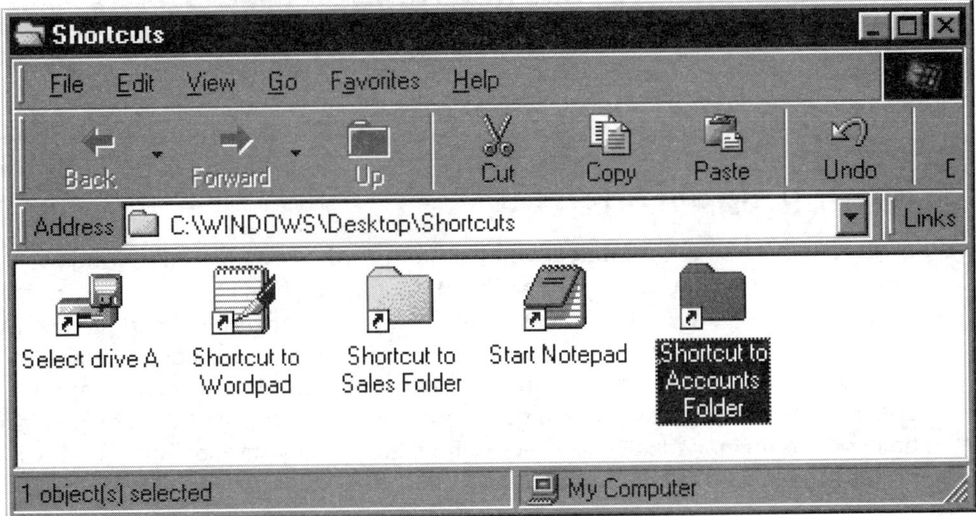

Figure 7.5

3 A copy of a shortcut can be placed at any other useful point, e.g. in a drive or folder to provide shortcuts. For example the **Sales** folder and **Accounts** folder on your practice diskette are used to store letters created in Wordpad and memos created in Notepad. It will be useful to have short cuts to these two applications if we want to create any new documents.

Open My Computer and display the window for the diskette drive.

Use the left mouse button to drag copies of the Notepad and Wordpad Shortcuts to the **Accounts** folder then the **Sales** folders – you will have to adjust the size of the windows to do this.

Open the destination folders to check that they have been copied – they should resemble Figure 7.6.

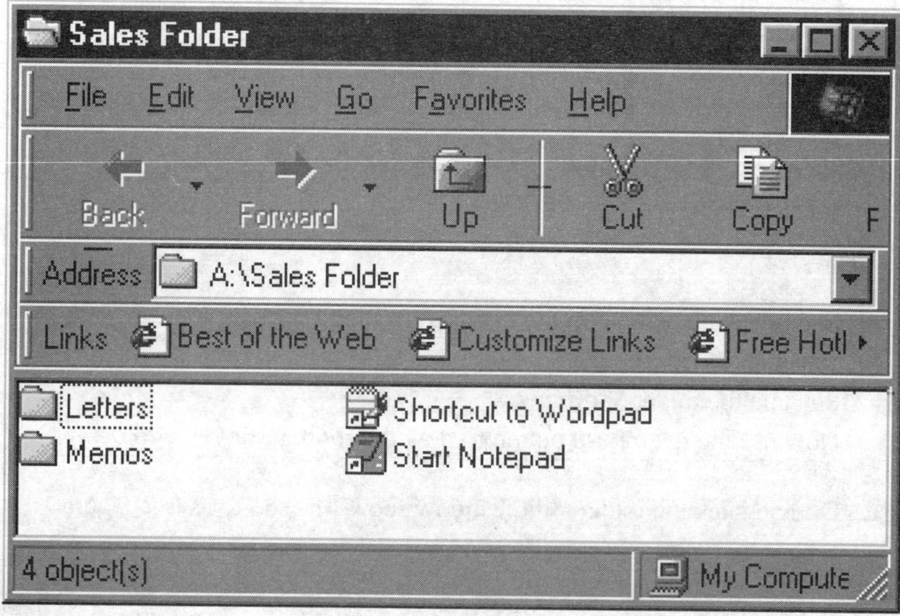

Figure 7.6

Startup applications

There may be an application that you tend to use when you first start Windows, e.g. a word processor, spreadsheet, or a Windows utility such as Date/Time. If you place an application in the Startup Folder it will be automatically started and ready for use whenever you start Windows. It can be either fully running in its own window, or displayed as an icon, ready to be opened. However, you should restrict startup applications to those that you will definitely need when you start Windows; it takes time to load up individual applications and therefore any startup application will prolong the time Windows takes to load.

As an example we will place Notepad in the Startup Folder.

Task 4: Creating startup applications

1 Click the **Start** button, then select the **Settings** and the **Taskbar and Start Menu** options. When the dialog box appears click the **Start Menu Programs** tab.

2 To find the application, click the **Add** button which calls up the Shortcut wizard (see Task 1 above).

You can type the name of the program that you want to start in the Command line box providing you know the path, e.g. **C:\windows\notepad.exe**, which involves some knowledge of MS-DOS syntax. If you prefer, click the **Browse** button then proceed as follows:

- the **Browse** dialog box appears
- make sure that the drive that contains the Windows folder is displayed in the **Look in:** box, if not click the down arrow and select it (see Figure 7.7)

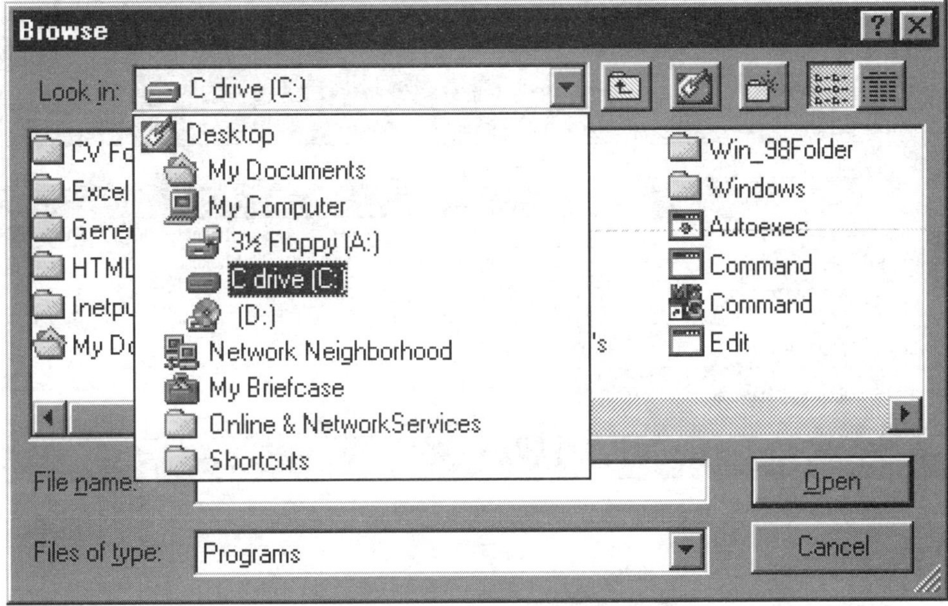

Figure 7.7

- find the Windows folder in the window display and double click it
- find the **Notepad** icon in the next window display (you may need to scroll it into view) and double click it
- you are returned to the **Browse** dialog box and the Command line box is now complete, e.g. C:\WINDOWS\NOTEPAD.EXE

3 Click the **Next** button and the Select Program Folder window is displayed.

Find the **Startup** folder icon and click it – you may need to scroll it into view. Do *not* choose the Start Menu folder.

Click the **Next** button again.

4 On the final dialog box you can rename the shortcut; accept the default offered and click the **Finish** button.

5 You are returned to the **Taskbar Properties** dialog box. We will start Notepad as an icon on the taskbar rather than an open window.

Click the **Advanced** button.

6 An Explore window for the Start menu is displayed – double click the folder icon for the Start menu if necessary.

Click the **(+)** sign next to the Programs folder to expand it.

Click the StartUp folder to open it – the **Notepad** shortcut icon is displayed in the right window (see Figure 7.8).

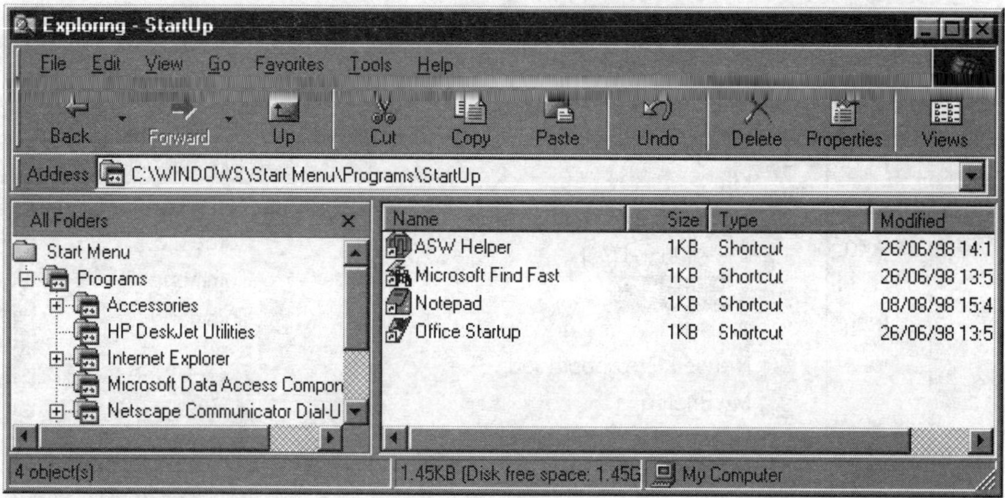

Figure 7.8

7 Right click the **Notepad** icon – a menu appears.

Select the **Properties** option.

The **Notepad Properties** dialog box appears. Make sure the **Shortcut** tab is selected.

8 Click the down arrow on the **Run:** box – see Figure 7.9 opposite – and select **Minimized**.

Click the **OK** button.

Finally close any dialog boxes remaining open.

9 To test the Startup application, exit from Windows and Re-start it.

The **Notepad** icon should start up automatically as a task button on the taskbar.

10 Add the **Paint** application to the **Startup** menu.

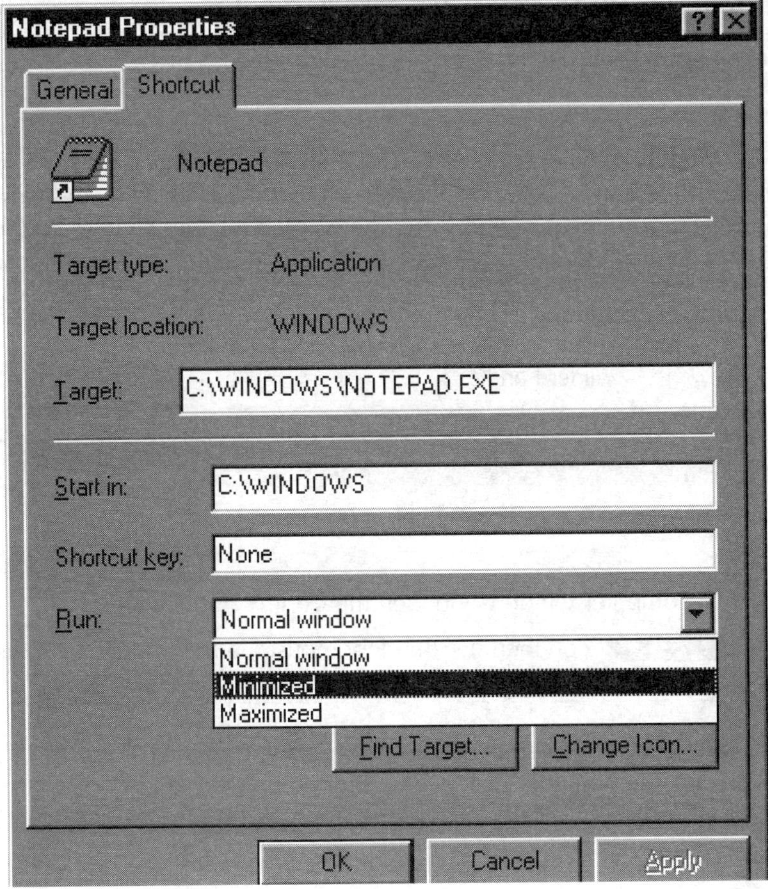

Figure 7.9

11 Removing an option from the **Startup** menu is simply a matter of repeating step 1 above then clicking the **Remove** button. You then need to locate the Startup folder in the Programs folder.

You may wish to remove Notepad from the Startup folder if you are sharing your PC with others who do not need this option.

12 You can add an option to the **Start** menu so that it is offered as an extra option when the **Start** button is clicked. It is simply a matter of using Explorer to find the file, folder or application that you want to add, then using the right mouse button to drag it onto the **Start** button.

Add the Paint program to the **Start** (not the **Startup**) menu in this way.

Check that the option is displayed when you click the **Start** button then remove it from the **Start** menu using the right mouse button.

Task 5: Adding quick launch buttons to the taskbar

The taskbar is a good place to place a shortcut as it is always in view. You can do this using the simple drag and drop techniques that you have already learned.

1 Various quick launch buttons should be installed on the Taskbar already – see Figure 7.10. These can be removed if you wish by right clicking them then selecting **Delete** from the pop-up menu. There are also slider handles on the taskbar to vary the amount of room used by tasks and quick launch buttons.

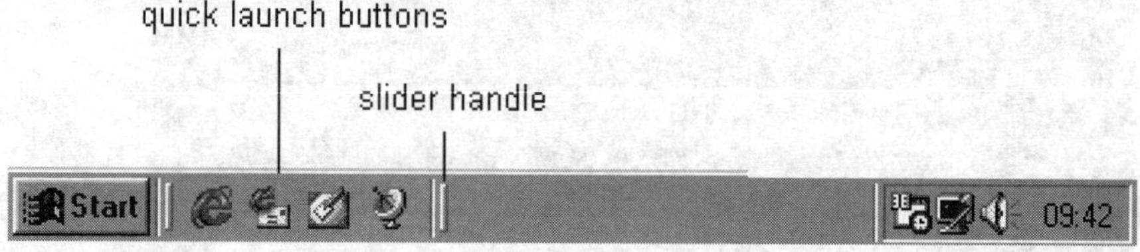

Figure 7.10

2 Open the My Computer window and then the Control Panel window.

Locate the **Internet** icon then use the right mouse button to drag a copy of it onto the taskbar.

3 You can now call up the Internet dialog box directly from the taskbar by clicking this new quick launch button. Delete it if you do not need it.

Printing

The usual way to print is to open the document and then select the **Print** option from the **File** menu. Instead, you can create a print shortcut on the desktop and print by dragging the document icon onto it. You can also form a print queue by dragging several document icons.

Task 6: Customising Printing

1 Open the My Computer window and double click the **Printers** folder.

2 Move the screen pointer onto the icon for your printer, hold down the right mouse button and drag the icon onto the desktop.

Release the mouse button and a menu appears. Select the option **Create Shortcut(s) here**.

3 A new object appears on the desktop **Shortcut to [...your printer]**.

You can rename the icon by right clicking it if you wish.

Close the Printers window.

4 To print a single document, insert practice disk 'a' in the diskette drive.

In the My Computer window double click the diskette drive icon.

Open the **Sales** folder.

Use the mouse to drag a text document from the diskette window on top of the **Printer shortcut** icon. The document will print immediately (one copy only).

5 Printing several documents can be useful when you are away from the computer. It is possible to check or change the status of print jobs when printing has started.

When you have finished this step continue with the next step as quickly as possible before printing is complete.

Hold down the *Ctrl* key and select four Notepad documents in the My Computer window.

Keep the *Ctrl* key pressed down, locate the cursor anywhere on the group of documents and drag them on top of the printer shortcut icon.

Release the mouse and then the *Ctrl* key. If a dialog box appears offering options to **Print** or **Cancel**, click **Print**.

A dialog box appears asking you to confirm that you are trying to print multiple documents. Click **Yes**.

6 To change print jobs before the first document starts printing, double click the printer shortcut icon: a printer window opens, displaying the remaining documents to be printed – see Figure 7.11.

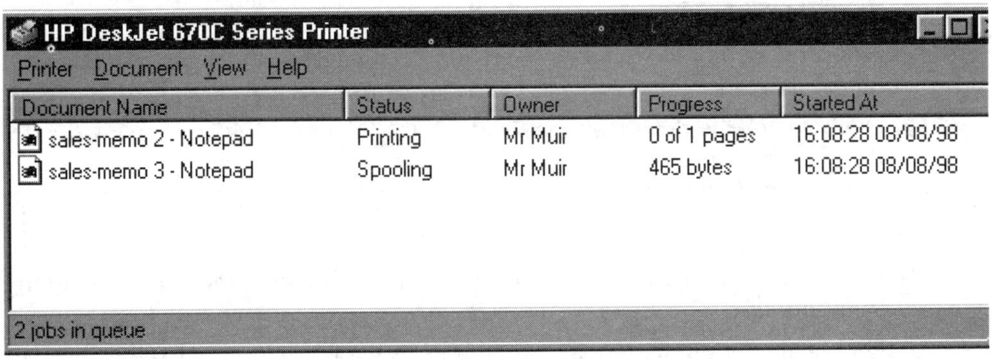

HP DeskJet 670C Series Printer

Printer Document View Help

Document Name	Status	Owner	Progress	Started At
sales-memo 2 - Notepad	Printing	Mr Muir	0 of 1 pages	16:08:28 08/08/98
sales-memo 3 - Notepad	Spooling	Mr Muir	465 bytes	16:08:28 08/08/98

2 jobs in queue

Figure 7.11

Open the **Printer** menu and select the **Pause Printing** option.

(!) All this may take some time, unless your PC is quite powerful, as you are printing from diskette and each document must be opened and queued.
The printer window shows the progress of your printing jobs, the length of each document and the time it was started. The Owner column is useful if your printer is shared by several networked users.

7 You can change the order of printing by dragging one document above another – try it. This will make you unpopular on a network and may not be available!

8 To pause an individual document, click one of the documents to select it, then select **Pause Printing** from the **Document** menu. A message appears in the status column.

Select this option again and the pause status is removed.

9 To cancel one of the print jobs, select the document then choose **Cancel Printing** from the **Document** menu. The document is removed.

10 The **Printer** menu can be used to start all the print jobs again or to cancel (purge) them all. We will do the latter.

Open the **Print** menu and select **Pause Printing** – it is de-selected and the remaining documents are printed.

11 Close the Printer window and the My Computer window.

12 To print using the **SendTo** option, right click the **Start** button and take the **Explore** option.

Open the **View** menu and make sure that the **Details** option is selected and the **as Web Page** option is deselected.

13 If necessary scroll the left hand side of the Window so that the various drive icons are displayed. If no drive icons are displayed then double click the **My Computer** icon.

Adjust the size of the window if necessary so that the printer shortcut is visible on the desktop.

Double click the drive icon that contains the Windows folder – usually drive C.

Open the Windows folder.

14 Double click the **SendTo** option – the contents are displayed.

Use the right mouse button to drag the printer shortcut from the desktop to the **Send to** folder.

Release the mouse button and a menu is displayed. Select the **Create Shortcut(s) Here** option. The printer shortcut is copied into the **SendTo** menu.

15 Double click the diskette drive icon in the left hand Explorer window to open it.

Open the **Accounts** folder and right click any document in the right hand window.

Select the **SendTo** option from the pop-up menu that appears.

Select the printer shortcut and the document is sent to the printer.

If anything, this is even more convenient than the 'drag and drop' method that we have just learned.

Summary of commands

Commands show the object to select first, followed by the command to choose from the menu, e.g. Start Button-Help means click the **Start** Button and select the **Help** command. Where a command is available from a particular window this is indicated in brackets.

Start-Program Files-Accessories	Open Accessories Folder
Start-Programs-Windows Explorer	Start Windows Explorer
Start-Settings-Taskbar & Start Menu Options	Change Taskbar properties
(Windows Explorer)	
File-New-Shortcut	Create new shortcut
File-New-Folder	Create new folder

unit 8

Object linking and embedding

Introduction

Object linking and embedding (OLE) allows easy transfer of data between Windows applications; for example you may have created a graph in an Excel spreadsheet and want to copy it into a word processed report in Word. Whenever the original graph changes you may want the version in the report to be updated too – even though a word processor and a spreadsheet are completely different applications.

Microsoft (the producer of Windows) have created the standard for this to happen – OLE.

What you should know already

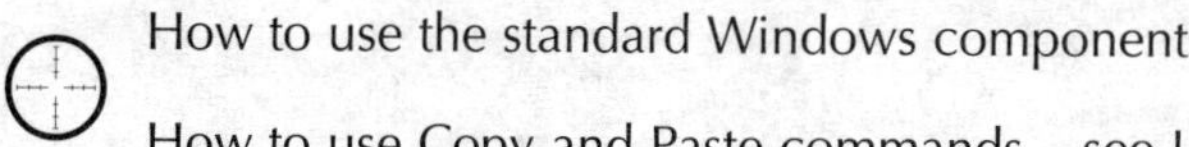

How to use the standard Windows components – see Unit 1.

How to use Copy and Paste commands – see Unit 5, Task 4.

What you need

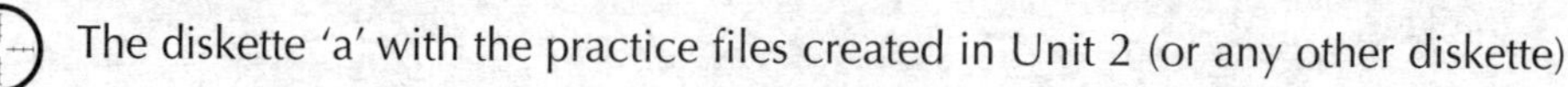

The diskette 'a' with the practice files created in Unit 2 (or any other diskette).

What you will learn in this unit

By the end of this unit you will be able to:

- copy an image from one application to another
- edit an embedded image
- save text as a 'scrap'
- link documents and edit their links.

Task 1: Copying, pasting and embedding

1 To copy and paste, open the Paint application. It is part of the Programs Accessories group.

Produce the simple image shown in Figure 8.1. The exact shape and size do not matter, it is made up of an empty ellipse inside an empty rectangle. Drawing them is simply a matter of clicking the shape to select the tool, then dragging on the Paint screen to draw the shape – see Figure 8.2 if you have not used Paint before.

2 Enclose the image using the **Select** tool (click the tool to select it, then drag to enclose the image).

Open the **Edit** menu and select **Copy**.

Figure 8.1

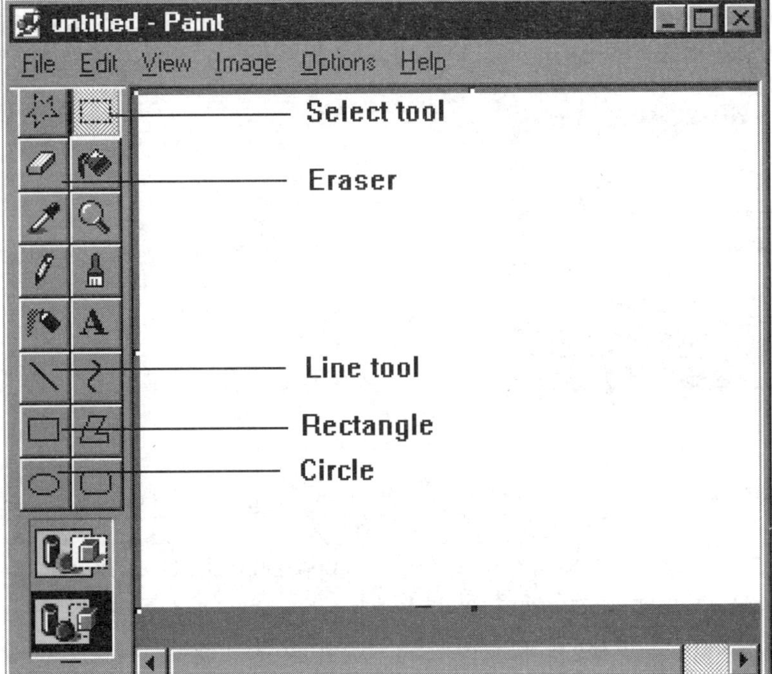

Figure 8.2

3 Save the Paint document on a diskette as **IMAGE**.

4 Exit Paint and open Wordpad. It is also part of the Programs Accessories group.

Type any few lines of text.

Now open the **Edit** menu and select **Paste**. The image is pasted into the Wordpad document.

5 Minimise the Wordpad document and open the Clipboard Viewer (if it is installed it is part of the Accessories-System Tools group). It contains the pasted image. Clipboard acts as the temporary storage area in main memory when data is cut or copied. It can only hold one chunk of data at a time: the next data to be copied or cut will overwrite the image.

Close the Clipboard Viewer.

6 To embed an object, exit from the clipboard viewer and return to the Wordpad document. Click the image to select it – the image is surrounded by a rectangle.

7 Try copying and cutting the image within the document. To do this, open the **Edit** menu and select **Cut** or **Copy**, locate the cursor where the image is to re-located, then open the **Edit** menu and select **Paste**.

8 If you need to edit the image you can change back to its 'home' application - Paint – automatically. This is called in-place editing.

Double-click the image – a Paint window opens, allowing you to edit the image.

Add a horizontal line to the image as shown in Figure 8.3 – use the line tool.

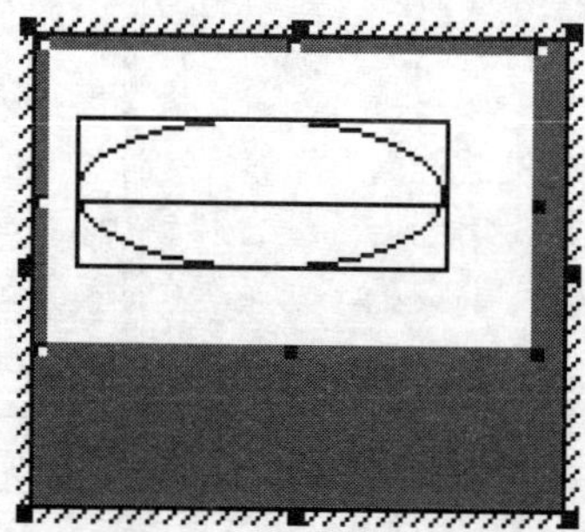

Figure 8.3

Click elsewhere on the window to return to the Wordpad document.

9 Now open the **File** menu and save the document on diskette as **DOC1**

Open the **File** menu again and select **Exit**

Now open the Paint document **IMAGE**. The original image has not changed – there is no link between the two.

10 If you have some text, such as an address, that you want to re-use many times, it can be dragged onto the desktop as a 'scrap'.

Open a new Wordpad document and type an address. Save the document.

Highlight the address and drag it onto the desktop, it appears as an icon.

Now close the Wordpad document without saving and try dragging the scrap into another document.

Rename the scrap (or delete it) by right clicking it.

Embedding

What we have just done is to create information in a *'source'* document (Paint) and insert it into a *'destination'* document from a different application (Wordpad). This information, the image, became an *embedded* object. Any changes can be made easily as an application window for the source application (Paint) opens automatically from within the destination document (Wordpad)

When you embed an object in a document you *copy* the object from the source to the destination document. Once this happens the original and its copy are not linked in any way – editing the copy does not affect the original.

Object linking

There are situations where you might want any changes to an original, e.g. a diagram or spreadsheet, to automatically update any copies of it that exist in other documents. In this case you can create a *link* to the original (you can link several documents to one original). In the examples that follow we use Paint as the *server* or source Application and Wordpad as the *client* or destination application. If you have Microsoft Office applications on your PC such as Excel, Word or Access you can try it with them.

Task 2: Creating object links

1 Open a new Paint document and create a simple map along the lines of Figure 8.4.

Bournemouth Rd

Main Site

Figure 8.4

Use the Line tool for the road, the Rectangle tool for the building – see Figure 8.2 above if necessary.

When you use the Text tool you will need to drag a suitably sized box for the text first.

2 Save the Paint document onto diskette as **MAP1**.

Exit and close **MAP1**.

3 Open a new Wordpad document and type the following text:

Below is a map showing the new site for the university building.

Leave a couple of blank lines.

Open the **Insert** menu and select **Object**.

Click the **Create from File** button – the dialog box changes to resemble Figure 8.5 on the following page.

4 Click the **Link** box – this creates the link.

Click the **Browse** button – we need to find the file **MAP1**.

Make sure that the diskette drive is selected in the **Look in:** box.

Select the **MAP1** icon and click the **Insert** button.

You are returned to the **Insert Object** dialog box. Click **OK** and you are returned to the Wordpad document

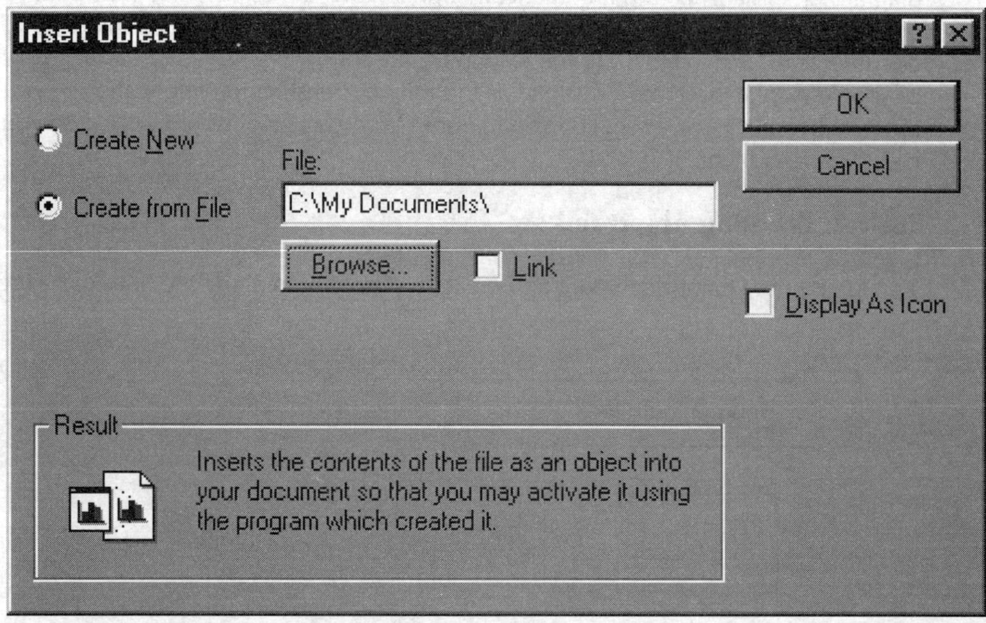

Figure 8.5

5 The map is inserted in the Wordpad document and is now linked to the original in the document **MAP1**.

Save the Wordpad document to diskette as **DOC2**.

6. To edit a linked drawing, double click on the map image: the Paint document **MAP1** containing the original map image is opened.

   Re-size and move the Wordpad window and the Paint window so that the map image is visible in both documents (drag the top window using the title bar).

   Amend the drawing by adding an IT Centre to the map as shown in Figure 8.6.

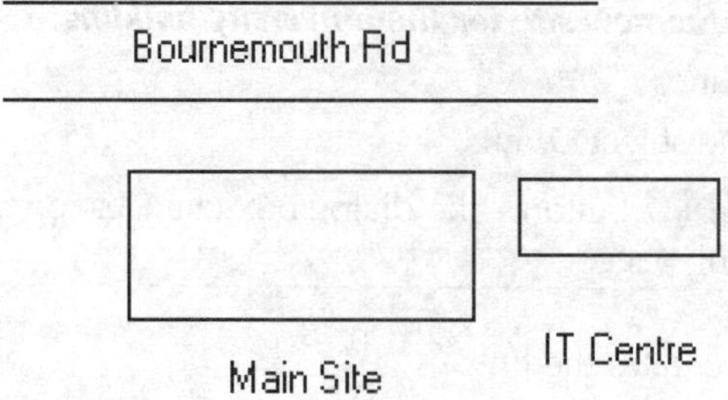

Figure 8.6

You will see that both images are linked and change at the same time.

7 Open the **File** menu in the Paint window and choose **Save** (this may take a long time as the links have to be saved too).

Open the **File** menu in the Paint window and choose **Exit**.

In the Wordpad document **DOC2** the linked image has also changed. Save the changes.

Task 3: Maintaining links

The links that we have established so far mean that any updates to linked objects are automatic, however you can make the links manual so that you can choose whether the linked object gets updated. You can also break or delete links and fix broken links, e.g. if the name of a linked document is changed.

At the moment, the linked object in the Wordpad document **DOC2** is updated automatically. We can change this default so that the update in optional.

1 Make sure that **DOC2** is still open

Right click anywhere on the map image – a pop-up menu appears.

Select the **Object Properties** option.

A dialog box appears, select the **Link** tab. The link to the Paint document **MAP1** is shown.

Click the **Update Manually** button.

Click **OK**.

2 Now double click on the map image; the Paint document **MAP1** containing the original map image is opened as before.

Arrange the Wordpad window and the Paint window as before, so that the map image is visible in both documents.

Amend the Paint image by removing the IT Centre from the map – use the Eraser tool (see Figure 8.2 above if necessary).

Open the **File** menu in the Paint window and choose **Save**.

Open the **File** menu in the Paint window and choose **Exit**.

3 In the Wordpad document **DOC2** the linked image has not changed. This is because the link is now manual.

To update the link repeat step 1, but this time click the **Update Now** button.

Re-set the Update to **Automatically** then select **Close** – the link is updated and the IT Centre image is also removed from the linked Wordpad document DOC2.

4 End this task by saving and closing the Wordpad document **DOC2**.

Task 4: Amending the original document

A linked object can be worked on in both the client and the server application. In the previous task we edited the map image from within the client application, Wordpad. But we can just as easily do it from the server application, Paint. As the object is shared rather than copied then all linked client documents will change as well.

1 Open the Paint document **MAP1** and make a change to the map image.
Save the changes and exit the document.

2 Now that the link is set to automatic the linked document will also be updated. Open the linked Wordpad document **DOC2** – you will find that the map is updated.

3 For the object linking to work, OLE needs access to both files. Experiment by moving or renaming the paint document.
End this task by closing all Wordpad and Paint documents.

Summary of commands

Commands show the object to select first, followed by the command to choose from the menu, e.g. Start Button-Help means click the **Start** button and select the **Help** command.

Edit - Copy	Copy selected section onto the Clipboard
Edit - Links	Maintain links between linked documents
Edit - Paste	Insert copied section into document
Insert-Object	Insert object into document from another file

Backing up and checking your system

Introduction

In this unit we will be creating backups of files and using the disk utilities Defragment, DriveSpace and ScanDisk. We will also learn how to compress a disk, check hardware components and schedule tasks.

What you should know already

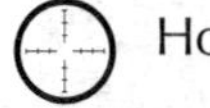

How to use the standard Windows components – see Unit 1.

What you need

Practice diskettes 'a' and 'b'.

What you will learn in this unit

By the end of this unit you will be able to:

- backup and restore data
- check disks and other system components
- defragment and compress disks
- schedule tasks.

Backing up

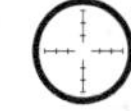

You already know how to copy files from one diskette to another and from hard disk to diskette (see Unit 5). However, to protect the programs and data on your PC you need to establish organised backup procedures. The hard drive or a diskette may fail, you may lose a box of diskettes, or the whole PC may break down. The cost to you (or your business) of lost data may be enormous, far exceeding the costs of the disks or hardware.

There are various backup methods, e.g. a regular backup of all files or an incremental backup of only those files that have changed. Often more than one set of backups of different 'generations' are kept. It is good policy to store the backups securely at a different location to the originals.

The backup media will vary depending on your needs and resources. Backup to diskettes is still used but the increasing size of data and program files on hard disk make this increasingly impractical. Backup to tape or zip drive is increasingly used by business and home users for mass offline storage. Backup to another hard disk is often used on networked PC's.

The Windows 98 Backup utility allows you define and save a backup set as a special file that defines which sets of files you want to back up; this file can then be run whenever you want to repeat the backup.

Task 1: Backing up your data

1 Click the **Start** button, then select **Programs** then **Accessories** and **System Tools**.

Backup should be located in this folder – see Figure 9.1.

Click this option to open the Backup application.

Figure 9.1

If you cannot find Backup it may not have been installed. If you have access to the Windows 98 installation CD-ROM then proceed as follows (otherwise omit this task or seek help).

Click the **Start** button, then **Settings** and **Control Panel**.

Double click the **Add/Remove Programs** icon.

Click the **Windows Setup** tab then scroll down to the **System Tools** option.

Click the **Details** button to check what is installed and from then on follow the instructions.

2 The first time you start Backup you see a Welcome screen. Make sure that the first option **Create a new backup job** is selected and click **OK**.

The Backup Wizard window opens. Select the second option **Backup selected files....** and then click the **Next** button (see Figure 9.2 opposite).

3 The next **Backup Wizard** dialog box is displayed (see Figure 9.3 opposite). Cancel this dialog box; the **Microsoft Backup** dialog box is now displayed.

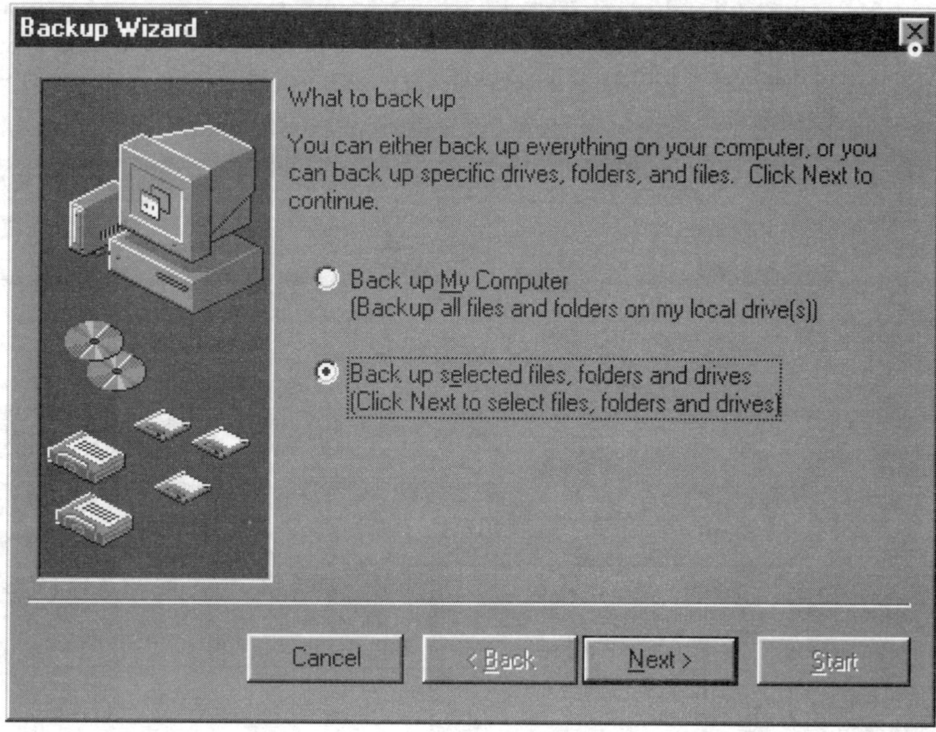

Figure 9.2

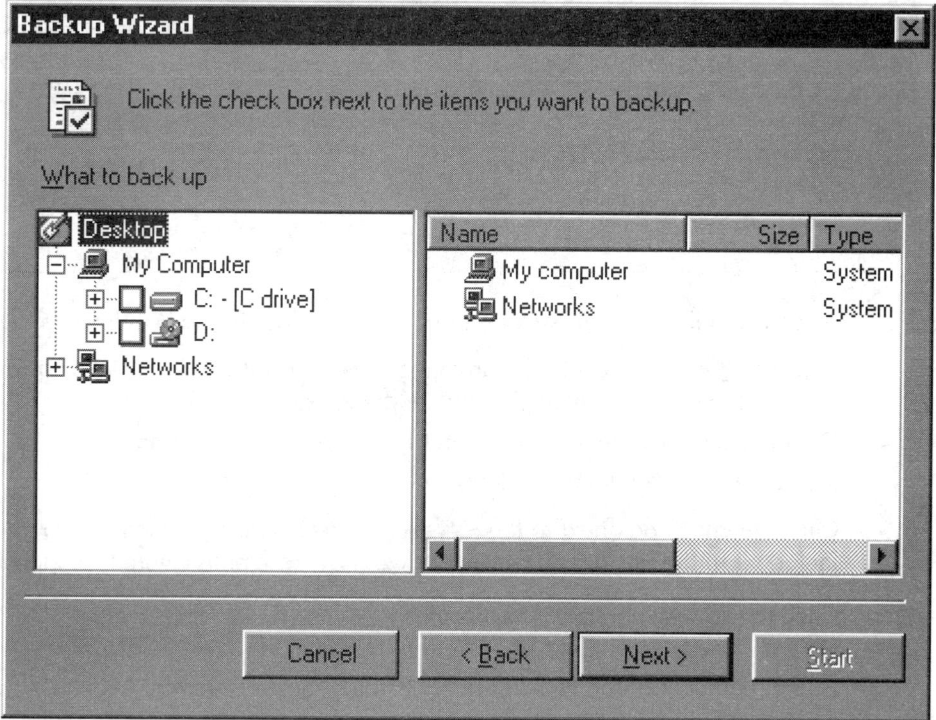

Figure 9.3

4 In the left hand pane are the drives for your PC. The display is similar to the Explorer window (see Figure 9.4). Next to each drive icon is the usual plus sign to display the folders, plus a checkbox which you click to include the drive in the backup.

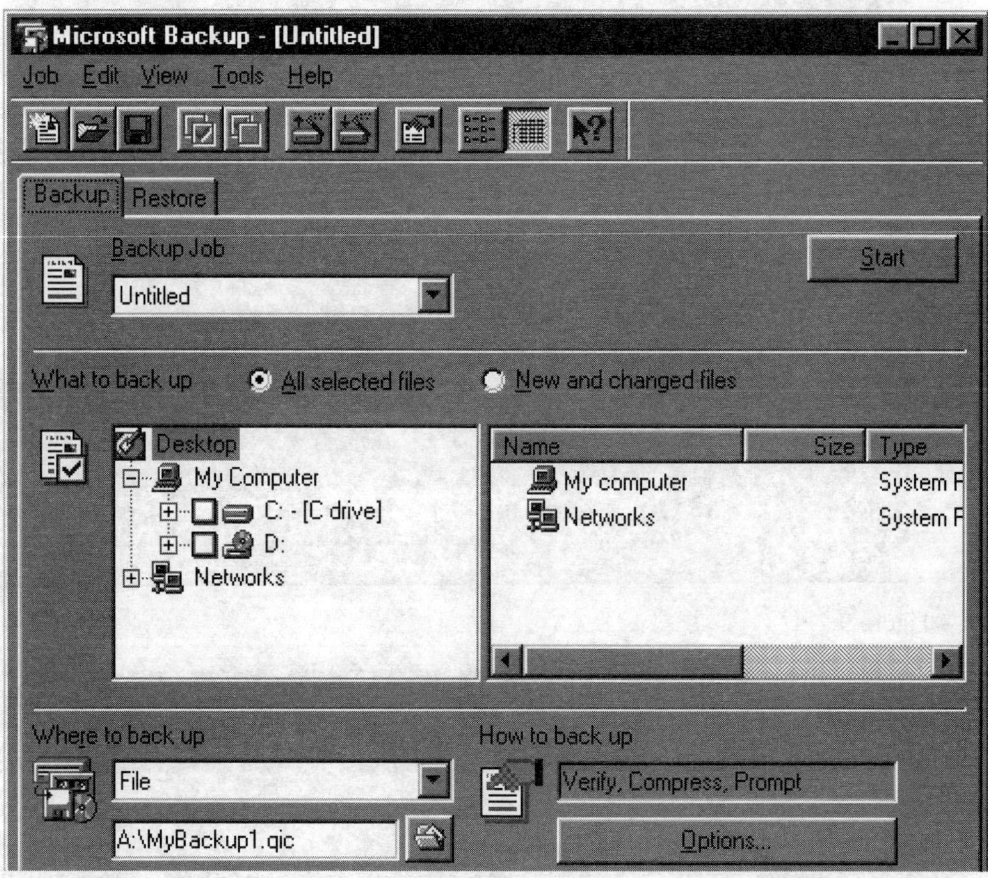

Figure 9.4

5 As an example, we will back up the **Fonts** subfolder in the **Windows** folder.

Click the **+** sign next to the drive icon that holds the **Windows** folder (usually C) – the folders are displayed in the left hand pane.

Double click the **Windows** folder in order to display its contents.

Identify the **Fonts** folder and double click to open it.

Click the check box next to the **Fonts folder** icon i*n the left hand pane* to include it in the backup. The window will now resemble Figure 9.5 opposite.

Click the **Next** button if necessary.

6 At the moment, all the files in the **Fonts** folder are selected for backup – about 5Mb of data to back up.

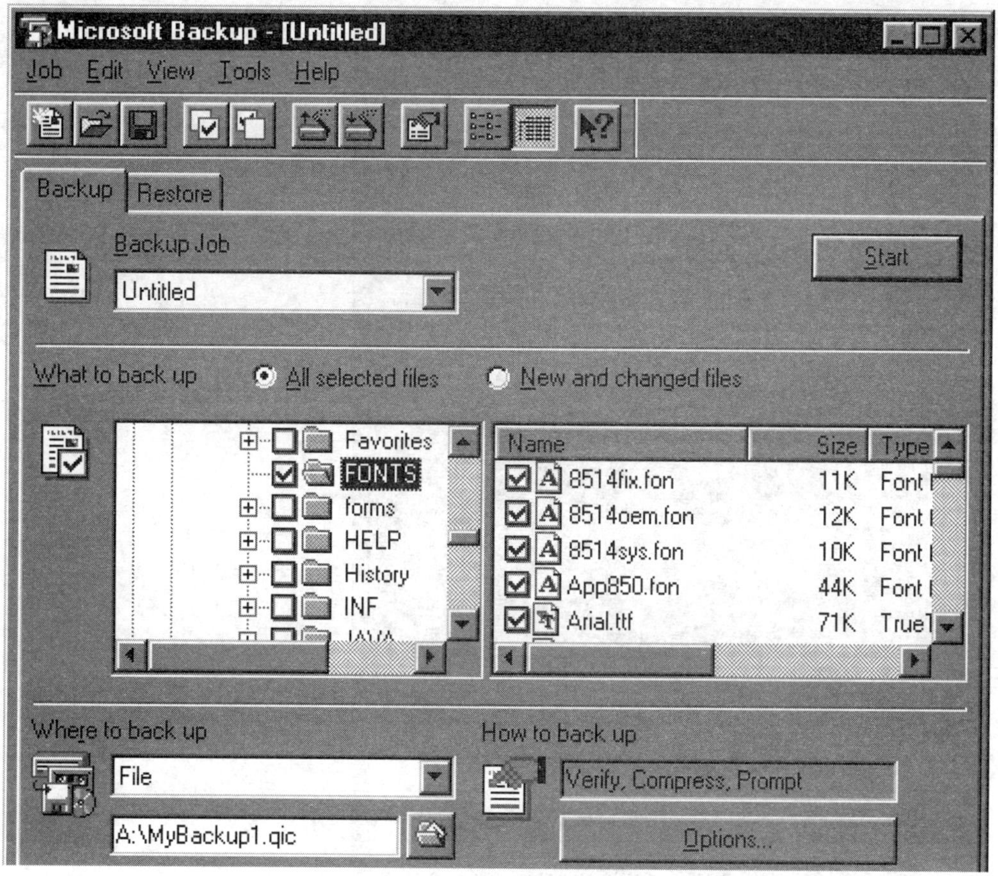

Figure 9.5

For illustration purposes we will choose a more limited number of files and exclude the True Type font files from the backup.

Click the **Options** button at the bottom of the dialog box.

7 The **Backup Job Options** dialog box appears; click the **Exclude** tab – see Figure 9.6 on the following page.

Click the **Add** button and a list of file types is displayed.

Scroll through this list and select **.ttf TrueType Font File** then click the **OK** button – it is added to the list.

The list should now resemble Figure 9.7 on the following page.

Click the **OK** button.

The Backup window is displayed again and only a few files are now shown to be included in the backup.

If the wrong files are selected repeat this step, click the **Remove** button and try again.

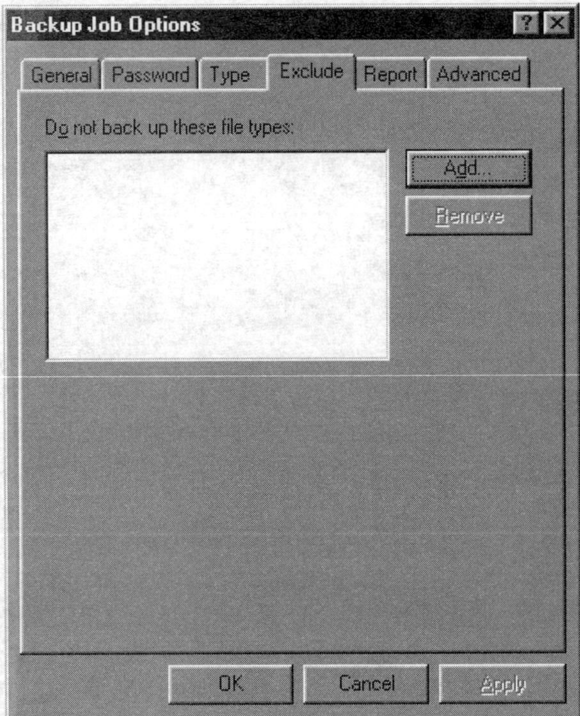

Figure 9.6

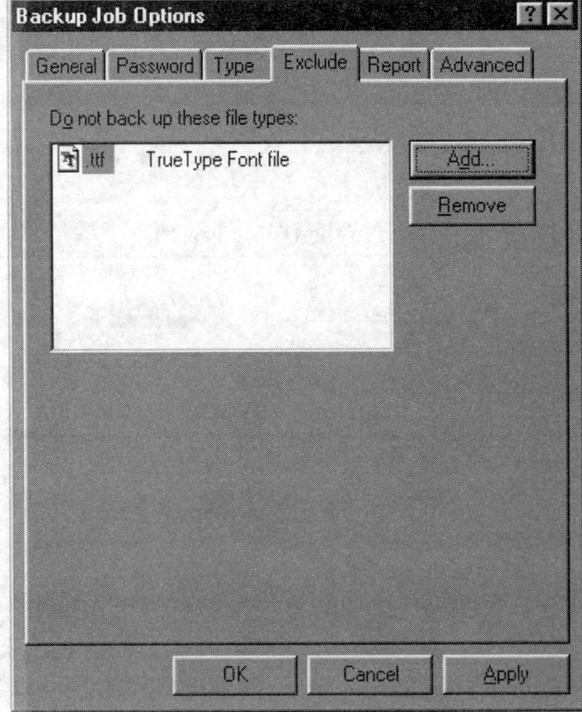

Figure 9.7

8 You must now give the backup a name and choose a destination drive for the backup. We will use practice diskette 'b'. Insert it in the disk drive now.

At the bottom left of the backup window there is a **Where to back up** section.

Leave the **file** option unchanged and click the button next to the drive box below.

A **Where to back up** dialog box appears – see Figure 9.8.

Alter the **Look in** box to **3 $\frac{1}{2}$ floppy (A:)**.

If necessary amend the name of the backup file to **MyBackup1**.

Click the **Open** button to return to the main backup dialog box.

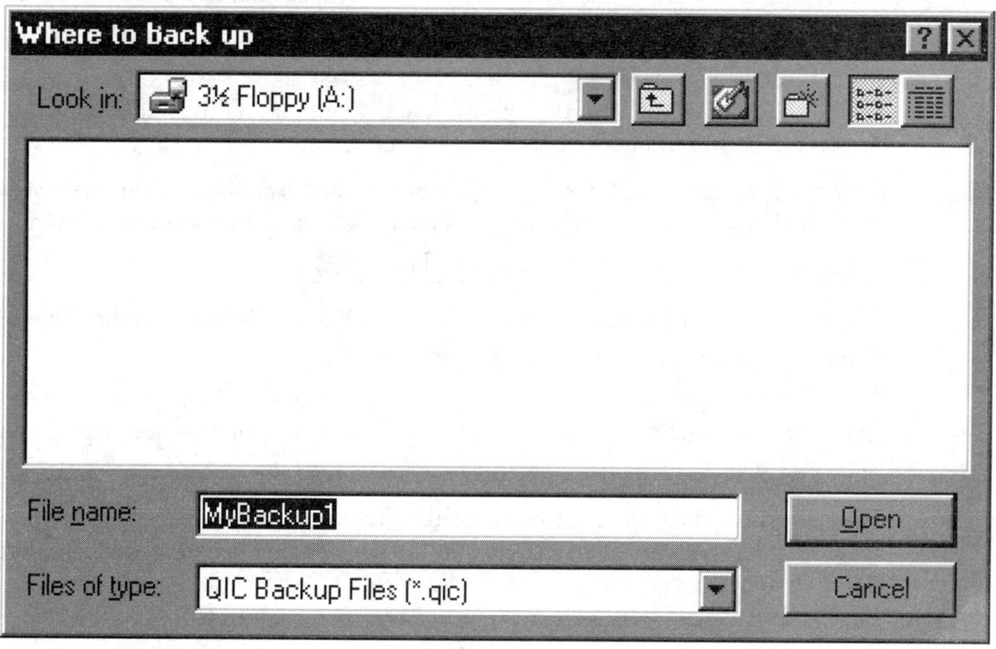

Figure 9.8

9 We have now selected files to backup, plus a destination drive and file name.

We must now save the backup job itself under a name before we can run the backup (you save the backup instructions as a named file so that it can be run whenever you want to backup the same set of files again).

Open the **Job** menu at the top of the dialog box and select **Save as**.

Name the backup job **backjob1**

Click the **Save** button and you are returned to the main backup dialog box.

Finally, click the **Start** button and the backup job starts; a dialog box reports its progress.

Notice that the files have been compressed to save on disk space. If you click the **Report** button, more details of the job are given.

Click the **OK** button to return to the main backup dialog box.

10 Let's review some backup options. Click the **Options** button.

A dialog box appears: make sure that the **Type** tab is selected.
We used the default – a full backup, i.e. all files selected. Keep this selection. Differential and incremental backups skip files that have not changed since their last backup.

Click the **General** tab. The default is to check that the backed up files are the same as the originals. Various types of compression are offered.

Review also the **Password** and **Report** tabs.

Click the **OK** button to return to the main backup dialog box. Close it.

11 If all goes well you will never need to use your backup. If you ever lose the data you must retrieve and run it.
This step examines the various options. Make sure that your backup disk, practice disk 'b' is still in the drive.

Click the **Start** Button, then select **Programs** then **Accessories** and **System Tools-Backup**. The Welcome screen appears. Make sure that the third option **Restore backed up files** is selected and click **OK**.

12 The **Restore Wizard** dialog box appears; check that the options are the same as Figure 9.9 opposite and click the **Next** button.
The **Select Backup Sets** dialog box appears next; check that the job is **backjob1**. This is the job which backs up certain files in the Fonts folder – see steps above.

Click **OK**.
The **Restore Wizard** dialog box shows the drive(s) in the left hand window; keep opening the drives and folders and the backed up files are displayed – see Figure 9.10 opposite.
You now have the option to restore all the files or select certain ones.

13 Press the **Next** button and the next dialog box asks you to confirm that you want to restore the files to their original location. This is the usual option when you are restoring to the same computer. An alternate location may be useful if you are restoring files to another computer with a different directory structure.

Click the **Next** button again.

14 The final **Restore Wizard** dialog box allows you to choose whether to overwrite any files that may still exist; you can choose whether any files with the same name are automatically overwritten, or only older versions with the same name. These options are important if files have changed since they were backed up and you do not wish to restore an earlier version.

As we have only just performed the backup there is no point in proceeding with Restore as nothing has changed. Click the **Cancel** button and exit Backup.

Figure 9.9

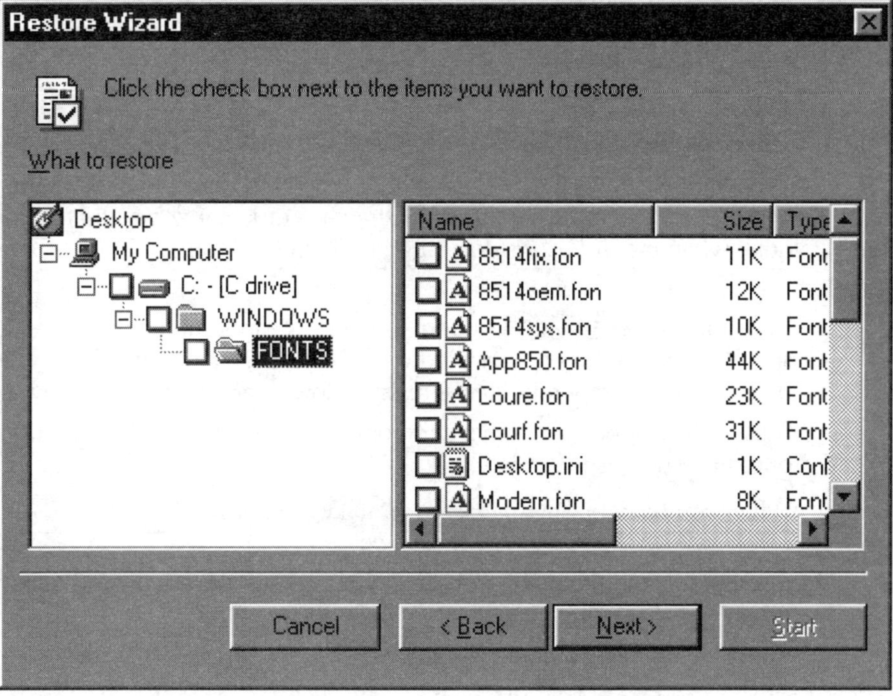

Figure 9.10

15 You may wonder where the backup file is stored.

Open **Explorer** and then open the drive containing the **Windows** folder. It contains the **Program Files** folder – open this and then open the **Accessories** and the **Systems Tools** folders. You will see that it contains a **Backup** folder.

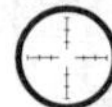

If desired you could create a shortcut to this folder (see Unit 7).

16 Providing you have the authority to copy files to the hard disk, back up the files in the **Accounts** folder on practice disk 'a' to the hard disk.

Save the backup set as a file and then restore them.

Checking and managing your system

The next few tasks are aimed at users who want to understand more about the technical aspects of their PC and its operating environment. A grasp of underlying theory can help you to use your PC more effectively and to solve problems for yourself. First a note of caution however: a little knowledge can be very dangerous, especially if it leads to casual and thoughtless tinkering with vital settings. This is never justified – especially on a machine that is shared with others! In many of these tasks, therefore, you will be observing and finding out about your system rather than changing it.

Task 2: Checking a disk

1 Open the My Computer application and right click the icon for your PC's hard disk, e.g. C drive.

Select **Properties** from the menu that appears.

2 The **Properties** dialog box opens; make sure that the **General** tab is selected.

The window shows the total capacity of the hard disk and the amount of free and used space. You can also label the hard disk, something that is normally done when the disk is first formatted (see Unit 3, Task 1).

3 Click the **Disk Cleanup** button; the Disk Cleanup utility calculates how much space it can free up on your hard drive by emptying the Recycle bin, and deleting other temporary files, e.g. ones downloaded from the Internet.

A list of files appears; you have the option of viewing the files before marking the ones that you wish to delete.

When you have finished click the **Cancel** button.

4 Insert practice diskette 'b', right click the diskette drive icon and open the **Properties** dialog box again.

Check the amount of free disk space.

Click the **Tools** tab – three disk utilities are offered. Click the **Help (?)** button, top right of the window and find out what each does.

- *Error-checking status* This uses the ScanDisk utility to check for and repair errors. It can detect sectors (parts of tracks) on the disk surface that are bad or about to fail and mark them so they are not used. This should be done periodically, especially when disks get older. ScanDisk will also automatically check your hard disk if the computer was turned off or crashed while files were still open and try to recover them.
- *Backup status* We have already used backup in Task 1.
- *Defragmentation status* As old files are deleted they leave scattered spaces free on disk. A new file may be fitted into a number of these spaces, i.e. fragmented, rather than as one contiguous block. Such files take longer to retrieve from disk, and need defragmenting to reorganise them, especially when data is being added and deleted frequently. The Defragmenter moves files around on the disk until all the parts of a file are stored next to each other. This should be done regularly on hard drives. We will do this in the next task.

5 To use ScanDisk, click the **Check Now** button. A dialog box appears – see Figure 9.11.

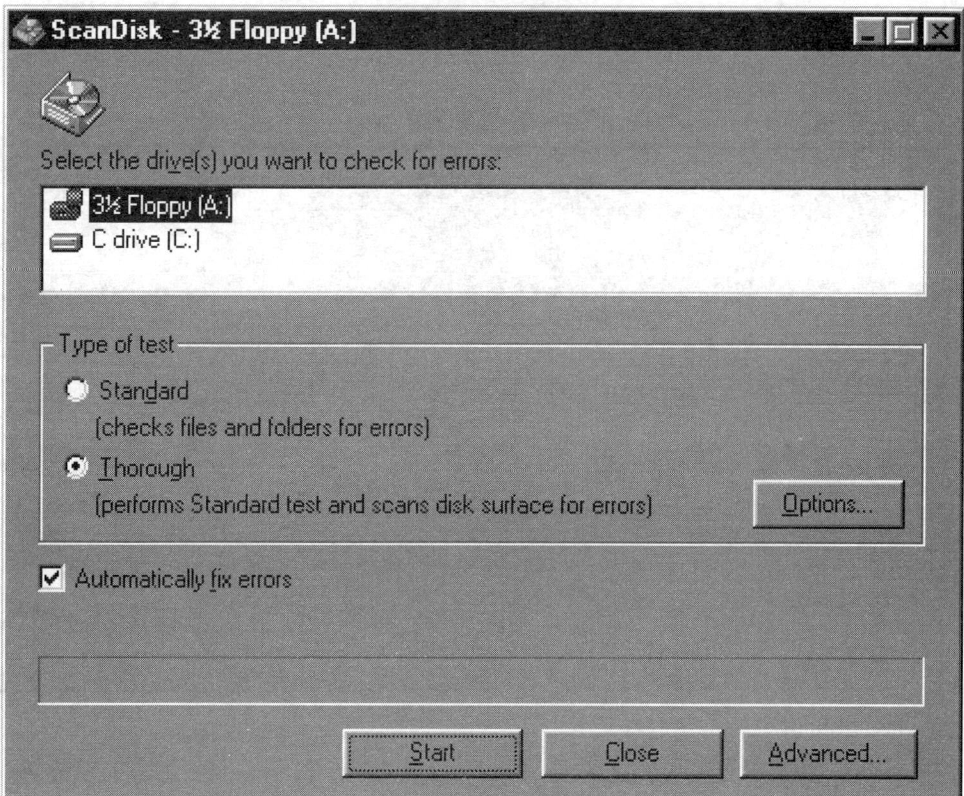

Figure 9.11

Make sure the diskette icon is selected, and select the **Thorough** option which checks the disk surface as well as files and folders.

Click the **Start** button.

The diskette is checked for errors – a slow process which you can cancel at any time. If ScanDisk detects an error you will be asked if you want it fixed, in which case click **Yes**.

Eventually a results window shows the number of bad sectors (if any) and other disk information.

Close the ScanDisk window.

Task 3: Defragmenting a disk

We will use the **Start** button to start this utility as it offers certain options not available from My Computer.

1 Close the My Computer window and click the **Start** button.

Choose the options **Programs-Accessories-System Tools-Disk Defragmenter**

A dialog box appears, perhaps telling you that your disk does not need defragmenting.

Select the **Drive A** option and click the **Settings** button. A further dialog box appears (see Figure 9.12).

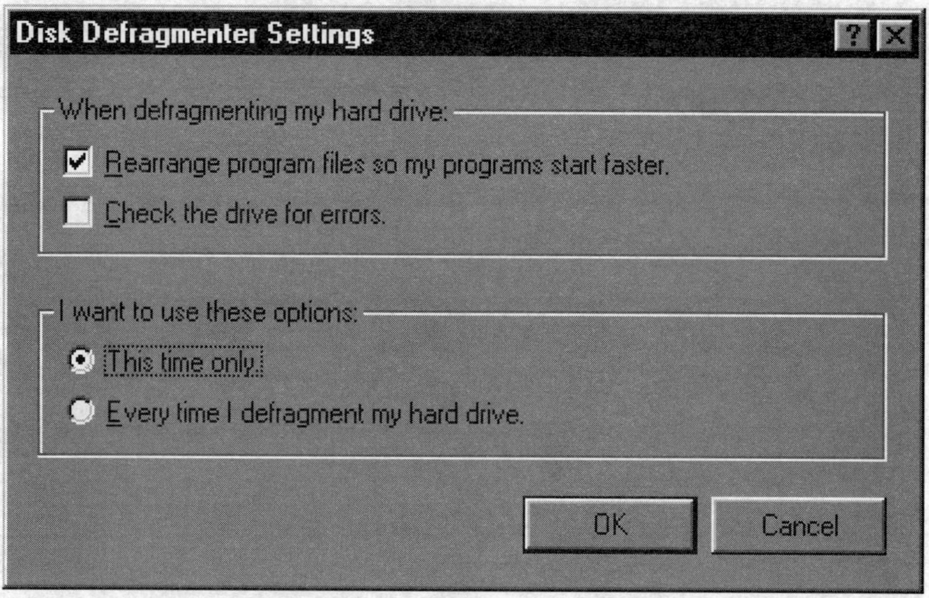

Figure 9.12

2 Leave the first option selected.

Deselect the second option **Check the drive for errors** (we have already done this using ScanDisk).

Select the third option **This time only**. The settings used will only apply to this session.

Click **OK** – you are returned to the **Disk Defragmenter** dialog box.

Click the **OK** button.

3 Click the **Show Details** button to see the defragmentation in progress.

Click the **Legend** button for an explanation of the defragment process – you can see which clusters are being moved.

When you are finished, exit from the Defragmenter (you can choose to exit at any time or run the process in the background while you are working with other applications).

DriveSpace

You can create more space on hard drives and diskettes using the Windows 98 DriveSpace utility – up to double the available disk space in many cases. This is achieved by compressing the disk. You can either compress an entire drive (including existing files), the free space, or part of a drive. The compressed files are only readable on a PC with Windows 98 installed. However, a compressed disk can be decompressed if you need to use it on a PC that does not have Windows 98.

When a drive is compressed another drive letter is assigned to the disk, e.g. drive C becomes drive H. Part of the drive remains uncompressed and is called the *host drive,* (H), the remainder of the drive is compressed into a single file: a *compressed volume file* or CVF (C). Diskettes can also be compressed in a similar way.

Read this before trying the next task!

Unless you are running short of disk space you do not need to use DriveSpace. Once you have used DriveSpace you must continue to use Windows 98 in order to access the compressed drive – the Windows Uninstall utility is disabled. This applies even to diskettes. So if you are sharing a PC with others you may decide not to go ahead with this task, or stop at step 5.

Task 4: Compressing disks using DriveSpace

1 Insert practice disk 'b' in the diskette drive.

Click the **Start** button and select **Programs** then **Accessories** and finally **Systems Tools**.

Select **DriveSpace**.

2 Select the diskette drive from the window that appears.

Open the **Drive** menu and select **Compress**. A dialog box appears showing the estimated compression gains.

Click the **Options** button.

3 The **Compression Options** dialog box appears offering three options.

Drive letter of host drive The default is H – you can change it if this letter has been used or will be used for another drive. If so, choose another letter.

Free space on host drive Leave this set at 0.00. You can choose to leave part of the disk uncompressed, normally because certain programs will not run on compressed drives. You would need to adjust the free space to hold these programs.

Use Double-Space Compatible format Select this option if you will use the diskette on a computer that is running Windows 95.

Click the **OK** button to return to the main dialog box and click the **Start** button.

---

4 A message box informs you that compression may take some time and offers you the option of backing up files. This is a wise precaution, although compression is very reliable you need to guard against accidents. You may also need uncompressed copies to use on a PC without the DriveSpace utility. However, we already have copies of the files on practice disk 'a' so we may safely skip this precaution in this instance.

Click the **Compress Now** button.

---

5 If you get the message:

'If you continue you will no longer be able to uninstall Windows 98
Do you want to continue?'

– click the **No** button, read the note at the start of this task and consider your options!

---

6 When compression is complete, a dialog box displays the compression statistics.

Return to the DriveSpace window for the compressed drive.

Exit to the My Computer window.

Right click the drive icon and select **Properties**. Click the **Compression** tab in the dialog box to see further information on space savings.

---

7 You may decide to *uncompress a drive,* e.g. a diskette may need to be decompressed to use it in another PC.

Select the drive in the DriveSpace Window.

Open the **Drive** menu and select **Uncompress**. A dialog box shows you the space available after the disk is uncompressed.

Click the **Start** button.

- *Adjusting free space* If you need more uncompressed space on disk (see step 3) open the **Drive** menu and select **Adjust Free Space**.
- *Compression agent,* also in the System Tools Folder, allows you to compress existing compressed drives even further.

---

8 Exit DriveSpace.

The System option

The **System** option in the Control Panel provides technical information and diagnostics about all aspects of your system, including the hardware. Some are too technical for a publication of this type but others can be used to provide useful supplementary information such as the type of central processing unit, hard disk types and memory.

Task 5: Checking your system

1 Click the **Start** button and select the **Settings** then the **Control Panel** option.

Double click the **System** icon.

The System Properties window appears displaying general information about your PC including the processor type (Pentium, MMX etc.) and the amount of RAM or main memory in megabytes (Mb).

2 Click the **Performance** tab. Various information is given on your PC's performance.

If you are unclear about the meaning of a technical term click the **Help** button **(?)** at the top right of the dialog box, then click the term itself.

Check the percentage of free System Resources; it will vary depending on the number of tasks and applications running. It is a good idea to check this if your PC appears to be running slowly. When you close a large application the percentage should increase.

Windows 98 configures your PC for optimum usage; there may be a window displaying additional information if your PC is not set up for optimum performance.

3 Click the **Device Manager** tab. A dialog box appears. Device Manager allows you to check and change the devices connected to your system.

Pictured in the window are a list of devices on your system (see, for example, Figure 9.13 on the following page).

To expand the information click the **+** sign next to the device. All the devices of that type (often only one) are shown.

To find out more about a device type click it and select the **Properties** option.

4 Click the **+** sign next to **System devices**. A list appears.

If a device is marked with an exclamation mark this indicates a problem.

Double click on some of these devices to find out more about them. Often the only information is that the device is working correctly.

Click the **–** sign to close the system devices list.

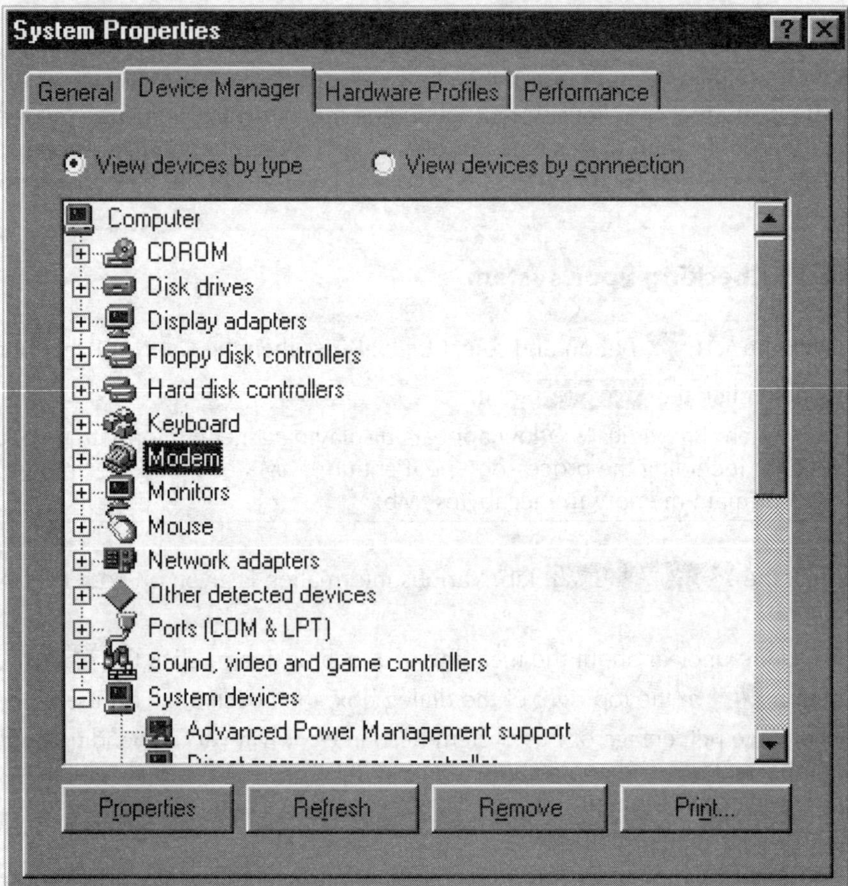

Figure 9.13

5 Exit from the **System Properties** dialog box and close the **Control Panel**.

Task 6: Checking the screen display

1 Click the **Start** button and select the **Settings** then the **Control Panel** option.

Double click the **Display** icon.

The Display Properties window appears, displaying general information about your VDU.

2 Click the **Background** . This dialog box allows you to choose a background pattern for your desktop.

3 Click the **Screen Saver** tab. A screen saver typically turns on a moving pattern if the computer is not used for a few minutes. You can use this dialog box to preview and change your screen saver and alter the length of time before it starts.

You can also require a password to be input before the screen saver display can be restored; this has the advantage of keeping your PC free from interference while you are away from it – providing that you don't forget it!

4 To save power, if your VDU is Energy Star compatible, you may be able to set it to turn off automatically if it has not been used for a certain period of time.

If the **Screen Saver** dialog box displays a section **Energy saving features of monitor** click the **Settings** button.

A new dialog box is displayed; make sure that the **Power Schemes** tab is selected. The Power Schemes section allows you to select a scheme for a certain type of use (home, portable etc.). Try out various schemes and the 'turn off' time changes too (see Figure 9.14).

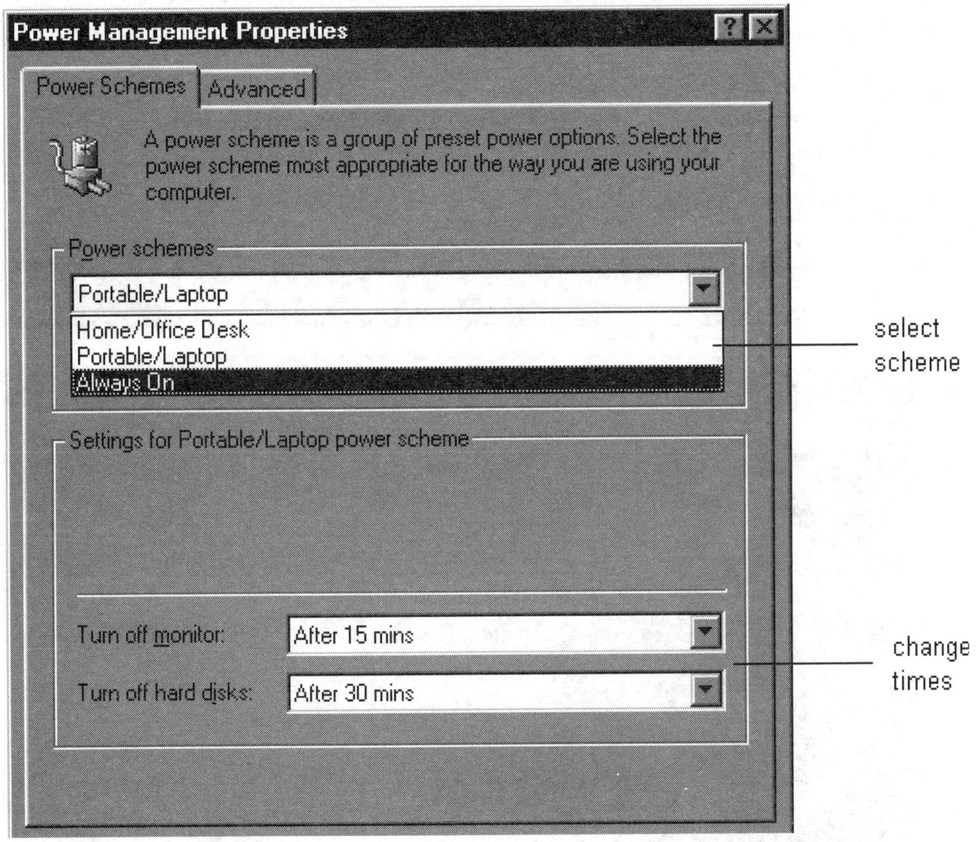

Figure 9.14

The 'turn off' fields can be changed too – these are the times the system waits to shut down if there is no keyboard or mouse input.

Exit from this dialog box.

5 Click the **Settings** tab. This dialog box allows you to change the VDU colour and resolution. How useful this is depends on the quality of your VDU; on low resolution monitors increasing the screen area will lower the colour depth (and vice versa).

6 Exit from the **Display Properties** dialog box and close the **Control Panel**.

Task 7: Scheduling tasks

In this unit you have learnt some standard maintenance tasks such as scanning, defragmenting and backing up disks. The Task Scheduler utility lets you schedule them to run regularly as background tasks at convenient times. You can schedule a task to run daily, weekly or monthly, at a specific time, or when the computer starts up.

1 Click the **Start** button and select **Programs-Accessories-System Tools** then **Scheduled Tasks**. The Task Scheduler window opens.

Double click the icon **Add Scheduled Task** and the **Scheduled Task Wizard** dialog box opens.

Click the **Next** button.

2 The next dialog box lists applications for you to schedule – see Figure 9.15.

For demonstration purposes choose **Calculator** and click the **Next** button.

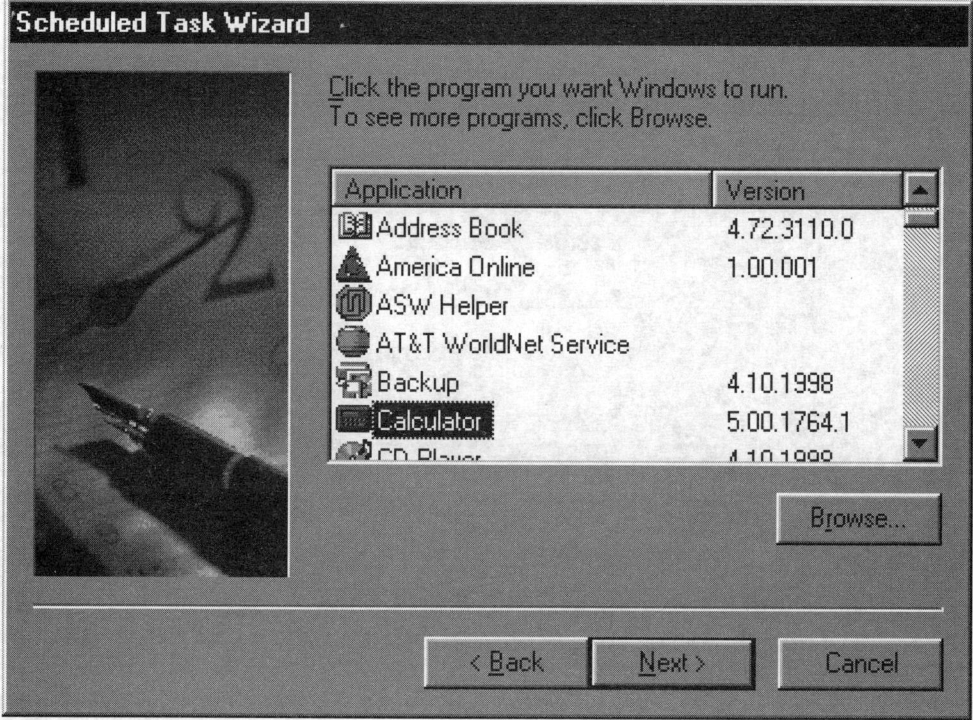

Figure 9.15

3 On the next dialog box select the **One time only** option and click the **Next** button.

4 The next dialog box lets you set the date and time for the Scheduled task; check the current time in the taskbar and schedule it for two minutes time.

Click the **Next** button.

5 The next dialog box confirms the task has been scheduled. Click the **Finish** button.

The Task Scheduler window now shows the task (see Figure 9.16).

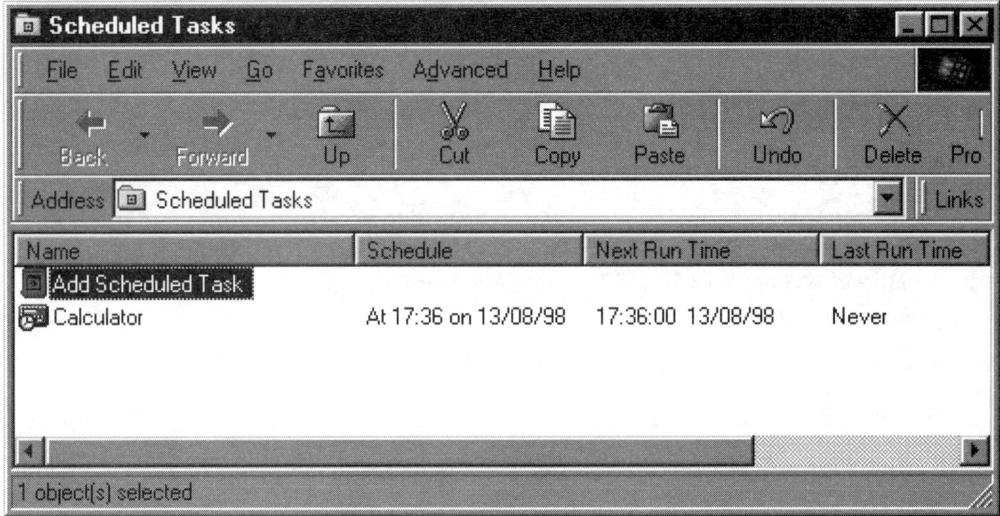

Figure 9.16

6 The Calculator application should now start at the time you have scheduled. Close it.

7 If you wish you can delete this task by right clicking the task icon and selecting the **Delete** command.

Close Task Scheduler now.

Task Scheduler is normally always running in the background – ready to carry out any tasks that you have scheduled. An icon appears on the taskbar to confirm this – see Figure 9.17.

Figure 9.17

If you turn off Task Scheduler it will not start automatically the next time you start Windows and any scheduled tasks will not run.

To turn it off open My Computer and then the **Scheduled Tasks** folder.

Open the **Advanced** menu and select **Stop Using Task Scheduler**.

You can also use this window to stop tasks that are running.

---

8 To start Maintenance Wizard, click the **Start** button and select **Programs - Accessories-System Tools** then **Maintenance Wizard**. Similar to Task Scheduler, Maintenance Wizard lets you schedule times to run the three utilities Disk Defragmenter, ScanDisk and Disk Cleanup – see Tasks 2 and 3 above.

Click the **Custom** option on the dialog box that appears, then click the **Next** button. The Wizard lets you set different times to run the three utilities, e.g. either daily, monthly, when the computer is started or when it is idle.

Proceed with the Wizard if you wish or cancel it.

Summary of commands

Menu commands show the menu name first, followed by the command to choose from the menu, e.g. Edit-Clear means open the **Edit** menu and select the **Clear** command. Where a command is available from a particular window this is indicated in brackets.

Start-Programs-Accessories-System Tools-Backup	Open Backup
Start-Programs-Accessories-System Tools-DriveSpace	Open DriveSpace
Start-Programs-Accessories-System Tools-Disk Defragmenter	Open Defragmenter
Start-Programs-Accessories-System Tools-Scheduled Tasks	Open Task Scheduler
Start-Programs-Accessories-System Tools-Maintenance Wizard	Open Maintenance Wizard
Start-Settings-Control Panel	Open the Control Panel
Start-Settings-System Tools	Open System Tools
(My Computer)	
File-Properties	Show properties of selected object

Section 2

Using Internet Explorer

Internet Explorer is Microsoft's own Web browser and forms a major part of the Windows 98 operating system. In the 1990's the use of the Internet and in particular the World Wide Web (WWW) have grown to a phenomenal extent and for many users represents their main area of computer use. Microsoft have therefore extended the 'look and feel' of a Web browser to the whole of Windows 98. As we have seen in Part 1 you can customise your desktop, windows and folders to give them the appearance of Web pages.

There are many publications offering full coverage of Internet Explorer and the Web; in this book I have concentrated on those aspects of most immediate interest to someone using the Web for the first time. These include:

- connecting to the Web
- browsing and searching
- saving and printing Web pages
- creating your own Web pages
- using email and newsgroups.

The tasks are based on single users connecting to the WWW via modem and phone line rather than via an organisational network.

A brief introduction to the Internet and Web

Internet and the World Wide Web

The Internet is not one network but an interconnected Web of many networks covering the whole globe. The networks are of many kinds – business, government, schools, charities, scientific and many private individuals who can all communicate with each other. The Internet is this system of physical connections – computer networks, telephone, satellite, cable and microwave links. Connected to the Net are many computer 'servers' that provide information; the most popular (but not the only) way to provide the information is via the technology known as the World Wide Web. If a computer system is providing information in this way then it is known as a Web site. There are many Web sites ranging from the private individual with one home page to major government or commercial Web sites with thousands of interconnected pages.

The Web, then, is the sum total of all these information sites on the Internet, plus all the Net users who connect to them. To browse or 'surf' the Web is to use a piece of software called a Web browser to look for information. This is what has made the Internet so popular: anyone can learn to browse using the graphical interface of buttons, icons, images, hyperlinks etc. Browsing is of course only one aspect of the Web, but it is the entry point to the delivery of many new technologies such as multimedia, interactive tv and Internet telephone.

Internet protocols and addresses

With so many different computer systems interconnecting it is vital that they all transmit and receive data using the same rules or 'protocols'. A communication protocol has been developed for the Net – TCP/IP (Transmission Control Protocol/Internet Protocol). This relates closely to Web site addresses or URLs (Universal Resource Locator); take a typical URL such as **http://www.bbc.co.uk**

The **http://** starts all Web site addresses and stands for 'hypertext transport protocol'. When your browser reads this part of the address it confirms that it will be connecting to a Web site that uses TCP/IP, hyperlinks and other Web features.

The **bbc** part is obviously the name of the organisation, **co** identifies it as a commercial organisation, there are many others, e.g., 'ac' identifies an academic organisation such as a university.

The **uk** part identifies the country; not all Web sites have this, e.g. **http://www.microsoft.com.**

Information access providers

Typically a private home user of the Internet and the Web will have the following facilities.

- Internet Explorer or some other browser (e.g. Netscape) installed on their PC.
- A modem connected to the PC. A modem is an electronic device that converts the messages from the PC from digital form (0's and 1's) to analogue (waveform) so the message can travel down ...
- ... a telephone line connected to the modem; this in turn is used to dial up ...
- ... an Information Access Provider or IAP, also known as an Information Service Provider. These are companies that link your PC to the Internet, e.g. CompuServe, America Online and Microsoft. When you subscribe to an IAP they provide you with other services such as electronic mail (email) and information services of their own such as news, financial information and sport.

Other features offered by the Internet Explorer Web browser

Channels If you subscribe to Channels you can automatically stay up-to-date with the latest content of a Web site; the content is updated by the content provider on a regular basis and regularly delivered directly to your desktop.

Security You can screen out objectionable or offensive content by setting your browser to display only the content you specify as suitable. You can also protect your computer from unsafe files, e.g. viruses, by setting levels of security for different areas of the Web. If you need to pay for goods or services on the Web, you can secure sensitive information.

Outlook Express is Internet Explorer's mail and newsgroup program. You can preview messages and download them for offline reading to avoid online connection charges.

Microsoft NetMeeting lets you hold conferences over the Web or a local area network, e.g. place calls over a network, talk or use video over the Internet, or work on a shared application with people at other locations.

FrontPage Express is a Web page editor used to create Web pages. It is compatible with Microsoft FrontPage, the full version of the editor.

Personal Web Server is a tool for publishing Web pages on your own computer to share with other users.

Task Scheduler allows you to schedule and run routine tasks – it starts each time you start Windows and runs in the background to carry out the tasks you want done at specified times, e.g. backups.

unit 10

Web browsing and searching

Introduction

In this unit you will use Internet Explorer to connect to various Web sites and learn how to browse and to search. You will find out how to store the addresses of your favourite Web sites and how to save and print information from the Web.

What you should know already

How to use the standard Window components – see Unit 1.

What you will learn in this unit

By the end of this unit you will be able to:

- connect to the Web and check your connection
- use standard Internet Explorer commands and features
- find out a Web site address
- browse the Web
- store Web addresses using Favorites
- use channels
- use a subject directory and a search engine
- save and print Web pages.

Task: 1 Connecting to the Web

Windows provides many points of access to the Web. The easiest are the icons provided on the desktop and the taskbar. Additionally you can gain access from folder windows, depending how your View options have been set up (see Unit 4, Task 1). If you are accessing the Web from work or college there may well be additional windows for you to use. What follows is a typical connection routine.

1 If you are using a new computer, or one that you share with others it is a good idea to check the initial settings *before* you use Internet Explorer.

Open the **Start** menu and select **Settings-Control Panel**

Double click the **Internet** icon. A dialog box appears.

2 First make sure that the **General** tab is selected. Make sure that the home page is set to **http://home.microsoft.com/** (this is the page we will be using in the tasks that follow).

Now click the **Connection** tab. Make sure that the option **Connect to the Internet using a modem** is selected. Click the **Settings** button.

The **Dial-Up Settings** dialog box appears. You can check the details of your Internet Access account, user name and password.

3 Ensure that the **Disconnect if idle...** option is set to a reasonable time, e.g. five minutes. This means that your computer will be automatically disconnected from the Net after five minutes if you make no key stroke or mouse movement, thereby saving on phone bills.

Click **OK** to exit from both dialog boxes.

Close the **Control Panel**.

4 Double click the **Internet Explorer** icon on the desktop. If the Microsoft home page is displayed then carry on with step 6.

Unless you or your organisation have already made the connection to your access provider, a dialog box may appear, similar to Figure 10.1. It is advising you that the *browser* software (Internet Explorer) on your PC cannot find the *Home Page* (at the Microsoft Web site) *offline*, i.e. on your local computer system, and needs to connect to the Net to access it.

Click the **Connect** button.

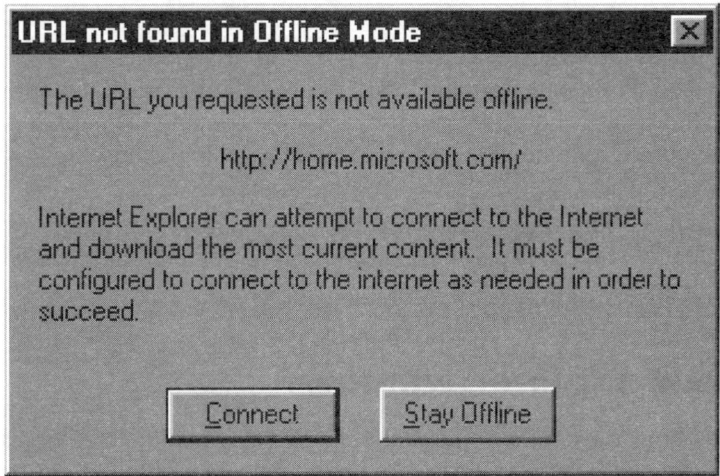

Figure 10.1

5 A further **Dial-up Connection** dialog box may appear for you to enter your user name and password. Do so and click the **Connect** button.

Your computer will then dial the number of your access provider, who then checks your user name and password and connects you, via their own communication links, to the Internet and the Microsoft home page.

Most access providers supply comprehensive Internet installation guides and help desks. These are your best guide; some obvious checks to make are:

- whether any shared phone line is already in use,
- that the cabling connections between the port at the back of your PC, any external modem, and the phone socket that you are using are secure
- with your IT services department, if you are connected via a local area network
- whether your username, hostname, password etc. need to be entered in lower case.

6 You are now connected, via Internet and the Web, to the Microsoft home page. If you do nothing you should be disconnected automatically in five minutes! A small icon, shown on the right of your taskbar, verifies your connection (see Figure 10.2).

Figure 10.2

Right click this icon and select **Status** from the pop-up menu – a dialog box shows your transmission speed and how long you have been connected.

7 This dialog box is the easiest way to make sure you disconnect – do so now. The connection icon disappears from the taskbar but the home page continues to be displayed offline; this is because your browser software (Internet Explorer) is still running on your PC and the Web page is still in the main memory.

8 Although the home page is still stored in your PC's memory, few if any of the other home pages will be. Experiment by clicking on some of the buttons. You will probably be prompted to reconnect – do so.

The Internet Explorer window

We'll take some time to examine some of the main features of the Internet Explorer Window before trying them out. Don't worry that the content of the Microsoft home page differs from Figure 10.4. Web pages tend to be updated regularly.

The Title, Menu and toolbars should be displayed; if not then use the next section to adjust the settings as follows.

If the Title and Menu bars are not displayed you may be in Full Screen mode; click the **Full Screen** icon to de-select it - see Figure 10.3.

Figure 10.3

If the Address Bar and the standard buttons are not displayed open the **View** menu and select **Toolbars**; make sure that all the options are selected.

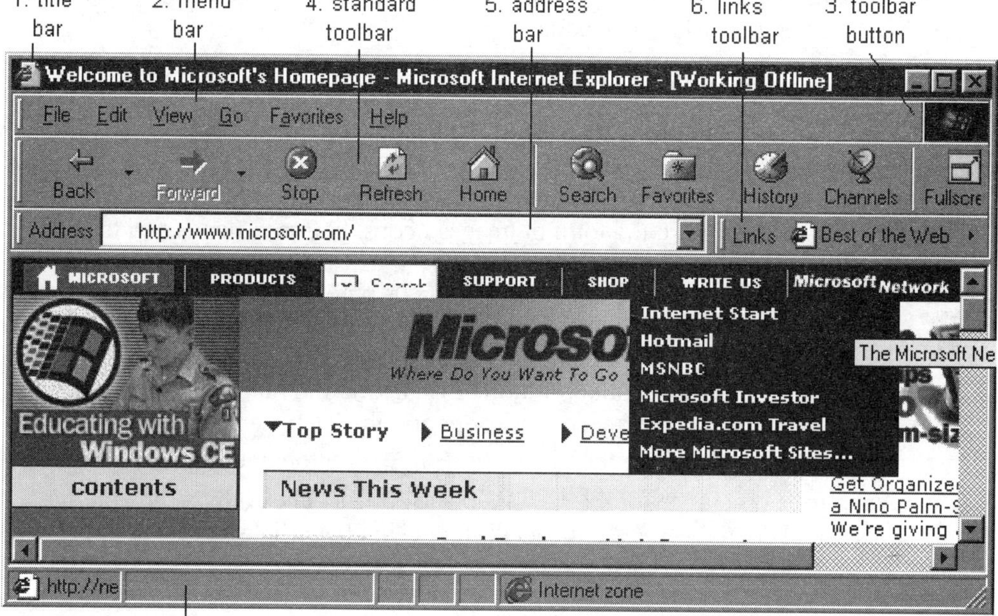

Figure 10.4

1 *The Title bar* shows both the name of the browser (Internet Explorer) and the title of the Web page currently displayed.

2 *The Menu bar* displays various menus – **File**, **Edit View** etc.

3 *The Toolbar button* is on the right of the Menu Bar; right clicking it lets you hide or display various toolbars.

4 *The Standard toolbar* displays a number of buttons – **Back**, **Forward**, **Stop** etc. We shall be looking at these in the next task.

5 *The Address bar* shows the Internet address of the current Web site and lets you type a new one. A down arrow lets you select recent ones to re-visit.

6 *The Links toolbar* is displayed to the right of the Address Bar. It provides direct links to a number of Web Sites, initially chosen by Microsoft. You can remove links and add your own.

7 *The Status bar* at the bottom of the window displays

- details of the site you are connecting to,
- progress of a page being loaded and
- the security status you are using.

The My Computer and Windows Explorer windows are now integrated with the Web too. This means that you can access the Web while you are using these utilities. Open My Computer and enter the Web address of the Microsoft home page (***http://home.microsoft.com***). The window displays the Web page; keep it open if you are carrying on with the next task.

Task 2: Basic browser operations

1 Move your cursor around the screen – it becomes hand-shaped, when it rests on a hypertext ('hot') link to another Web site; notice also that the Status Bar shows the Net address of the site. These links have been created by the Web page designer and can take the form of images, icons, buttons, menus and text.

2 To browse, click one of these links. The Status bar shows the address of the site you are trying to link to. It also shows the progress of the connection. This will depend on many factors including the speed of your PC and modem, the traffic on the networks, the location of the Web site, and the number of other users trying to connect to your access provider and the Web site. If a particular link fails or is taking too long then click the **Stop** button and try another link.

When the home page for the new Web site appears click a hyperlink on this page too. When this page appears keep clicking hyperlinks until you have browsed about five pages.

3 Try using the **Forward** and **Back** and **Home** buttons. Click the **Back** button on the Toolbar once to return to the previous Web page selection.

Now click the **Home** button to return directly to Microsoft's home page (or whichever home page you have selected – see step 2).

The **Forward** button will retrace your steps – try this (note that the **Forward** and **Back** buttons are dimmed when you can go no further).

If you wish to view different Web sites at the same time you can start up Internet Explorer again from the desktop and use the second browser window to visit another site.

4 Click the **History** button – a list is displayed of the Web sites that you have visited. Click the icons to open or close the list for each day/week.

If you click one of the Web site addresses you will be connected to it (do not do this yet). We will looking at how to change the History settings in Task 5.

5 Open the **Help** menu and select the option **Web Tutorial**.

Try out the section on browsing the Web.

Remember to disconnect if you are not carrying straight on with the next task.

Web site addresses

Task 3: Connecting using the Web site address

If you know the Web site address you can simply type it in the address box, then press the _Enter_ key and connect directly. There is no need to browse or search for it. We will try this and learn some shortcuts along the way.
The structure of a Web address (also known as a Universal Resource locator or URL) is discussed in the introduction to Section 2. Upper or lower case can be used when typing an address.

1 If necessary, open the Internet Explorer home page, making sure that you are online (see Task 1 above).

2 We will connect to the Yahoo Web site which provides a subject directory and search engine (see Tasks 6 and 7). The full address is **http://www.yahoo.com** However with the latest version of Internet Explorer you do not need to know the full address – often only the name, e.g. Yahoo, will do.

3 Type ***yahoo*** in the address box (simply highlight the existing address and over-type).

Press the _Enter_ key – you will be connected to the Yahoo Web site. The rest of the address is inserted for you. If you are offered a list of Web sites instead – see step 5 below – you will need to select the one that you want.

4 Now try this again inserting ***excite*** in the address box – this time you are connected to Excite's Web site **http://www.excite.com/** which provides similar search services to Yahoo.

5 Where several Web sites share a similar name using the short form of the address is not so straightforward. e.g. 'Alta Vista' is a US place name used in many Web addresses, including the search and information site **http://www.altavista.digital.com**

Insert ***Alta Vista*** in the address box and press _Enter_.

Your browser compiles a list of Web sites containing this name and displays them – see Figure 10.5 on the following page – you must locate the site you want and click the name to connect (all the names listed are 'hot' links).

See the next task for other ways of dealing with incomplete Web site addresses.

6 Now click the down arrow button on the address box. A history list of the sites visited is displayed and can be selected to re-visit the sites.

7 We have visited three of the most popular search and information sites: Yahoo, Excite and Alta Vista. Try connecting to some others – Lycos, WebCrawler, InfoSeek and Hotbot. Search sites offer you a range of information, e.g. news, maps, directories, email and newsgroups.

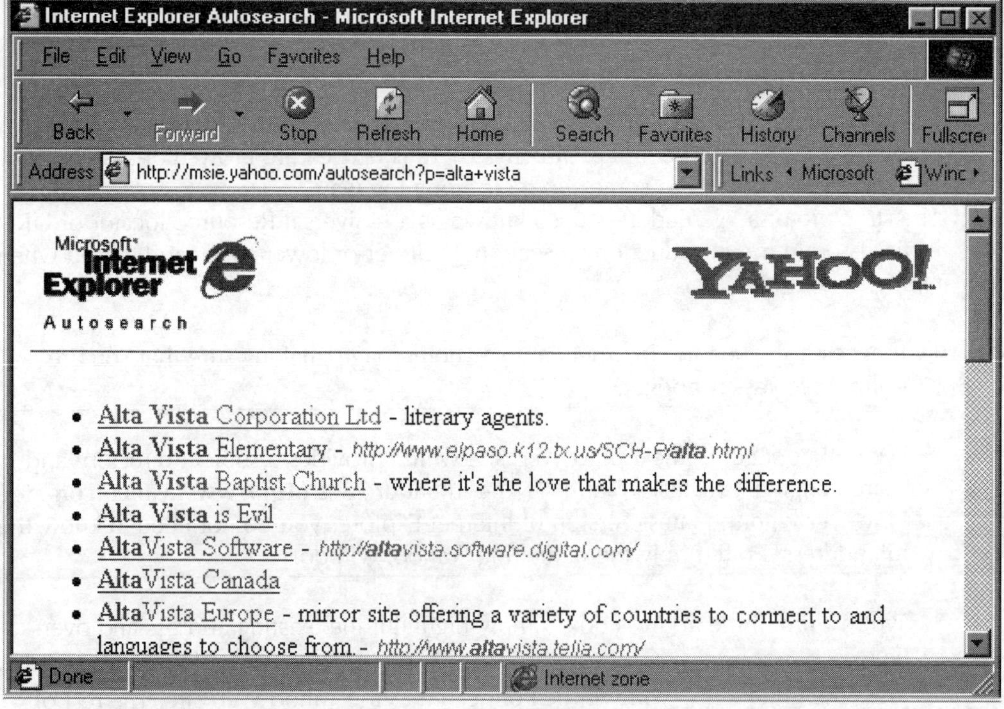

Figure 10.5

Task 4: Finding the correct Web site address

We have already seen in the previous task that you don't need to type the full Web site address. Often merely typing the name of the organisation or individual, e.g. Yahoo, will be enough. In this task we will review other ways of dealing with incomplete Web addresses. Quite often you will type a Web address only to get a message that the site could not be found. Sometimes this is caused by a problem beyond your control, e.g. the Web site is off-line or there is a connection problem. However, often the address is slightly incorrect; in such cases you can use Internet Explorer to search for similar names.

1 AutoComplete will complete an address as you type it, based on addresses of sites that you have already visited. If necessary open the Internet Explorer home page, making sure that you are online. See Task 1 step 6.

2 Highlight the present address in the Address box if necessary. Start typing a Web address in the Address bar, entering the letters **www**.

The AutoComplete feature may well suggest a match at this stage, highlighting it in the Address bar, e.g. **www.yahoo.com.** Don't press the _Enter_ key yet: if you do you will be connected to this Web site.

3 Carry on typing till you have typed **www.e** - again AutoComplete will probably suggest a match – probably **www.excite.com.**

You can turn off AutoComplete if you wish – open the **View** menu and select **Internet Options**. Make sure that the **Advanced** tab is selected and click the **Use AutoComplete** checkbox to clear it.

4 To search for the correct address, open the **View** menu and select **Internet Options**. Make sure that the **Advanced** tab is selected.

Scroll down to the section **Search when URL fails:**

Make sure that the default option **Always ask** is selected (this ensures that Explorer will ask you if you want it to search for close matches when an address fails).

Click **OK**.

5 Let's try locating the correct address for Woolwich plc.

Simply type **www.woolwich** in the Address box and press *Enter*.

A dialog box will ask you if you wish to search, click **Yes**.

Explorer then uses the Yahoo AutoSearch service which locates a number of close matches (see Figure 10.6 on the following page) for the Woolwich group of companies.

6 Try a similar search for Shell Petroleum; you can do this from any Web page.

Try locating the correct address for the Automobile Association using **www.aa** in the address box. This is not so successful as many organisations use the letters 'aa' somewhere in their address.

Task 5: Recalling your favourite Web sites

We have already seen that the **Forward**, **Back** and **History** buttons let you re-visit Web pages. The capacity of these lists is limited, however, and will eventually be overwritten, especially if you share your PC with others. Internet Explorer lets you keep a list of *Favorites* (called Bookmarks in Netscape Navigator), organise them into folders and delete unwanted ones. Explorer also provides some 'favorite' folders of its own.

1 If necessary open the Internet Explorer home page, use the down arrow button on the address box to return to the Yahoo Web site.

2 Open The **Favorites** menu and select **Add to Favorites**.

A dialog box opens offering three options.

Make sure that the first option **No, just add the page to my favorites** is selected; the other two options are only appropriate when you need informing of the latest changes to a Web page – see step 8 below.

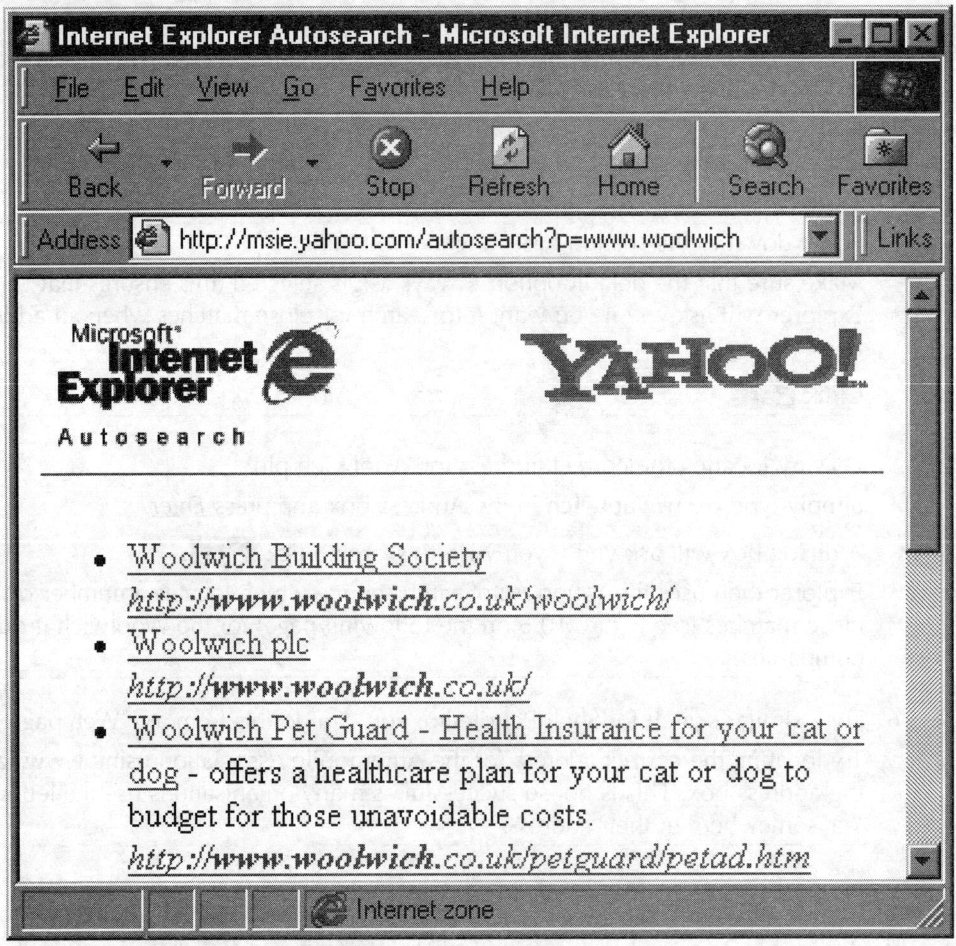

Figure 10.6

3 To organise your Favorites, it is a good idea to store links to related Web sites in the same folder. Click the **Create in** button on the dialog box.

Make sure that the **Favorites** folder is highlighted – see Figure 10.7 opposite.

Click the **New Folder** button and enter the folder name ***Search Pages***.

Click **OK** and the new folder is added to the Favorites folder.

Finally click **OK** and the Yahoo home page is added to your 'favorites' - open the **Favorites** menu and check that it appears on the menu.

4 Repeat these operations to add some other Web sites to the **Search Pages** folder. Use the sites that you visited in the previous task, e.g. Excite, Alta Vista, Lycos, WebCrawler, InfoSeek and Hotbot.

The **Organize Favorites** option on the **Favorites** menu allows you to re-organise folders. To cut, copy, paste or delete a favorite simply right click it and select the appropriate menu option.

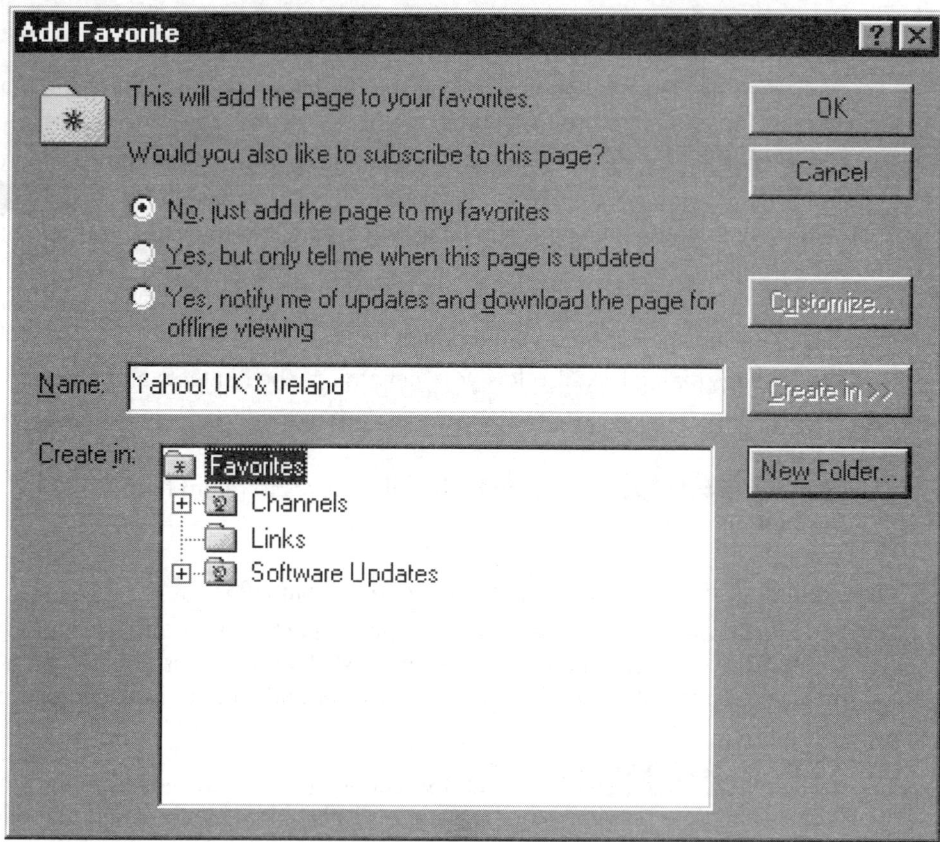

Figure 10.7

5 You may re-organise the History List. In Task 3 we saw that you can easily find Web sites that you recently visited using the **History** button. An address file is kept for each site and they are stored in the History subfolder (part of the Windows folder).

Open the **View** menu and select **Internet Options**.

A dialog box is displayed – make sure that the **General** tab is selected. If hard disk space is limited you can either reduce the number of days history files are kept from the standard 20 days or delete the list of sites using the **Clear History** button.

6 You may review the cache size. When you are connected to the Web the content of the Web pages that you visit is downloaded (copied) to your PC. It is kept in the Temporary Internet Files subfolder, part of the Windows folder. This cuts down on access time as the next time that you visit the site Internet Explorer will retrieve the page from the cache rather than from the site (which involves communication delays). However, this means that if the page has changed since you last viewed it, you will see the older version.

Click **Settings** on the **Temporary Internet files** section of the dialog box.

The **Settings** dialog box offers a number of options to update the content of a cached Web page, as follows.

Every visit to the page will ensure you see the latest version of the page but increases loading and browsing time.

Never gives the fastest loading time, but you may miss important recent information if the Web page is updated frequently. However, clicking the **Refresh** button when you are viewing the page will connect to the site and display the latest content.

Every time you start Internet Explorer is the default setting and the best compromise between speed and updated content.

The **Settings** dialog box also lets you view the cache contents and change the cache size.

---

7 Click the **Cancel** buttons on both dialog boxes to return to the Internet Explorer window.

---

8 Explorer also offers its own set of favourites – **Channels**.

You can choose to subscribe (at no cost) to a selected group of information providers, e.g. BBC, Vogue and New Scientist. The content is updated on a regular information by the information provider and can be displayed on your desktop.

- Click the **Channels** button and select one of the providers from the **Channel Bar**. When the provider's home page is displayed locate the button labelled **add active channel** or similar and click it. A dialog box appears offering you three choices. The first option is the default – not subscribing to it but calling up the page when needed. The second option **only tell me when this page is updated** informs you when the information is updated by a red 'gleam' next to the site name on the **Favorites** menu. The third option **notify me of updates and download the page** transfers the Web site information to your computer. If you take this option the transfer may take some time.

Take option 2 for the moment.

- You can modify your subscription as follows; take some time to explore these options.

  Open the **Channels** menu again if necessary and right click the channel you have just subscribed to.

  Select **Properties** from the pop-up menu.

  Click the **Subscription** tab to check details of the subscription or to cancel it.

  Click the **Receiving** tab to change the subscription type, or to add a password.

  The **Schedule** tab allows you to change the time interval to update the information.

  You can also select times for downloading when your computer is not busy.

- Although not strictly a 'channel', the Microsoft Web site offers updates to its various products, including Windows 98. Click the **Start** button and select the options **Settings-Windows Update**.

Browsing vs. searching

Web browsing can be an enjoyable and effective way of gaining information. There is such a wealth of information on many areas, e.g. news, IT, entertainment, that you will inevitably find something of interest. If used as a sole way of information gathering, however, it is restrictive in several ways.

- *Browsing* (or 'surfing') simply means clicking the 'hot links' provided by the page designer. These link you to other pages, either at the same or at different Web sites. The quality of these links will vary, depending on the designer's skill and commercial or knowledge bias, e.g. you might wish to compare different suppliers' products but why should a commercial Web site provide links to a competitor's pages?
- Following hot links often wastes time; it can lead you up blind alleys to sites of marginal relevance or poor quality.
- You may well miss sites and pages to which no links have been provided.

Using a reputable search site such as Yahoo can give us other ways to locate useful sites rather than happen upon them while browsing. In the next task we will use Yahoo's subject directory to locate information about the Internet; don't worry if some of the links have changed when you come to try it; topical Web pages are changed frequently.

Task 6: Using a subject directory

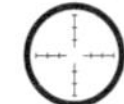

1 If necessary open the Internet Explorer Home page, making sure that you are online (see Task 1 above).

2 We will connect to the Yahoo Web site. Use the **Favorites** menu or the **Address Box** to do this.

You will probably be able to do this off-line because of Explorer's History feature –see Task 3. Connect to your Access Provider when prompted to do so.

3 Click the **UK and Ireland sites only** button. Excluding overseas Web sites will speed the searching and loading of Web pages.

Scroll down the Yahoo home page; it provides a directory of major subject categories: Arts and Humanities, News and Media etc. Each one is a hot link, taking you to a further list of categories and so on.

4 Click on the **Computers and Internet** section When the next page loads scroll down the list of categories and locate the section on **Internet**.

5 Choose a topic of interest from the next list to appear, e.g. **Information and Documentation** and click this topic.

6 When the next page appears choose the topic **How to search the Web** (or similar).

7 Look at the top of the next page: Yahoo shows you the different levels of the subject index you have used:
Top:Computers and Internet:Internet:World Wide Web:Searching the Web:How to Search the Web

8 Use the **Back** button to retrace your steps, notice that the links that you have already used have changed colour as a reminder. Use the **Forward** button to go forward again (note that the **Forward** and **Back** buttons are dimmed when you can go no further) .

9 Finally, scroll down the page – a list of relevant Web documents is given (see Figure 10.8). To visit the site simply click the hypertext ('hot') link – usually in blue.

- Choose the Best Search Engine for Your Information Needs
- FAQ - Internet Research
- FAQ - Web and Internet Search Engine
- Guide to Effective Internet Searching - progresses through 48 topics for beginning to intermediate Web users.
- Hints & Tips for Searching the Internet
- How to Search for Medical Information - Rhode Island reference round table presentation on medical information for the layperson.
- How to Search the World Wide Web: A Tutorial and Guide for Beginners
- **How to Use Yahoo!@**
- Index - Understanding And Comparing Search Engines

Figure 10.8

Useful tips

'FAQ' means 'frequently asked questions' - a popular and effective way of answering basic user queries.

Save any site that appears useful as a Favorite – see Task 5 above.

Use the **Stop** button to cancel any Web site taking too long to load. Repeatedly clicking a hyperlink will not speed up the loading of the page!

Use the **Forward** and **Back** buttons to re-visit pages and sites.

Remember that anyone can put information on the World Wide Web; you need to evaluate the content and the reputation of the Web site for yourself.

Exploring Web sites

- Go back to the Yahoo home page and use the News and Media section to find information on some topic of interest, e.g. UK employment.
- In Task 4 we visited some other search Web sites, e.g. Excite, Alta Vista, Lycos, WebCrawler, InfoSeek and Hotbot. Each one tends to organise its search index in a different way. Try one or two of these sites; for purposes of comparison try locating the information on searching the Web that we found before using their subject categories.

Searches using search engines

We have already located information on the Web by browsing and using a search directory. A third important way is using a search engine, offered by major search sites such as Excite, Alta Vista, Lycos, WebCrawler, InfoSeek and Hotbot.

A search engine maintains a huge index to Web sites and the information that they contain; most also provide some sort of evaluation of the sites. When you enter a search term, e.g. networks, the search engine displays a list of all Web sites containing it. Because no one search engine can catalogue all the sites on the Web it is a good idea to use more than one if you want a truly comprehensive search (or use an all-in-one type search site). When the index is compiled by human indexers, e.g. Yahoo, you tend to get fewer results but of a higher quality – better for a quick trawl of fairly common topics. When the index is automatically compiled by computer, e.g. Excite, you will tend to get more results, but often of marginal relevance. This can be better if you are searching for an unusual topic.

Tips for searching

At its simplest, a search engine merely provides a text box for you to enter a search term, e.g. 'cars, 'computing', or 'weather', and then compiles a list of all known Web sites containing this word. However, due to the wealth of information on the Web far too many sites would be listed to visit. We should refine the search using the features provided by the search engine. Here are some ideas for you to use when you search.

- Every search engine uses a slightly different set of search features. It is therefore important to read the Help pages – links from the home page labelled 'About', 'Search Help', 'How to' etc.
- Use the most specific words that you can to avoid targeting too many sites, e.g. use the term 'mobile PC' rather than simply 'PC' or 'computer' if this is your interest. Fewer, but more relevant sites will be listed. On the other hand if you

over-specify your topic you may well get no relevant sites listed, e.g. 'mobile pc rental'. In this case you should try again, omitting one or more of the terms.

- Use the Boolean operators AND, OR and AND NOT to specify if you want to search on all the terms or any of them.
- Use AND or the '+' sign to narrow your search; AND means both terms must be present, e.g. 'job and description'
- Use OR to broaden your search as it can search on similar terms, e.g. 'resume OR CV'. You may find sites that would be missed by only searching on one of the terms.
- Use AND NOT or the '–' sign to exclude certain terms; say you are interested in spreadsheets but not Excel then you can specify 'spreadsheet and not Excel' to search for sites that include the first term but not the second.
- When the search combines different Boolean operators, clarify the logic by use of brackets, e.g. '(resume OR CV) AND design' will find pages either containing both the words 'resume' and 'design' or both the words 'CV' and 'design'.
- Use the asterisk 'wild card' operator to allow for various word endings, e.g. 'comput*' will find pages containing the words computer, computers or computing.
- Use double quotation marks to search for an exact phrase, e.g. "electronic commerce".
- Use **t:** to restrict searches to document titles only; this tends to increase the relevance of documents listed, e.g. t:Windows 98.

Task 7: Using a search engine

1 If necessary, open the Internet Explorer home page, making sure that you are online.

We will choose the Lycos search engine as it offers a good range of search features; other search engines work in a similar way. Don't worry if some of the pages and information have changed in the examples we are using.

2 You can enter the Lycos Web address directly (www.lycos.com) or choose different engines using Internet Explorer's **Search** button on the toolbar. Try this.

The home page for the search engine is displayed; click the **UK and Ireland sites only** button.

3 Let's see how you can progressively refine a search for information on the Car Industry in Europe. First enter the term ***car*** in the search box and press the **Find** button – see Figure 10.9 opposite.

The search engine locates literally thousands of Web sites containing the term car.

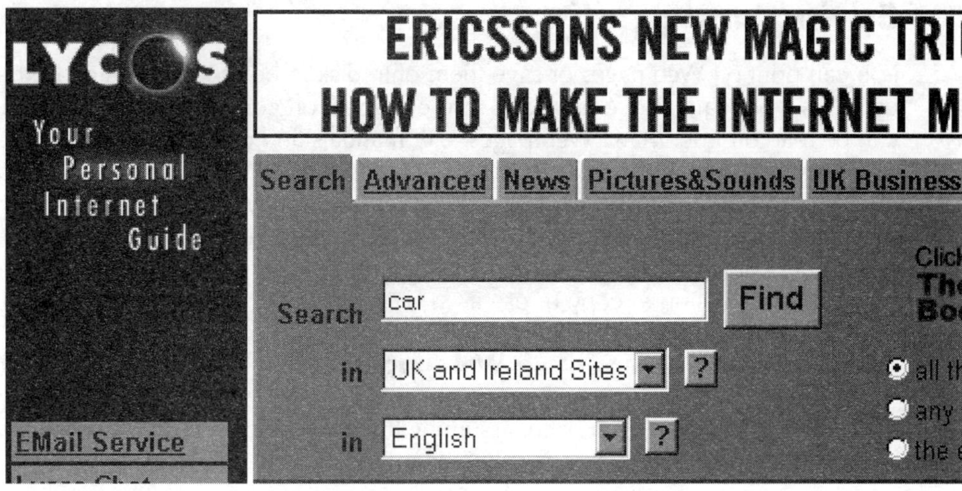

Figure 10.9

4 Scroll down the results page but do not click any of the links yet; at the bottom of the page you can refine your search; enter the search terms ***car +industry*** to specify that both terms must occur (there must be a space after the word 'car' but none before the word 'industry').

Press the **Find** button again – fewer sites are listed but still far too many to visit.

5 Now click the **Back** button and amend the search term to "car industry" using quotation marks to search on the exact phrase, i.e. both terms adjacent in this order. This cuts down considerably on the number of sites located.

6 Finally amend the search to ***"car industry" +europe*** – this will give you a more manageable number of sites.

7 Visit some of the sites and check them for relevance – simply click on any link to open the associated Web page.

Let's try locating the search terms in the text; this works in the same way as a word processor and is useful for locating the relevant sections of a Web document. Open the **Edit** menu, and select **Find (on this page)**.

Enter the text you want to find, e.g. ***car industry***.

Change any options if necessary, e.g. case, whole word.

Click the **Find Next** button.

8 Now use another search engine for a search of your own choice. Select a topic that is fairly specific or you may be overwhelmed by the number of Web sites listed. Some search engines let you display the most recent information added, e.g., in the last week or month. Try using this.

When you have found a Web page that you wish to save or print continue with the next task.

Saving and printing

You can print off Web pages or save them onto disk to be processed later. Both are useful as a permanent reference and also cut down on connection charges as they can be read off-line. Many Web pages, e.g. manuals and guides, are designed to be saved or printed in word processor-compatible format. Other pages may give you unpredictable results if you attempt to print unusual fonts, icons or graphics, and may need some post-processing before they look presentable. Bear in mind that the copyright of any copied material remains with the creators of the Web page and you may need permission to copy or use it.

Task 8: Saving and printing Web pages

1 To save the current Web page, assuming that you are currently displaying a Web page in Internet Explorer, open the **File** menu and select **Save as**.

Make sure that a diskette is in the drive.

The **Save HTML Document** dialog box appears – see Figure 10.10 opposite.

Select the drive **3 $\frac{1}{2}$ floppy (A:)** from the **Save in:** box.

Give the page a suitable file name.

---

2 In the **Save as Type:** box you have the choice of two formats.

HTML is the universal format for Web pages. Keep this if you intend to view the saved page again using a Web browser such as Internet Explorer.

Text file is the better format if you intend to incorporate the Web page into a word processed document.

Save the document as an HTML file.

---

3 Copying part of a Web page into a document is a simple copy and paste procedure. Open a new Web page.

Open a word processor, e.g. Wordpad or Word, using the **Start** button on the taskbar.

Select a block of text on the Web page using the usual dragging technique.

Open the **Edit** menu on the *Explorer* menu bar and select **Copy**.

Activate the word processor window.

Open the **Edit** menu on the *word processor* menu bar and select **Paste**.

You may need to re-format the text.

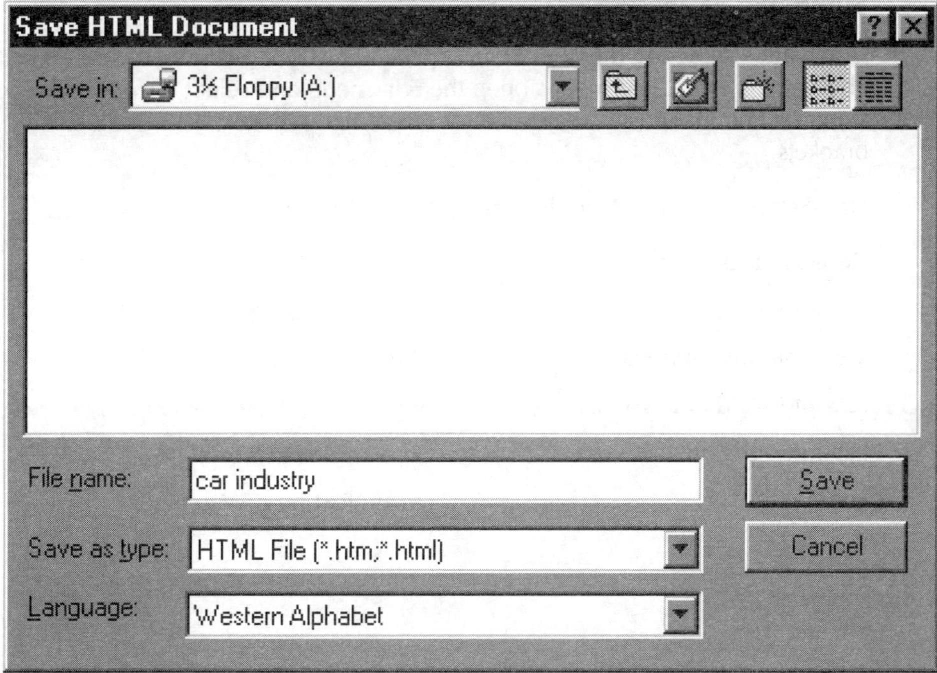

Figure 10.10

4 To print the contents of the current Web page, find a Web page divided into different frames.

Open the **File** menu again and select **Page Setup** – you can alter the page orientation, margins, headers and footers.

The default code for the header **'&w&bPage &p of &P'** prints the page name, centres the text, and prints the page number.

The default code for the footer **&u&b&d** prints the page address and the date.

Make any changes you wish and click **OK**.

---

5 Click one of the frames on the Web page.

Open the **File** menu and select the **Print** option. The **Print** dialog box opens, offering the usual choices of number of pages, number of copies etc.

You can choose to print all the frames on the Web page, or only the frame that you have selected. If you print all frames then you can opt to print them as laid out on the Web page or on separate sheets.

Choose an option and click **OK** to print.

Summary of commands

Commands show the menu or Window name first, followed by the command to choose, e.g. Edit-Clear means open the **Edit** menu and select the **Clear** command. Where a command is available from a particular window this is indicated in brackets.

Start-Settings-Control Panel-Internet	Check Internet connection settings
(Internet Explorer)	
View-Toolbars	Show/hide toolbars
View-Internet Options	Check Internet Settings
Favorites-Add to Favorites	Add Web address to Favorites list
Favorites-Organize Favorites	Copy or delete a favorite
Edit-Find	Locate text on a Web page

unit 11

Creating Web pages using FrontPage Express

Introduction

FrontPage Express is a Web page editor that allows you to create and edit Web pages in a similar way to using a word processor or desktop publishing package. There are more powerful Web page editors on the market (including Microsoft FrontPage Editor with which it is compatible), however FrontPage Express can be used to produce perfectly adequate and attractive Web pages without needing to learn any special language such as HTML or Java.

In this unit you will learn the basic editing formatting and linking features and produce your personal Web Page. In the next unit you will learn more advanced Web page features such as adding tables, forms and images.

What you should know already

How to use the standard Window components – see Unit 1.

What you will learn in this unit

By the end of this unit you will be able to:

- create your own home page
- use FrontPage Express commands and features
- format a Web page
- view a Web page in Internet Explorer
- link pages.

Creating a Web page

FrontPage Express provides you with the template for a personal Home Page which you can adapt to suit yourself. A 'Wizard' guides you through a series of simple steps to achieve this.

Task 1: Creating your own Home Page using a Wizard

1 Click the **Start** button on the taskbar. Select the **Programs** then the **Internet Explorer** option.

Select **FrontPage Express** from the menu.

2 Initially you get a blank window. Open the **File** menu and select **New**.

The following dialog box appears; FrontPage Express allows you to create a number of standard Web pages and forms. Click each option and read its description.

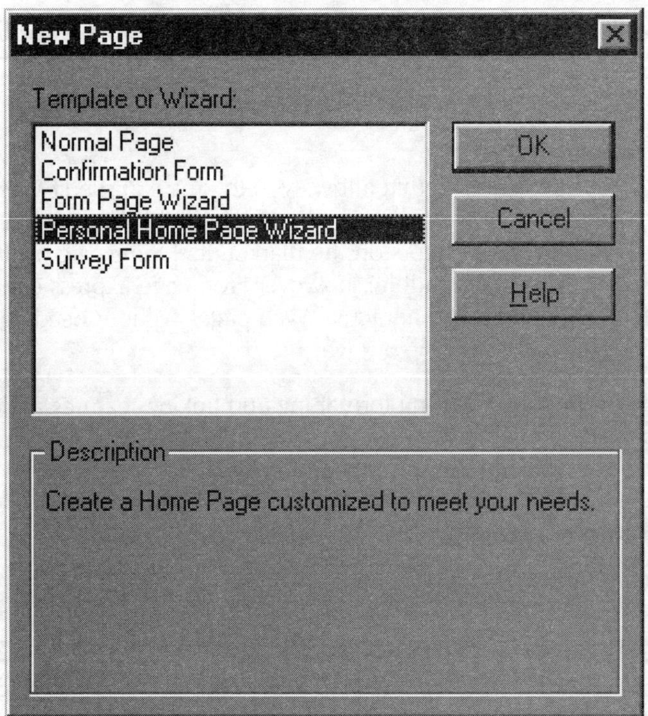

Figure 11.1

3 Select **Personal Home Page Wizard** and click **OK**.

The 'sections' page appears next. You can choose the sections that you wish to include, depending whether the Home Page is for work, college or home.

Select all the sections for the moment; you can always delete them later.

Click the **Next** button.

4 Carry on through the steps of the Wizard, choosing options relevant to you; at each stage you have the option to go forward, back or to cancel.

On the final dialog box click the **Finish** button. The page outline is created; all you need to do now is to save and edit it.

Scroll down the page; you will find the information that you have just supplied.

5 To save your Web page, open the **File** menu and select **Save as**.

A dialog box appears, allowing you to save the front page to a Web site, your organisation's Web server, your desktop or to disk. For the moment we will save it to disk as an HTML file. It can then be opened and edited like any other file.

6 Click the **As File** button – a further dialog box appears as in Figure 11.2. Select a suitable drive and folder from the **Save in** box, e.g. diskette or hard disk (remember you can create a new folder when you save – see Figure 11.2). Give the file a suitable name, e.g. **Home Page 1**.

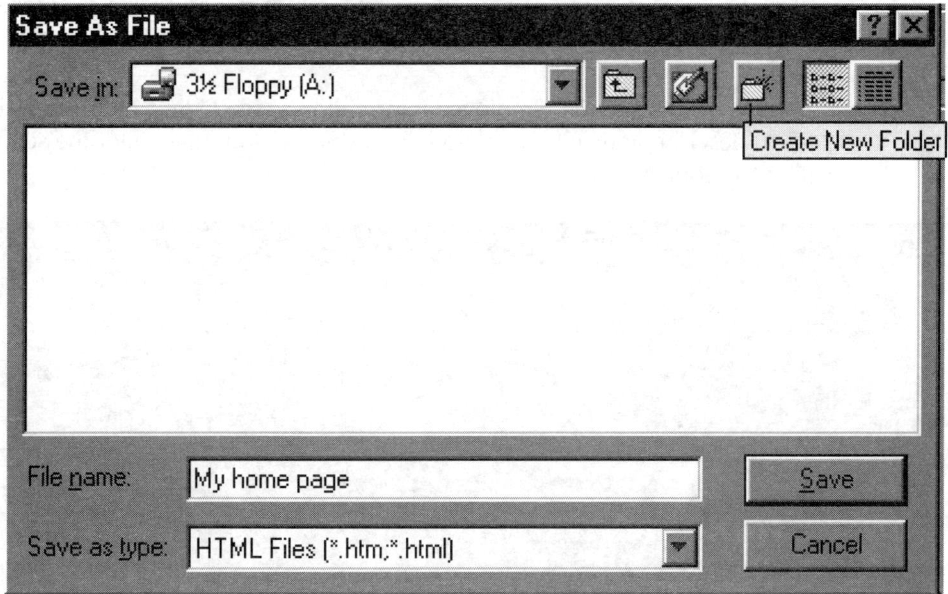

Figure 11.2

7 Your file is now saved and open ready for editing. Close the file, leaving FrontPage Express open.

Task 2: Opening and editing a Web page

We have now created a template for a personal home page, using a FrontPage Express wizard. In this task you can personalise it with your own details.

1 Open FrontPage Express if necessary, then open the **File** menu and select **Open**. The **Open** dialog box appears.

The **Other Location** tab should be selected, also the **From File** radio button.

Click the **Browse** button then select the appropriate drive/folder and file name.

Click the **Open** button and your Web page is opened, ready for editing.

It is important to realise that the hyperlinks do not work in edit mode, they have to be viewed through a Web browser, e.g. Internet Explorer. The formatting and layout, however, look the same as they will actually appear.

2 Open the **View** menu and make sure that all the FrontPage Express toolbars – Format, Standard and Forms – are selected.

Move the screen pointer over each button; as usual a screen tip explains the function of each.

3 You can carry out the operations of Cutting Copying and Pasting using the **Edit** menu or the buttons on the Standard toolbar.

Scroll down the Web page – you will see that comments and hints are included to guide you. We will amend this text then format it later.

4 Scroll down to the section 'Employee Information' – see Figure 11.3. Amend the details to describe yourself, e.g. if you are a student you might alter the section heading to 'Course Information' etc.

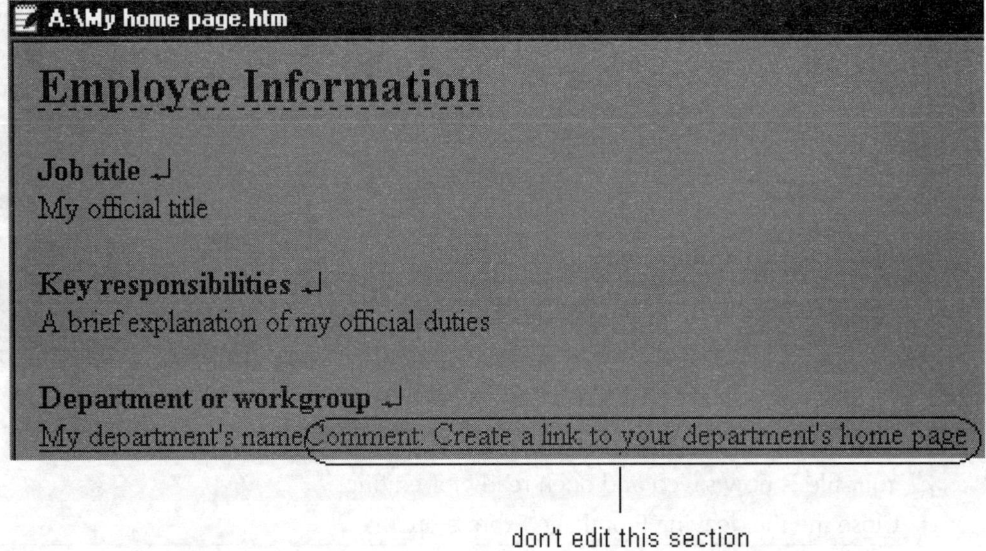

Figure 11.3

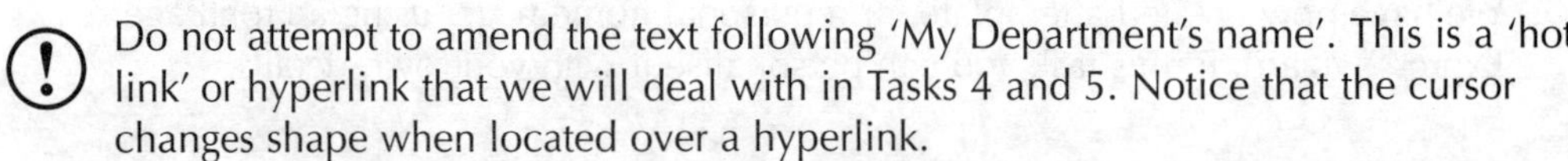

Do not attempt to amend the text following 'My Department's name'. This is a 'hot link' or hyperlink that we will deal with in Tasks 4 and 5. Notice that the cursor changes shape when located over a hyperlink.

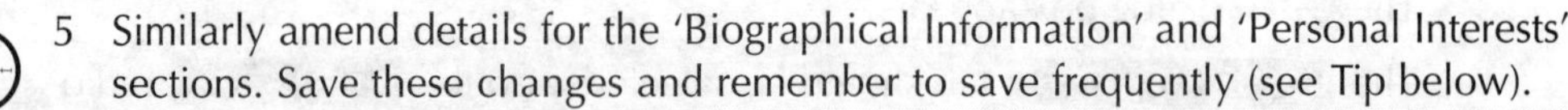

5 Similarly amend details for the 'Biographical Information' and 'Personal Interests' sections. Save these changes and remember to save frequently (see Tip below).

6 Styles, fonts and colours can be amended either using the Format toolbar or by opening the **Format** menu and selecting **Font**. We will try both.

Select a section heading, e.g. 'Personal Interests' so that it is highlighted.

Click the down arrow on the **Style** box (see Figure 11.4) and experiment with various styles.

Use the **Edit-Undo** command (or **Edit Undo** button) to reverse unwanted changes. Failing this you can always close the Web page without saving unwanted changes – though you may lose amendments that you would have preferred to save as well.

7 While the text is still selected click the down arrow on the **Font** box and experiment with different fonts.

Use the other buttons on the Format toolbar to alter the text size and colour, underlining etc.

Figure 11.4

8 Select another block of text, open the **Format** menu and select **Font**.

A dialog box is displayed; the selected text should be visible too – if necessary use the title bar to drag the dialog box to one side.

Now experiment with various selections; the sample part of the dialog box shows you the selection.

Click the **Apply** button on the dialog box and the selection is applied to the selected text on the Web page (even if you click the **Cancel** button later).

9 If you are proceeding to the next task save your latest changes and leave the FrontPage Express application open.

Task 3: Viewing your Web page in Internet Explorer

To see how your Web page will appear to someone else you have to use a Web browser; it is good idea when you are developing the more complex aspects of a Web page to have the Internet Explorer Web browser open as well as the FrontPage Express Web page editor. You can then 'flick' from one to the other to check the effects of changes. If your page is stored on a local drive or server then there is no need to be connected online.

1 Open Internet Explorer; if you are prompted to connect take the offline option.

Open the **File** menu and select **Open**. The **Open** dialog box appears.

Click the **Browse** button then select the appropriate drive/folder and file name.

Click the **Open** button on both dialog boxes and your Web page is opened, ready for browsing.

2 Click the buttons on the taskbar; you can view the same file using two different applications – FrontPage Express and Explorer.

Make sure that the Internet Explorer browser window is open and scroll through the document, clicking the 'hot links'. The internal ones that take you to a different part of the page will work; links intended to connect to external Web sites will generate error messages as they have not been set up yet.

3 To view the effects of changes, activate the FrontPage Express window.

Make a small change to the text of your Web page *without saving it*.

Activate the Explorer window and locate the text you have just changed; you will see that the change has not been updated in the browser application.

Activate the FrontPage Express window and save the change now.

Activate the Explorer window again; the change is still not displayed.

Click the **Refresh** button and Explorer will show the change.

If changes made in edit mode (FrontPage Express) are not visible in browser mode (Internet Explorer) you have probably forgotten one of the two steps above – saving the change and clicking the **Refresh** button. If you cannot edit or save a Web page then you are probably not in edit mode at all but browsing; this is a common mistake. You cannot edit any page (whether yours or someone else's) while you are browsing, i.e. using Internet Explorer or Netscape.

For the next tasks you should have the Internet Explorer Web browser open as well as the FrontPage Express Web page editor.

Creating links

Using FrontPage Express you can insert links to other Web sites, pages on your own Web site, or simply to other parts of the same page. The links, i.e. what you click, can be text, icons or images.

Task 4: Inserting links on the same page

1 You can create links to other locations on the same page, e.g. to the top of the page, or to and from a table of contents. Microsoft calls intra-page links bookmarks; they are also referred to as anchors.

Make sure that you are viewing your home page in FrontPage Express not Explorer. Scroll through the page and you will notice the hyperlink text 'Back to Top' has been used several times; it is identified as a hyperlink by the standard blue underlined text.

2 We will insert a bookmark to take you from the table of contents to the email section.

Insert a blank line after the last item in the Contents section of your Web page.

On this new line type the text ***Email Me*** (see Figure 11.5).

Highlight this text then open the **Edit** menu and select **Bookmark** – a dialog box appears.

The bookmark name should be **Email Me**, the text you have just selected. Click **OK**.

You have now created a bookmark, i.e. a named section of a Web page.

Contents

- Employee Information
- Current Projects
- Hot List
- Biographical Information
- Personal Interests
- Contact Information
- Comments and Suggestions
- Email me

Figure 11.5

3 Scroll down to the **Contact Information** section and highlight the text 'Electronic Mail Address'. Open the **Insert** menu and select **Hyperlink**.

Click the **Open Pages** tab in the dialog box that appears, make sure that your home page is selected in the **Open Pages** section, then click the down arrow on the **Bookmark** section and select the bookmark **Email Me** – see Figure 11.6.

Click **OK** and the bookmark is selected.

Save your changes.

4 To test the Bookmark, activate the Explorer window to browse your home page and click the **Refresh** button.

Now go to the **Contact Information** section and find the text 'Electronic Mail Address'. It is displayed in hyperlink format.

Click the link and you are taken to the **Contents** section.

5 Activate the FrontPage Express window and create a bookmark hyperlink that takes you in the opposite direction, i.e. from the **Email Me** entry in the **Contents** section to the **Email** section.

If you use the same piece of text 'Electronic Mail Address' to act as a bookmark then you may need to give the bookmark a specific name. You can use the **Edit** menu to edit or remove a bookmark or hyperlink.

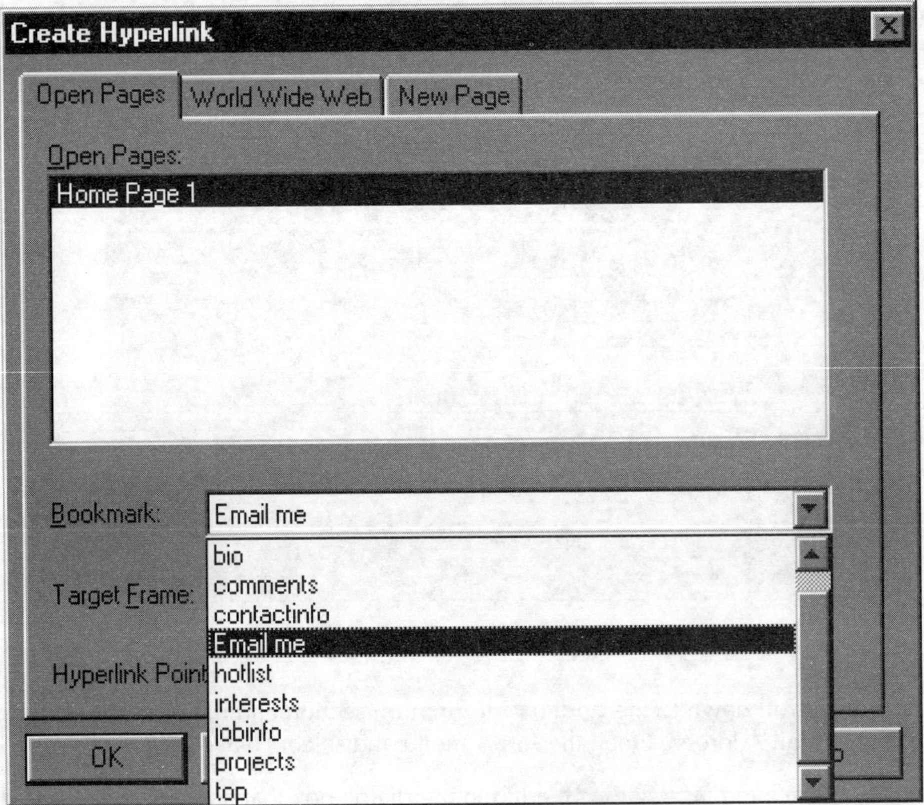

Figure 11.6

Task 5: Linking to another page on the same site

Links between pages are vital, especially in larger Web sites. Once users start to feel frustrated or lost they are likely to give up or try another site.

1 Scroll down to the bottom of your home page in FrontPage Express; insert a blank line and type the text ***Details about this page***.
  Highlight the text.
  Open the **Insert** menu and select **Hyperlink**. Click the **New Page** tab.
  Complete the details as shown in Figure 11.7 opposite.

2 Click **OK** and the **New Page** dialog box appears; select **Normal Page** and click **OK**.
  We will use this page to store details of the home page and its creation; enter text on the new page along the lines of Figure 11.8 opposite.

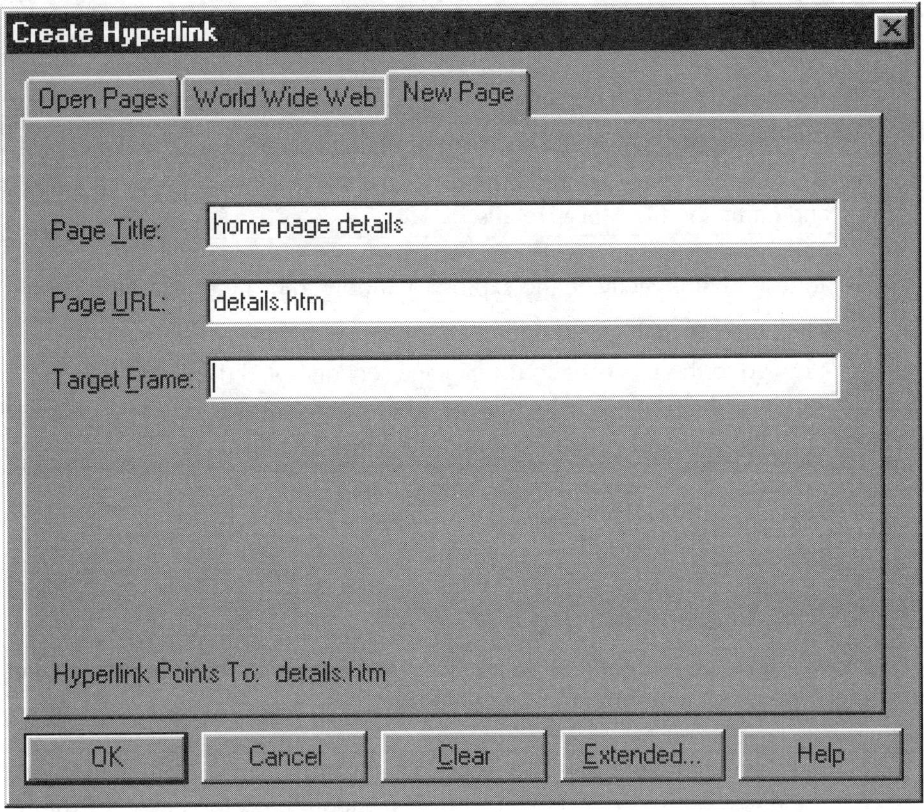

Figure 11.7

Figure 11.8

3 ■ The 'Last Modified' date can be automatically updated. Open the **Insert** menu and select the **WebBot component** option. Select **Timestamp** from the dialog box.

■ To insert the horizontal line use the **Insert** menu.

- The text is presented as a series of indented bullet points; experiment with the lists and indent buttons on the Format toolbar for this and similar effects

4 To save your new page, open the **File** menu and select **Save as**.

Click the **As File** button – a further dialog box appears.

Save the new page on the same drive and folder as your personal Home Page and name the file **More Details**.

5 To test the link, activate the Explorer window to browse your Home Page.

Click the **Refresh** button.

Now go to the **Details about this page** section – it is displayed in hyperlink format – blue underlined.

Click the link and you are taken to the **More Details** page.

6 Activate the FrontPage Express window and create a hyperlink that takes you back from the **More Details** page to the Home Page.

Task 6: Creating moving text

Moving text can be useful as an attention-grabbing feature; it should be used sparingly if it is not to annoy or distract the user.

1 Make sure that your personal home page is open and you are viewing it in the FrontPage Express Web page editor. You should have the Internet Explorer Web browser open as well.

2 Insert a blank line at the bottom of the page. Open the **Insert** menu and select the **Marquee** option.

A dialog box appears. You can experiment with the speed, direction, size and other characteristics of the moving text.

Complete the copyright message as shown in Figure 11.9 opposite.

3 Test whether the Marquee is working in Explorer.

HTML, Java and ActiveX – a brief overview

If you are new to computing and the Internet you may well wonder how HTML – Hypertext Markup Language – fits into Web page creation. HTML is a way of marking up a text with tags so that it can be published on the Web and viewed by a Web browser. In this task we will be looking briefly at some HTML code to understand how it relates to the appearance of a Web page. We will not be learning HTML.

Task 7: Looking at HTML

1 Make sure that the **More Details** page is open and you are viewing it in the

FrontPage Express Web page editor. You should have the Internet Explorer Web browser open as well.

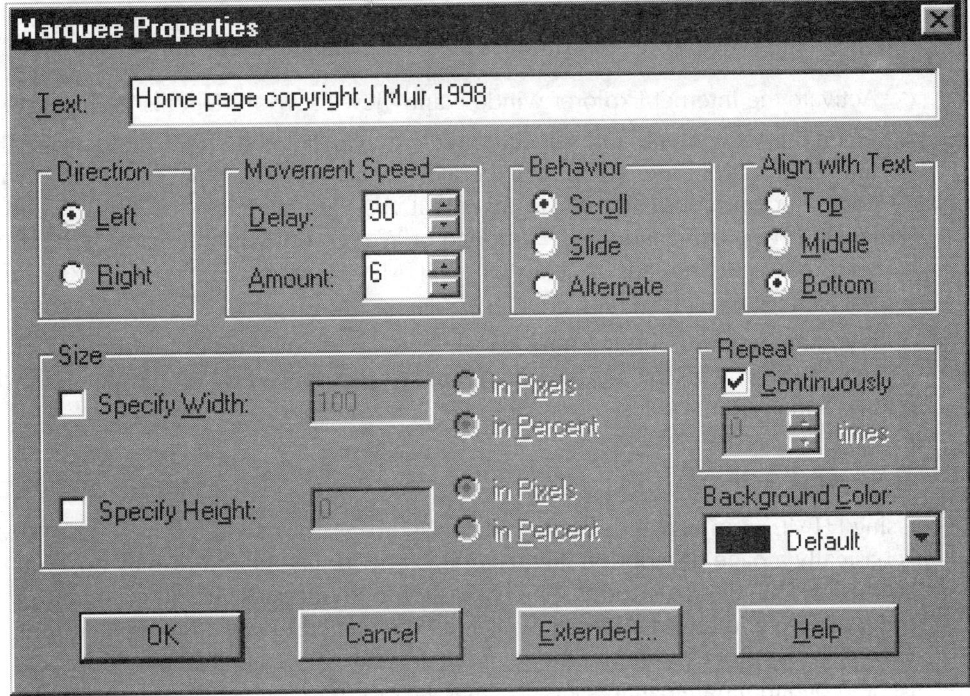

Figure 11.9

2 Open the **View** menu and select the option **HTML**. A window opens showing the HTML code that 'lies behind' the Web page display. Let's look at some of its features.

- The first two lines of code are probably **<html>** and **<head>** These are HTML 'tags' and always appear in pointed brackets. They mark up the various sections of the page so that your Web browser knows how to display it:

  <html> confirms to the browser that it is about to read an HTML document,

  <head> marks the start of the heading – the name of the page that appears in the title bar, in this case **More Details**.

- **</head>** – tags starting with a forward slash mark the end of a section of the page. Locate the main document body section, starting with <body> and ending with </body>

- The **<p>** and **<font>** tags determine new paragraph and font sizes – notice that they also need </font></p> to show when this page feature ends.
  Close the HTML code window.

HTML is in essence a simple programming language that controls the layout and appearance of a Web page. A Web page editor such as FrontPage Express makes it unnecessary to learn HTML, you merely create your page and the editor generates the HTML for you.

In fact it is the browser, e.g. Internet Explorer, that is doing most of the work; it interprets the HTML code and displays it as a fully-featured Web page.

3 Activate the Internet Explorer window and view the **More Details** Web page.

Open the **View** menu and select **Source**. You can see the HTML code again, this time displayed in the Notepad text editor. As it is your own page on your own computer you could edit it (assuming that you have the knowledge!). You can key in HTML using Notepad, Wordpad or Word – but you must save it in a form your browser can read, basically as an HTML (.HTM) or simple text (.TXT) file, not as a Word (.DOC) file.

If you are interested in learning HTML there are many tutorials on the Web. Do a search using, e.g., the Yahoo search engine. The terms 'HTML' and 'tutorial' will find some suitable sites.

Java and ActiveX

Using HTML or an HTML editor to create Web pages has certain limitations. HTML is basically a page description language. It is fine for layout and display and you can also use HTML to create forms which a visitor to your pages can fill in to place an order or give you information. However, if you wanted to use animation on the Web page, or process the input to generate a result immediately, you would need to use a programming language such as Java. Java is used to create applets: small programs that the Web page user can download to their own computer and run from their own Web browser. This offers the ability to create Web pages with active content.

Microsoft's own browser Internet Explorer supports Java, but they have also launched their own competing technology, ActiveX, which performs a similar function of adding live content and interaction to Web pages. Some ActiveX controls are provided with FrontPage Express – see the Help text for this application. There are many Web sites on ActiveX and Java; two you can try are:

Java – http://www.zdnet.com/cc/chat.html

ActiveX – http://www.activex.com

The Active Desktop

3.1 ⇨ 98 The Active Desktop is a major new feature of Windows 98. It is designed to incorporate elements from the Web and provide an extra layer to the normal Windows desktop. We have already seen in Unit 10, Task 5 that you can use the Active Desktop to display information channels; it can also be used to run Java and ActiveX components. For example, you could use it for constantly updating share prices, news, weather or sports. Your desktop can be customised to reflect your needs and interests.

In the next task we will download an active component from Microsoft's own Web site and run it.

Task 8: Installing Active Desktop components

1 Right click the desktop and select the options **Active Desktop - Customise my Desktop** from the pop-up menu that appears.

Make sure that the **Web** tab is selected

2 Select the option **View my Active Desktop as a Web page** and click the **New** button.

A dialog box asks you if you wish to visit Microsoft's Active Desktop Web site.

Click **Yes** to automatically connect to this site.

Browse the items on offer and select one to download.

3 You will be asked to confirm the download; do so and the utility should run on your desktop.

To disable an active component repeat step 1 above and deselect the item that you want to turn off.

Summary of commands

Commands show the menu or Window name first, followed by the command to choose, e.g. Edit-Clear means open the **Edit** menu and select the **Clear** command. Where a command is available from a particular window this is indicated in brackets.

(FrontPage Express)

Edit-Bookmark	Create/Edit bookmark
File-New	Create a new Web page
File-Save as-As file	Save Web page to local drive
Format-...	Format Web page
Insert-Horizontal line	Insert a horizontal line
Insert-Hyperlink	Insert a hyperlink
Insert-Hyperlink-New page	Insert a hyperlink on a new page
Insert-Marquee	Insert moving text
Insert-WebBot	Insert a WebBot
View-HTML	View HTML code behind page being edited
View-[toolbar]	View/hide toolbars

(Internet Explorer)

File-Open-Browse	Find a Web page on local drive
View-Source	View HTML code behind page being browsed

unit 12

Forms, tables, security and newsgroups

Introduction

In this unit we will learn how to incorporate tables, forms and images into Web pages. We will then examine the Internet Explorer built-in security features. The unit also gives you practical tasks on subscribing to newsgroups.

What you should know already

How to use the standard Window components – see Unit 1.

How to use Windows Explorer, FrontPage Express and Internet Explorer – see Units 10 and 11.

What you will learn in this unit

By the end of this unit you will be able to:

- create Web page tables and forms
- include images in a Web form
- set Web security features
- use Outlook Express to subscribe to newsgroups.

Tables and forms

Task 1: Creating a table

In the this tasks we will create a Web page showing a table of holidays.

1 Make sure that FrontPage Express is open. Open the **File** menu and select **New**. Select **Normal Page** from the dialog box that appears and click **OK**.

2 Start your Web page with a suitable company name and title as in Figure 12.1 opposite.

3 Insert a horizontal line as shown, then position the cursor where you want the table to start.

4 Open the **Table** menu and select **Insert Table** – a dialog box appears. Complete it as shown in Figure 12.2 opposite.

Untitled Normal Page
Sunfilled Holidays
Special Summer Breaks

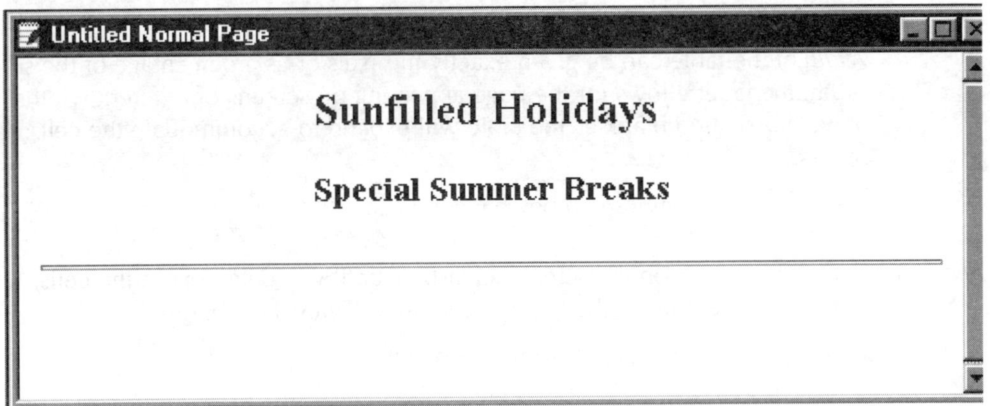

Figure 12.1

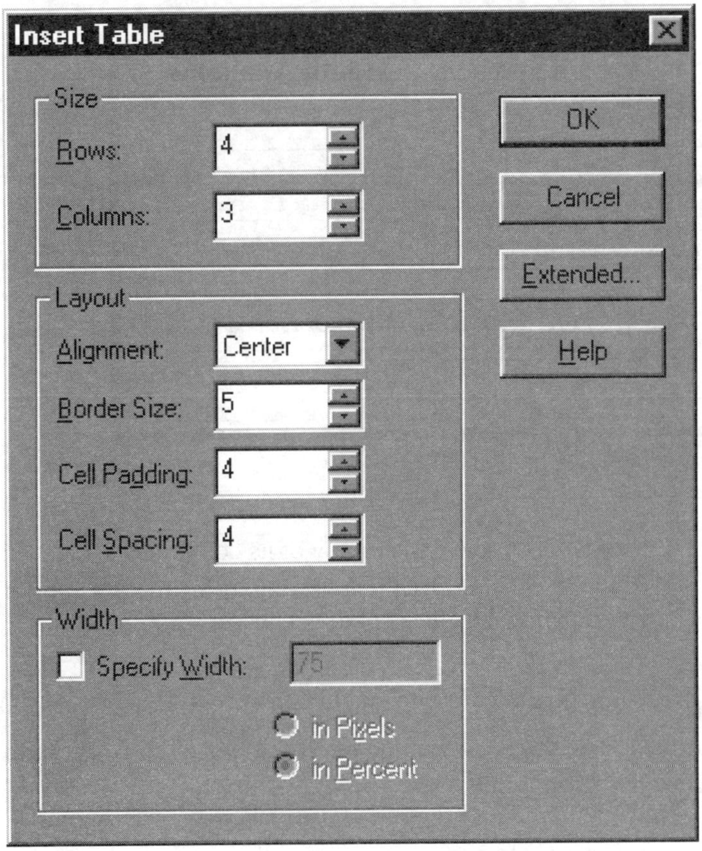

Insert Table
Size
Rows: 4
Columns: 3
Layout
Alignment: Center
Border Size: 5
Cell Padding: 4
Cell Spacing: 4
Width
Specify Width: 75
in Pixels
in Percent
OK
Cancel
Extended...
Help

Figure 12.2

Alignment affects the table's position on the page – left, right or centred.

Border size is the thickness of the border round the table.

Cell padding is the amount of space between the text you enter and the table cells.

Cell spacing is the spacing between the cells in the table.

Width of the table can be given exactly in pixels or as a percentage of the screen width; the latter allows for the page appearing on screens of different widths. Leave this section blank as the table will expand to accommodate the cell entries.

Note that these settings can be changed later.

5 The table appears on the screen 'squashed' until you enter text in the cells; complete the entries in the table as shown in Figure 12.3 below.

- Use the *Tab* key to move from cell to cell
- Use the **Edit-Undo** command to reverse an unwanted change to the table.
- Centre and embolden the column headings as shown.

Area	**Type**	**Month Available**
Llandudno	Caravan	July
Anglesey	Farmhouse	June, July
Snowdonia	Guest house	September or October
Carmarthen	Hotel	August

Figure 12.3

6 You can alter the properties of the table or any of its components, e.g. cells, cell borders and text, by right clicking. Try the following, using the **Apply** button on the dialog box to preview the effects of the changes.

- Right click the table and select **Table Properties**; use the **Custom Colors** section of the dialog box to colour the table border.
- Use the **Custom Background** section of the dialog box to colour the cell backgrounds. Click the **OK** button.

7 To change cell properties, select the first row of cells as follows:
locate the cursor on any cell in the first row; open the **Table** menu and take the **Select Row** option.
The row of cells is selected; right click the table and select **Cell Properties**; use the **Custom Colors** and **Custom Background** options as before to emphasise the column headings.

8 We will insert a fourth column to hold the holiday prices.

Select the third cell in the top row; open the **Table** menu and select **Insert Rows or Columns**. Make the appropriate selection from the dialog box and a fourth column is inserted: complete it as shown in Figure 12.4.

Area	Type	Month available	Price per Week
Llandudno	Caravan	July	£220
Anglesey	Farmhouse	June, July	£280
Snowdonia	Guest house	September or October	£170
Carmarthen	Hotel	August	£300

Figure 12.4

9 Use the **Insert** menu to amend your table as follows:

- Insert 2 rows in the middle of the table to hold further holiday details.
- Add a caption to the table.
- Try splitting one of the cells into two rows.

10 Save your Web page as a file to the same drive/directory as your other Web pages. Call it **Special Deals**.

View the page in Internet Explorer.

Task 2: Creating a form on a Web page

A form is a Web page containing sections, responses etc. that the user has to complete and send back to you, e.g. a survey, registration or order form. Although you can create a form on a blank page it is easier to adapt a FrontPage Express template. Whether you will actually be able to use the form 'for real' depends on whether you have the application Personal Web Server installed.

Check now on your desktop for an icon labelled **Publish**. Open this icon and check that it is the application Personal Web Server. If it is not present then Personal Web Server is probably not installed and you will need the Windows 98 CD. If so proceed as follows:

- put the CD in the drive
- click the **Start** button and select **Run**

- in the **Run** dialog box, type **d:\add-ons\pws\setup.exe** where d: is the letter of your CD drive
- click **OK**.

From then on follow the directions in Personal Web Server setup. Unless you are familiar with Web servers choose the default settings when prompted. Remember that you will have to re-start your PC to fully install Personal Web Server.

Personal Web Server is a desktop Web server that can be used to 'host' a Web site, i.e. it will manage users' access to a linked set of Web pages on your PC. The PC can either be at home or part of an 'intranet' at work. An intranet is a set of Web pages that form an internal information system only available on the organisation's internal network. A good source of information on intranets is the Intranet Journal, available on the Web; try searching for it.

Even if your Web site is not on your computer system but hosted by an Internet Service Provider (ISP), Personal Web Server can be used to develop and test the pages.

1 Activate FrontPage Express. Open the **File** menu and select **New**; select **Form Page Wizard** and click **OK**.
  The first step of the Wizard is displayed. Click **Next**.

2 The second step of the Wizard suggests a name for the form page; accept this and click **Next** again.

3 Click the **Add** button on the third dialog box; a further dialog box displays the choices shown in Figure 12.5 opposite. You can select the best type of form for your needs. Click each option in turn for a brief description (you can also use the **Next** and **Back** buttons to preview each form).

4 First choose **personal information** from the list; you can also edit the prompt for the question. Click the **Next** button.

5 The next step of the Wizard supplies a typical set of data items for the type of form that you have chosen (see Figure 12.6 opposite).
  Select all of them – they can be amended or deleted later.
  Now click the **Next** button then click the **Add** button again
  Select **Contact Information** to add this to your form too.
  Click the **Next** button again.

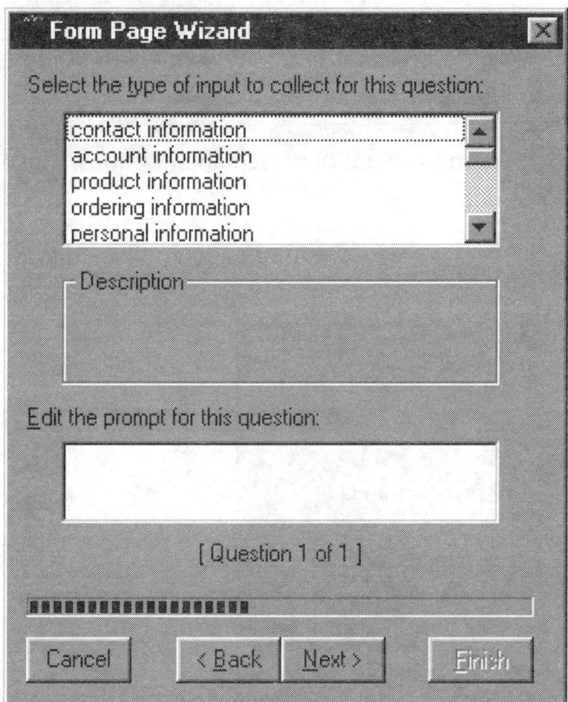

Figure 12.5

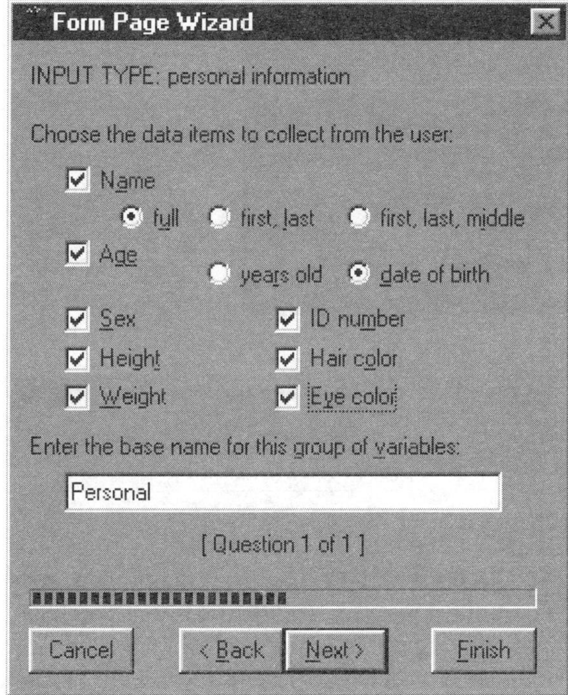

Figure 12.6

6 Again select all the data items supplied and click the **Next** button.
The next dialog box shows you the questions currently defined for the form
Accept them by clicking the **Next** button.

7 The next dialog box offers you various types of presentation options. Make your choice and press the **Next** button.

8 The final dialog box lets you specify where the information collected from users will be stored (see Figure 12.7).

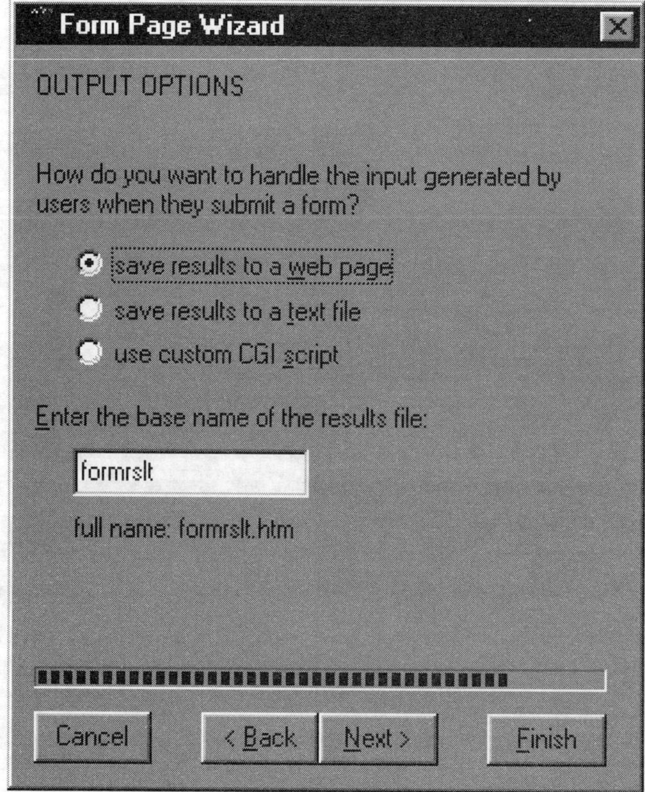

Figure 12.7

Choose the first option, **Save results to a Web page**, and press the **Next** then the **Finish** button.
The new form appears in FrontPage Express ready for editing.

Task 3: Editing a Web form

1 Scroll through the form that you have just created; the fields that you have selected in Form Page Wizard appear on the form; each element of the form can be edited, formatted, copied, pasted or deleted – refer back to Unit 11, Task 2 if necessary. You might, for example, decide to change some of the prompts for the user's address to UK format.

2 The data entry boxes where the user enters information are called form fields. Each one can be validated, so that only certain data values are allowed – e.g. numeric, alphabetic, a certain length or within a certain range of values.

Right click the form field for the name (not the text next to it) and select the option **Form Field Validation**.

Click the down arrow on the **Data Type** box and set the field contents to **text, letters** with a suitable minimum length.

3 To determine form field properties, right click one of the drop down menu boxes, e.g. for hair or eye colour. Select **Form Field Properties** from the pop-up menu.

The dialog box allows you to add, change or re-arrange the order of options – try this, e.g. add another hair or eye colour.

4 The Forms toolbar in FrontPage Express allows you to add other elements to the form, e.g. buttons and scrolling text boxes (see Figure 12.8).

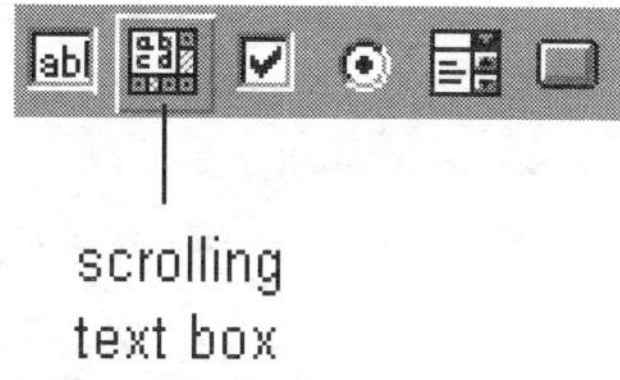

Figure 12.8

Add a scrolling text box as follows.

- Locate the cursor before the **Submit Form** button at the bottom of the form.

  Use the <u>Enter</u> key to insert a few blank lines. Type the title ***Further Details*** on a blank line.
- Click the space on the form just below this title.
- Click the **Scrolling text box** button on the Forms toolbar – the scrolling text box is placed there.

Your form should now look like Figure 12.9.

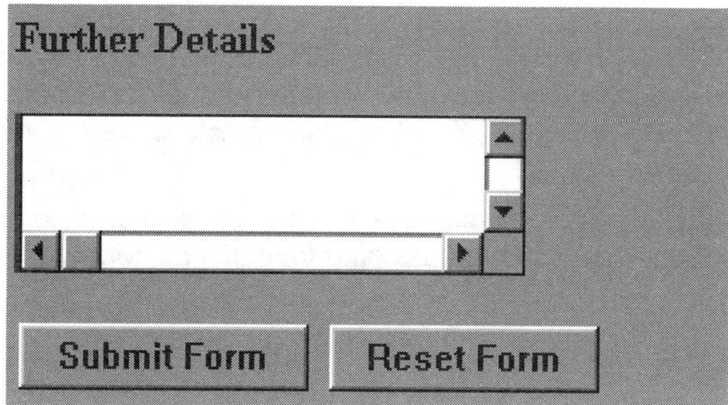

Figure 12.9

5 Right click anywhere on the form and select **Form Properties** from the pop-up menu. Notice the **Form Handler** section of the dialog box that appears – see Figure 12.10. It confirms that the form uses the WebBot Save Results Component to automatically save the information that the users enter into the form. You can also use this dialog box to give the form a new name.

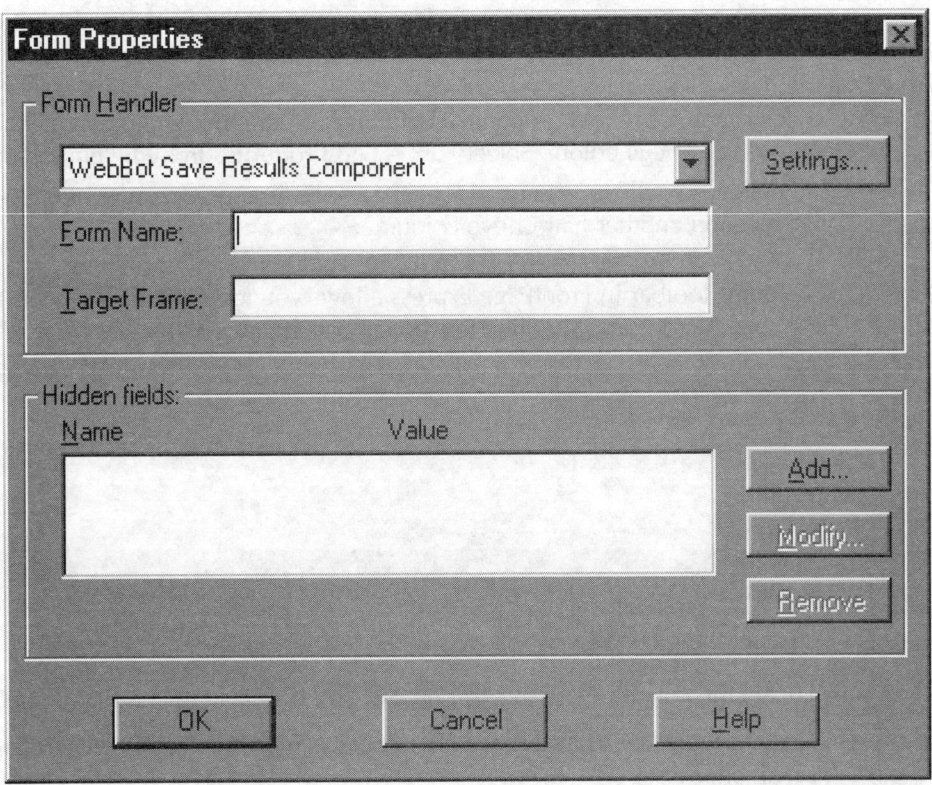

Figure 12.10

A WebBot is a small program or application that automates a task such as saving. You have already used the Timestamp WebBot in Unit 11, Task 5 to update the date and time on a Web page.

6 Click the **Settings** button on the dialog box and the further dialog box shown in Figure 12.11 opposite appears; use it to select a drive and folder where the Web page that holds the user's responses will be stored. Make a note of it for future reference.

You can also use the lower part of the dialog box to add other information to the output page, e.g. the user's name and the date and time that the form was completed.

Click **OK** on both dialog boxes to return to the form.

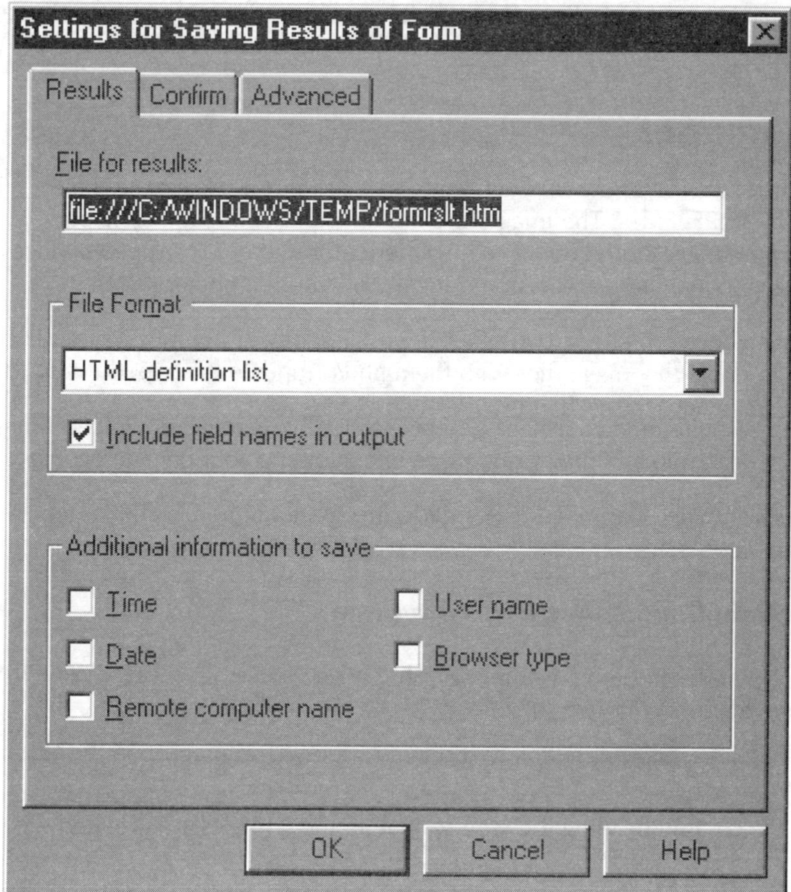

Figure 12.11

7 Open the **File** menu and select **Save as**. Click the **As file** button on the dialog box.

On the **Save As File** dialog box give the page a suitable name and select a drive and folder where the form page will be stored.

8 To test the Web form, make sure that the Internet Explorer Web Browser is open as the active Window.

Opt to work offline if you are prompted to connect to the Internet.

From the **File** menu select **Open**. Click the **Browse** button on the dialog box that appears.

Select the drive/folder where the form page is stored and open the form page.

9 The form should now open; as a test, complete all the details as appropriate and click the **Submit Form** button. The form responses should now be stored to the drive/folder you chose in the previous task.

10 FrontPage Express' New Page Wizard also provides templates for a confirmation form and a survey form. Create one of these forms and edit and test it.

Using images

Images are not stored as part of your page; they are stored as separate image files, usually GIF or JPEG files. The image files are linked to your page by hyperlinks; you can link to an image stored on a site anywhere on the Web. For speed of access, however, the image files can be stored locally on your computer system.

If you move your Web pages to another drive, directory or computer system you will need to move the image files with them and/or update the hyperlinks to them.

Images increase the time your page will take to load; excessive download times cause user frustration and may result in people avoiding your page altogether.

The next task covers still images not videos and sound, although similar techniques apply to them.

Task 4: Including images in a Web page

1 We will start by inserting a simple graphic image into a Web page. We will use one provided in Windows 98.

Right click the **Start** button and open Windows Explorer; open the **Windows** folder.

Click the column heading for **Type** so that all the GIF files are grouped together.

2 Select the files **HLPGLOBE.GIF** and **BACKGRND.GIF** and copy them into the folder/drive where your personal Web page is stored. Check that they are copied to the correct location.

3 Now activate the FrontPage Express window and open your personal home page created in unit 11. Click the Web page at the point that you want the image to be inserted.

Open the **Insert** menu and select **Image**. Click the **Browse** button and select the file **HLPGLOBE** that you have just copied.

4 Click the **Open** button and the image is inserted into your Web page.

Click the image – selection rectangles appear; they can be dragged to change the shape and size of the image. Try this.

5 A small image such as HLPGLOBE makes an ideal hyperlink to another Web page. Right click the image and copy it to another part of the Web page, e.g. the 'Hot List' of Web sites.

Click once to select the image then open the **Insert** menu and select **Hyperlink**.

Make sure that the **World Wide Web** tab is selected and the hyperlink type box is set to **http:**

Now enter a Web site address in the URL box, e.g. ***www.bbc.co.uk***

Click the **OK** button.

6 An image can be used as a background to a Web page. Not all colours and designs are suitable, however; some images are too intrusive and make the foreground text difficult to read.

Right click on the Web page and select **Page Properties**.

Click the **Background** tab to select it – see Figure 12.12.

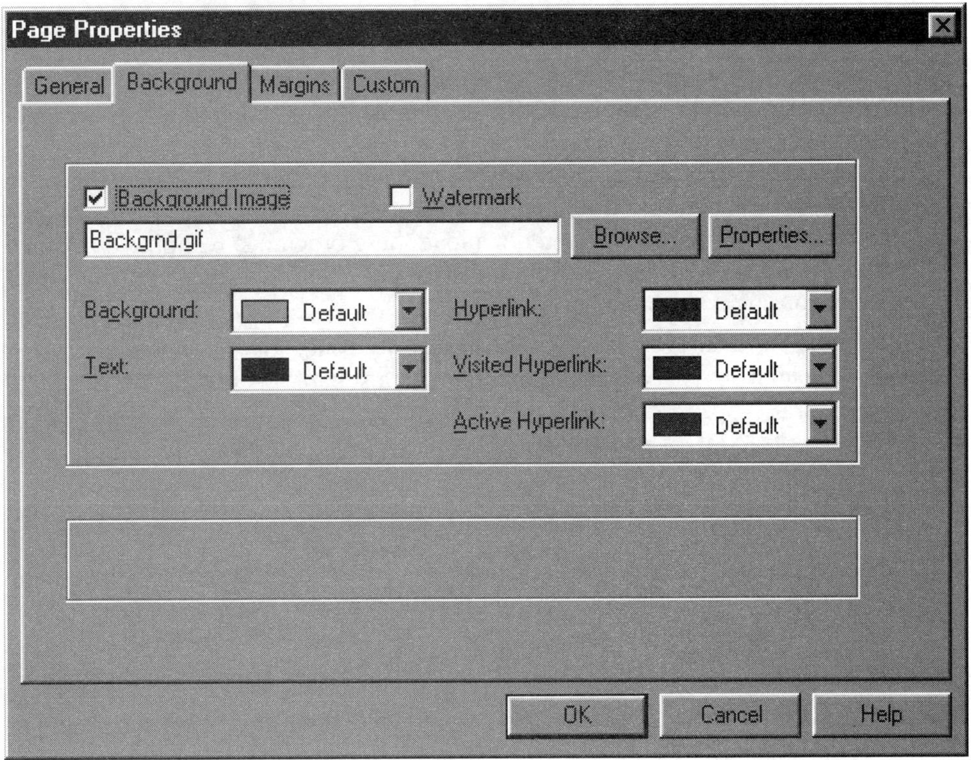

Figure 12.12

Click the **Background Image** box to select it then click the **Browse** button.

Click the **Browse** button on the next dialog box and select the file BACKGRND.

Click **Open** then the **OK** button – the Web page now has a background.

7 Now test that your Web page displays the image and the background in Internet Explorer – remember to save changes before displaying the page. Check that the hyperlink from the image is working correctly.

8 You can copy images found on a Web page anywhere on the Web by simply right-clicking the image and copying it to your local drive. Many sites contain images which you may legally copy.

- The Yahoo search engine will lead you to many of these. Start with the subject category **Computers and the Internet**, then **World Wide Web**, then **Page Creation**, then **Design and Layout**.
- When you have located a suitable image right click it and select the option **Save Picture as**. Select a suitable drive/folder to store the image.

Check the size of the images that you intend to link to a Web page; the larger the image (and the more images that you use) the longer your page will take to load.

Security

Web pages originally contained only text (HTML code) and graphics; downloading them to your computer was fairly safe. Web pages now incorporate *active* elements, i.e. executable programs of various types are incorporated into them e.g. Java applets, ActiveX controls, and graphics viewers of various kinds. When you request information a Web site will often download these programs, without your knowledge or permission. They may contain viruses or alter the settings on your computer system, causing it to malfunction.

Internet Explorer allows you to establish security zones for your computer system so that you can assign a Web site to a zone with a suitable security level.

Whenever you attempt to open or download information from a Web site, Explorer checks the security settings for the site's zone and displays a status message.

Task 5: Security on the Web

1 Open Internet Explorer offline. Open the **View** menu and select **Internet Options**.

Click the **Security** tab on the dialog box.

2 Click the down arrow on the **Zone** box to view the list of zones shown in Figure 12.13 opposite.

Select each zone in turn and note how the security ratings change.

- *Local Intranet zone* The default for an organisation's internal intranet is set to medium; i.e. Explorer will warn you before running any content from Web sites included in this zone in case it could be damaging.
- *Trusted sites zone* The default setting here is low. Select this option and click the **Add sites** button. A dialog box appears; the idea is that you can add the addresses of sites that you trust (sites from which you can download or run programs from without damage to your computer or data files) to avoid being interrupted by warning messages. Obviously caution is necessary here. Cancel this dialog box.

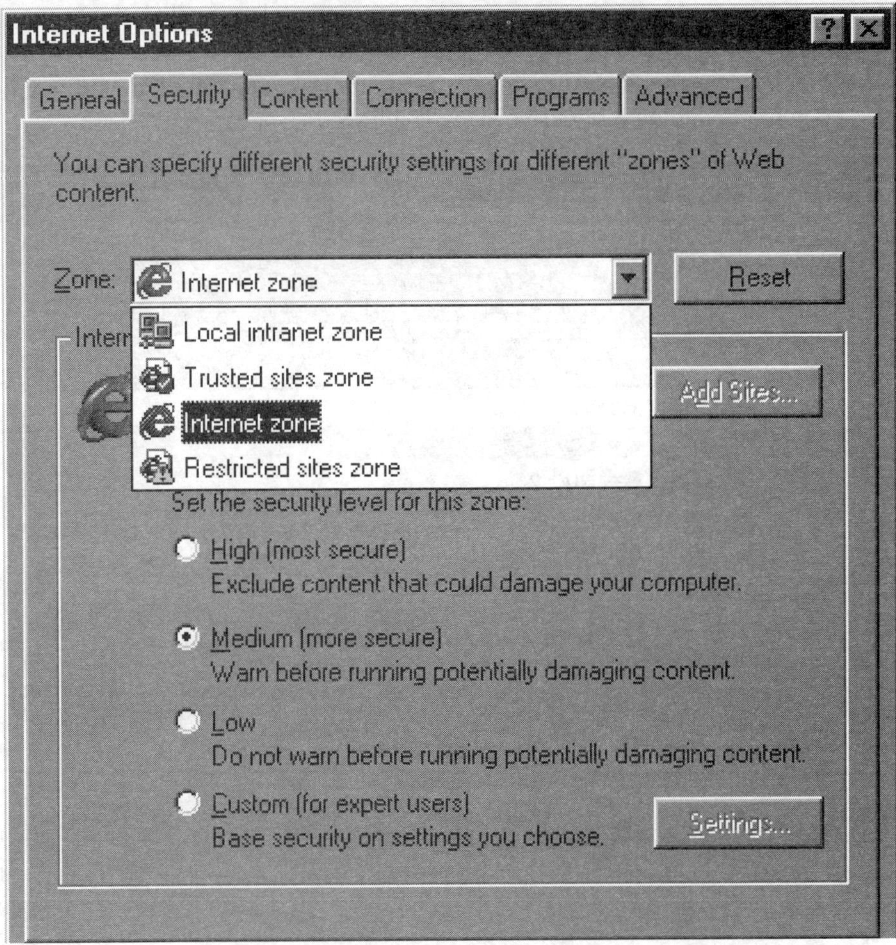

Figure 12.13

- *Internet zone* This zone will contain the vast majority of sites: all the ones not on your computer system or an intranet, or sites that have been assigned to the other three zones. The default security level is medium.
- *Restricted sites zone* This is for sites you feel you can't trust: sites where downloading or running files could damage your computer system. As with trusted sites you can assign sites to this zone. The default security level is high.

The *Custom* setting allows you to create your own zone settings.

3 To block sites, click the **Content** tab on the **Internet Options** dialog box.

In the **Content Advisor** section click **Enable**. You are now required to supply a password. Do so and remember it!

4 A separate **Content Advisor** dialog box should appear – if not click the **Settings** button. This dialog box allows you to exclude Web sites that contain 'adult' content considered not suitable for children. It is based around

the four categories of language, nudity, sex and violence. Click the **Language** category.

Now try re-setting the rating level – at the moment it is set to level 0 – only Web content containing inoffensive slang is allowed – see Figure 12.14.

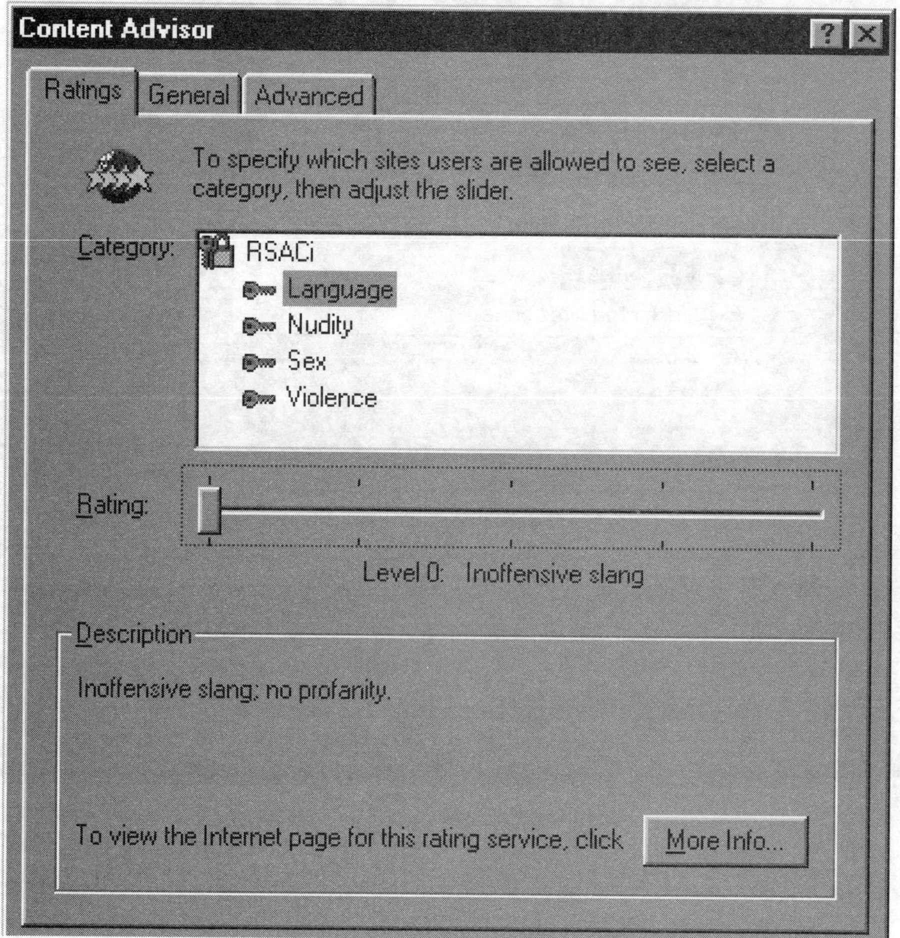

Figure 12.14

5 As you move the sliding control a description appears below; look at the ratings for the other three categories as well. As these ratings are relatively new and based on a voluntary code of conduct not all Web sites use them. This means that sites without a rating will be blocked by default, irrespective of content.

6 Close the **Content Advisor** dialog box; you are returned to the **Internet Options** dialog box. If you wish to disable the Content Advisor, click the **Disable** button and supply the password.

Close the **Internet Options** dialog box.

Newsgroups

Outlook Express provides a newsgroup service; a newsgroup is simply a number of email messages on a related topic stored on a central computer or server. Your Internet service provider will give you access to a news server in addition to the other services they provide; one news server can store messages for thousands of different newsgroups. Newsgroups cover nearly every subject imaginable from the highly serious, technical and academic to the recreational, bizarre and semi-legal.

Some newsgroups are maintained by companies and groups that monitor them closely but generally there is little monitoring or control. You can join or 'subscribe' free of charge to as many newsgroups as you wish; messages can then be read and sent by any subscriber to the group.

Outlook Express maintains folders to store your newsgroup messages and a number of time-saving tools to help you manage them. The Web is also a good source of information on newsgroups.

Task 6: Subscribing to newsgroups

1 To install Outlook Express, click the **Start** button and select **Programs** then **Internet Explorer** from the menu.

Finally select **Outlook Express**.

2 The Outlook Express window opens. Click the **Read News** icon.

If this is the first time you have used this option a 'Wizard' will prompt you for a name and email address. Supply them.

3 You will then be prompted for the news server supplied by your information access provider. Check on this; you may need to read the documentation or contact your access provider for the name. (See also Unit 13, Task 1, steps 1 and 2.)

The 'friendly name' that you are asked to supply next will be used to create a folder to store newsgroup messages; call it, e.g. **News**.

4 Select the connection method next; for the home user it is usually via telephone.

5 Once the settings are made you are connected to your service provider's news server and a message invites you to subscribe to newsgroups.

Click the **Yes** button and a list of available newsgroups is downloaded; as there are thousands of newsgroups it will take some minutes.

When completed a dialog box appears; drag the column divider as shown in Figure 12.15 on the following page to see the full names of the newsgroups.

Scroll through them and you will see that it would take far too long to browse through the list and pick out ones of interest (even if the names were fully informative).

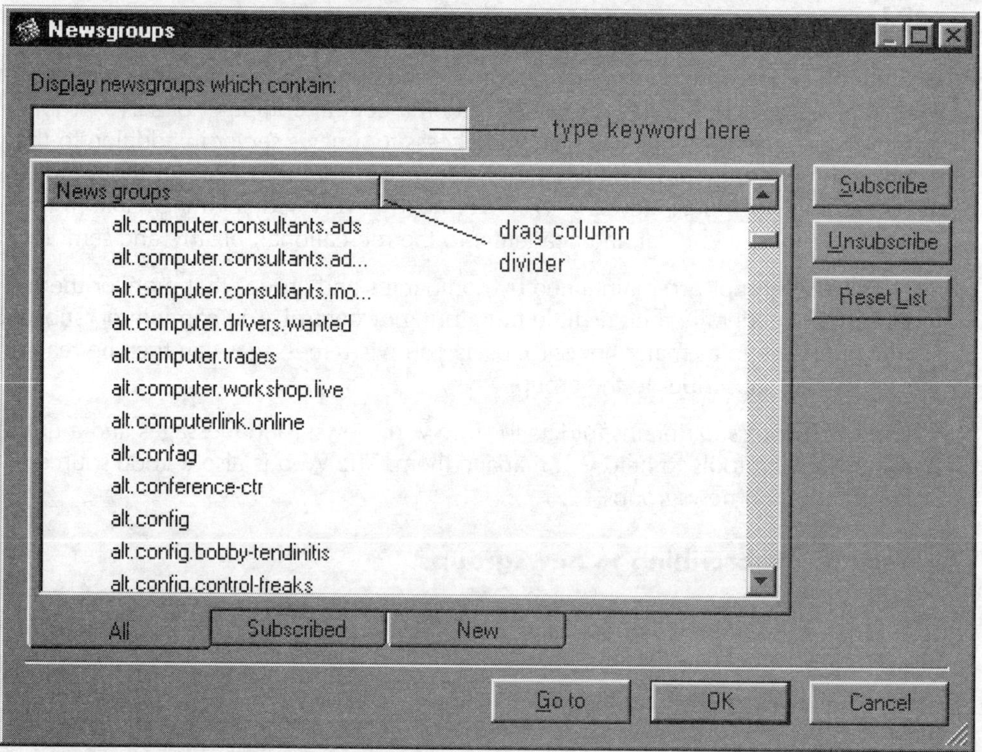

Figure 12.15

6 To find relevant newsgroups merely type all or part of a word (or words) in the field at the top of the dialog box – see Figure 12.15.

As you type the list is filtered – however your success depends on using one or more appropriate keywords. Try the following.

- Type the word ***car*** and newsgroups are selected not only for cars, but also cartoons, childcare, career – any newsgroup name containing these three letters.
- Type the words ***car sport*** and the list is reduced but still contains many irrelevancies.
- Try the keywords ***auto sport*** instead and the search is more successful – mainly because you used the US term 'auto' rather than 'car' in your search.
- Find a list of newsgroups using a keyword search on a topic of interest to you.

7 You can preview a newsgroup before deciding if you want to subscribe to it. Often the quality or the subject matter of the messages posted may be disappointing; some newsgroups are almost inactive while others are very active with hundreds of messages (which may take a long time to download).

Select a newsgroup and click the **Go to** button at the bottom of the dialog box.

A dialog box similar to the one shown in Figure 12.16 appears.

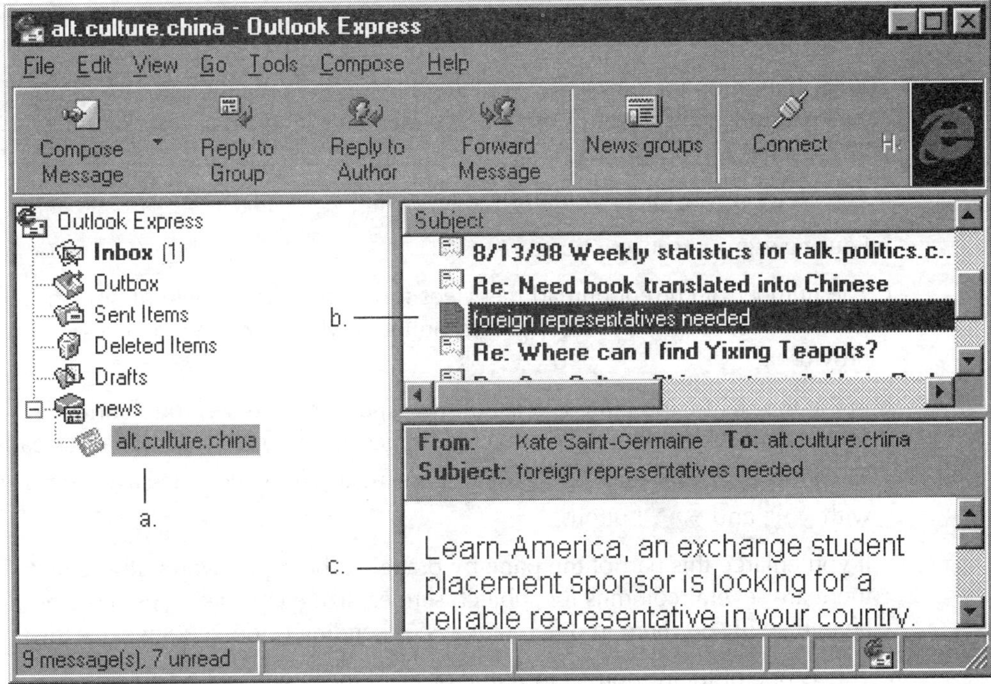

Figure 12.16

Pane 'a' shows the newsgroup alt.culture.china temporarily added to my **News** folder (see step 3 above).

Pane 'b' shows some of the messages currently stored in the inbox for this newsgroup; click on any of these messages to read its content – see pane 'c'. If you are offline then pane 'b' may be blank.

Click the **News groups** button on the toolbar to return to the list of available newsgroups.

8 Subscription to a newsgroup is free; once you have identified newsgroups of interest to you, you merely click the **Subscribe** button to join. This means that you can participate by both responding to messages and sending new messages, queries etc. of your own. However you can also become the unwilling recipient of junk email, and other unwelcome messages. If this is an issue for you then read step 12 before subscribing!

9 Select newsgroup(s) of interest to you and click the **Subscribe** button. A newspaper icon appears next to these newgroups.

You can select a block of Newsgroups by using the *Ctrl* or the *Shift* keys on the keyboard.

To cancel a subscription select the newsgroup(s) and click the **Unsubscribe** button.

To view a list of all newgroups you must remove any keywords from the field **Display newsgroups which contain:**.

10 Let's assume that you are now a member of several newsgroups. Click the **OK** button on the **Newsgroups** dialog box and the main Outlook Express News window is displayed. Compare the elements labelled a - f in Figure 12.17 with the ones in your window.

a The **News** server folder contains the following.

b Four newsgroup subscriptions.

c The number of current unread messages for each is also shown (if none are shown check that you are connected online to your information access provider).

d In the top right hand pane is a list of messages for the newsgroup currently selected. Messages that have attracted replies are grouped together as 'threads'. Click the **Open** and **Close** buttons next to threaded messages, marked with **+** and **-** buttons.

If you enlarge this part of the pane by dragging the border you will see that there are several columns for subject, sender, size etc. Clicking the column heading will sort them in different ways (ascending or descending). Try this.

e This is one of the responses to d, the original message. To read a message simply click it.

f The **News groups** button takes you back to the list of newsgroups.

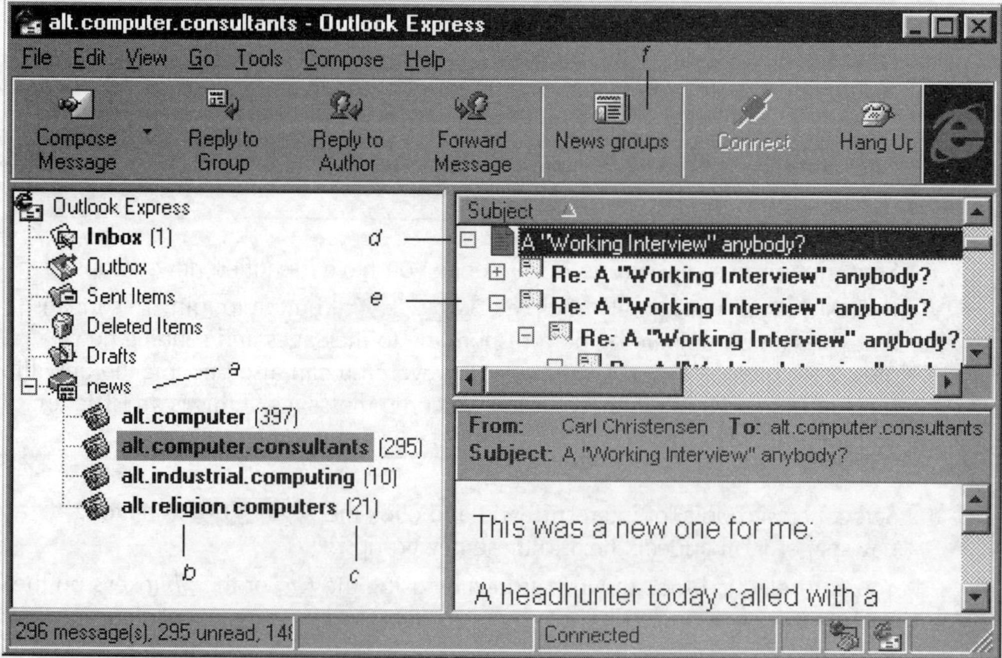

Figure 12.17

11 To search for messages, select a newsgroup with a substantial number of messages in the Inbox.

Open the **Edit** menu and select **Find Message**. A dialog box appears (see Figure 12.18). You can search by date, sender's name or subject.

Enter a suitable subject and click the **Find** button.

The first message is displayed – keep pressing the F3 function key at the top of the keyboard to display further messages.

Figure 12.18

12 You can choose to filter out messages that you consider either offensive, too large to download, or advertising 'junk mail'.

Open the **Tools** menu and select **Newsgroup Filters**.

Click the **Add** button on the **Newsgroup Filters** dialog box.

To filter out advertisements complete the second dialog box as shown in Figure 12.19 on the following page.

Make sure that you have selected an appropriate newsgroup in the **Group(s)** box.

Enter the filter term ***sell*** as shown.

Click the **OK** button – you are returned to the first dialog box. Click the **Add** button again and filter out the word 'sale' too.

Check the filter is correct and then click the **OK** button.

13 To use the filter, open the **View** menu and select the **Current View** option.

Make sure that the **Filtered messages** option is selected (ticked).

Scroll down the list of messages for the Newsgroup to which you have applied the filter; the excluded messages will appear in blue.

Now de-select the **Filtered messages** option – when you scroll through the list again the filtered messages should be hidden.

Finally re-select the **Filtered messages** option.

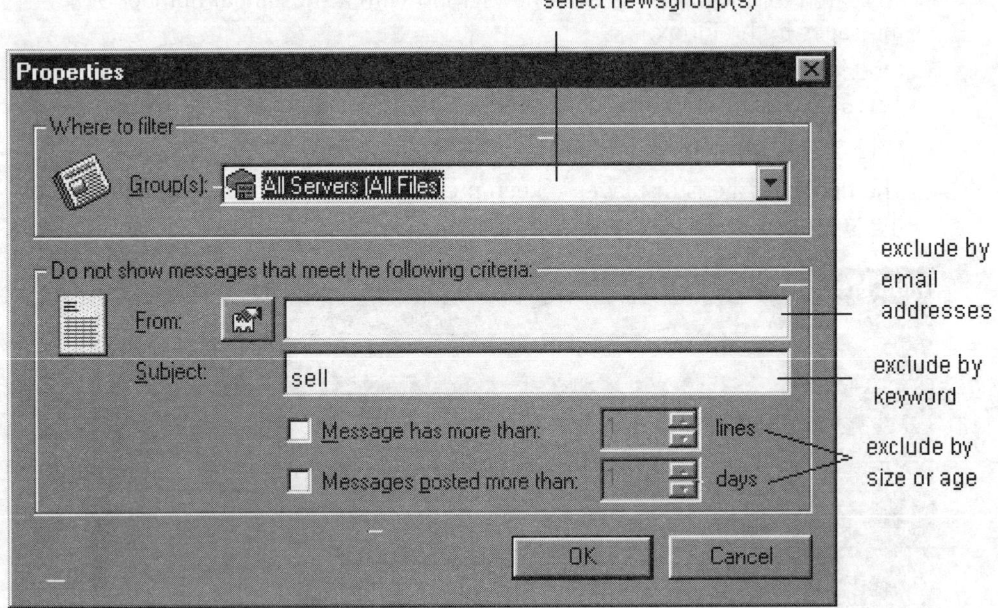

Figure 12.19

14 Right click a message in the list and select **Properties** from the menu. On the dialog box choose the **Details** tab. You should be able to find out the sender's email address and other details. If the window is blank it may be because you are offline and the details are not available. Close the dialog box.

15 Right click one of the newsgroups listed in the right hand pane. Select **Properties** from the menu.

The **Download** tab contains options covered in Task 7; click the **Local Files** tab.

You are offered the options of either deleting complete messages or deleting the main text of the messages only, or compacting files. You can also reset the information stored.

Cancel the dialog box.

Task 7: Downloading messages

1 To save connection charges when you are reading newsgroup messages you can download the message headers only and mark the ones you want to read offline. When you re-connect Outlook Express will then retrieve the message text for the marked messages only.

2 Display the list of newsgroups that you have subscribed to – see Task 6 if necessary.

Right click the icon for one of the newsgroups. Select **Mark for retrieval** from the menu. You now have the options to download new headers only, or the full text of messages (see Figure 12.20).

Select the first option **New Headers**.

3 Open the **Tools** menu and select **Download this Newsgroup**.

Choose **New headers** from the dialog box that appears.

If you are prompted to connect now, do so.

Figure 12.20

4 When the download is complete disconnect again; click the **Hang Up** button.

5 Now review the headers of some recent downloaded messages; when you find one that you wish to download in full text then right click it and select **Mark Message for Download** from the menu. A down arrow mark appears next to the message.

6 When you have finished open the **Tools** menu and select **Download this News group**. Set the options on the dialog box as shown in Figure 12.21.

If you are prompted to connect now do so.

When the download is complete then disconnect again; click the **Hang Up** button.

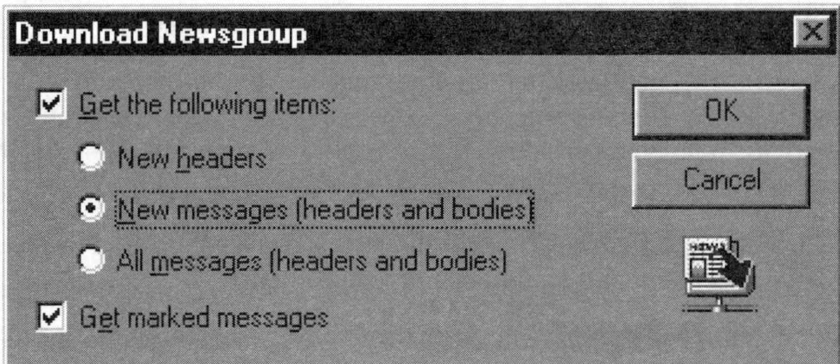

Figure 12.21

7 You will find that the text of the marked messages is now available offline.

Task 8: Responding to newsgroup messages

Before you send out newsgroup messages you may wish to consider whether to hide your email address (see step 3). This will prevent programs that automatically compile email address lists from using it, e.g. for advertising purposes. It will mean, however, that other newsgroup members will not be able to reply to you automatically by simply clicking a 'reply' button. You can, however, include your email address in the text of your message.

1 There are four reply buttons on the toolbar (read Task 6 step 8 first).

Compose Message – this is to create a new message.

Reply to group – this will send a reply to all the newsgroup members; use this with caution; many newsgroups have their own rules and conventions and send rude messages to contributors whom they consider time wasters! To avoid being 'flamed' in this way read some of the mail to get an idea of the newsgroup's ethos. If the newsgroup provides any 'FAQ's' (frequently asked questions) messages then read these too.

Reply to Author – this will send a private reply only to the author of the message. Many authors do not provide their true email address to avoid junk mail so this option may not be available (see step 3 below).

Forward message – this will send a message to an email address, whether or not they subscribe to this newsgroup.

2 First make sure that you are in the correct newsgroup and have selected the correct message, then click one of the above buttons. The two **Reply** options are fairly straightforward; if you click the **Compose Message** button then a new message window similar to Figure 12.22 opposite appears. Use it as a guide to creating a new message.

3 Open the **Tools** menu and select the **Accounts** option. Click the **News** tab.

Select a news account (you may have only one) and click the **Properties** button; the dialog box shown in Figure 12.23 opposite appears.

- Select the **General** tab if necessary. The User information section contains your email address, name etc. that will appear in your newsgroup messages or replies. You can amend this information if you wish, e.g. to 'anon' if you wish to remain anonymous.
- Click the **Server** tab – this allows you to change your news server (if you have access to more than one) and your logon.
- Click the **Advanced** tab – this contains technical settings for more advanced users.

Close the dialog boxes.

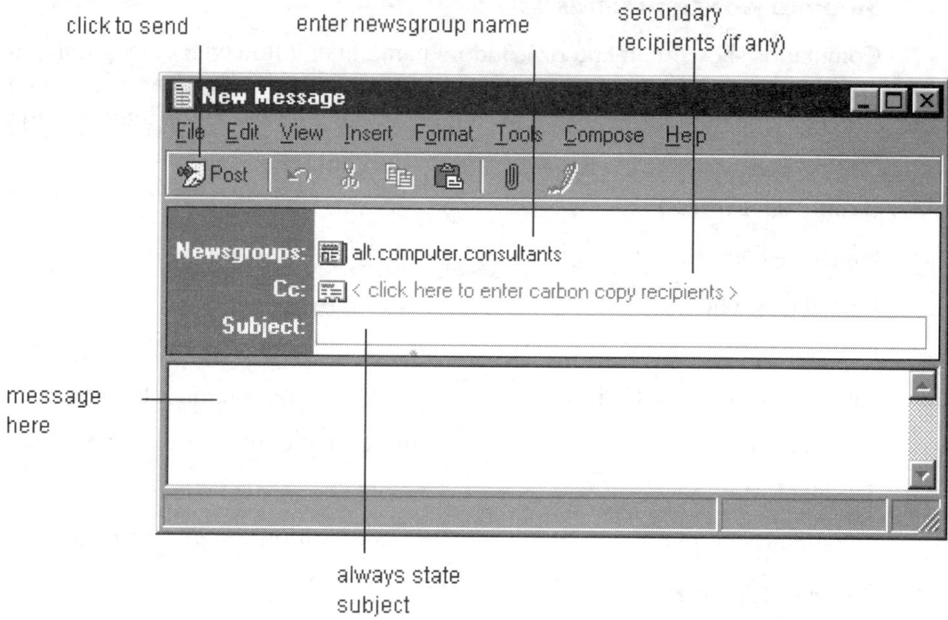

Figure 12.22

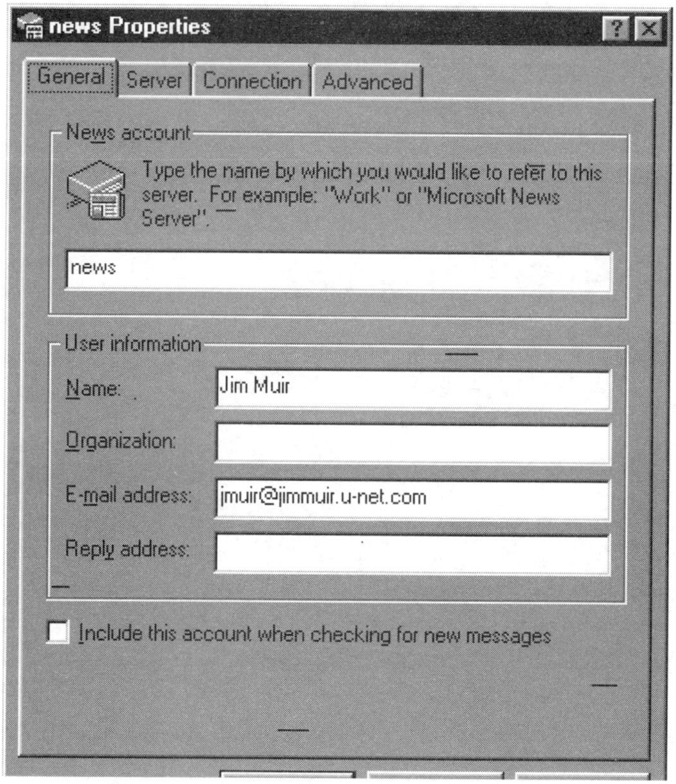

news Properties

General | Server | Connection | Advanced

News account

Type the name by which you would like to refer to this server. For example: "Work" or "Microsoft News Server".

news

User information

Name: Jim Muir

Organization:

E-mail address: jmuir@jimmuir.u-net.com

Reply address:

Include this account when checking for new messages

Figure 12.23

Summary of commands

Commands show the menu or Window name first, followed by the command to choose, e.g. Edit-Clear means open the **Edit** menu and select the **Clear** command. Where a command is available from a particular window this is indicated in brackets.

(FrontPage Express)

File-New-Form Page Wizard	Create a Web-based form
Insert-Hyperlink	Insert a hyperlink
Insert-Image	Insert an image into a Web page
Table-Insert Rows or Columns	Insert rows or column into table
Table-Insert Table	Insert a table into a Web page
Table-Select Row	Select a row in a table
View-Internet Options	Change various Internet settings

(Internet Explorer)

File-Open-Browse	Find a Web page on a local drive

(Outlook Express)

Edit-Find Message	Search for newsgroup messages
Tools-Accounts-News	Change news account settings
Tools-Download this newsgroup	Download newsgroup messages
Tools-Newsgroup Filters	Filter incoming messages
View-Current View-Filtered messages	Turn filter on/off

unit 13

Email using Outlook Express

Introduction

In this unit we will learn how to manage your email using Microsoft's Outlook Express. Outlook Express in a compact version of Microsoft Outlook, the full version of Microsoft's newsgroup and email software. Even if you are presently using an email service such as Eudora from another Internet access provider, there is normally nothing to prevent you trying Outlook Express too. Your Access Provider normally only supplies you with an Internet connection to their mail server. You can choose to install the email software you prefer in order to manage this connection. The only exceptions may be in the case of Full Service Providers, which restrict you to their own email service.

What you should know already

How to use the standard Windows components – see Unit 1.

What you will learn in this unit

By the end of this unit you will be able to:

- connect to the Outlook Express email service
- compose, read and reply to email messages
- format an email message and select stationery styles
- attach signatures and business cards to email
- secure and encrypt email messages
- organise email into folders and create mailing lists
- conduct an email search.

Email with Outlook Express

In Unit 12 we used Outlook Express to manage newsgroups. Its other main function is to send and receive electronic mail messages. You can:

- organise email messages into folders
- automatically filter messages into different folders
- filter out unwanted messages
- store and retrieve email addresses using the Address Book
- format and personalise your messages
- send and receive messages in a secure format.

You can usually (see Introduction on previous page) use Outlook Express even if Microsoft is not your Internet access provider (IAP). To create an email account with Outlook Express you may need to know the following, make sure that you have them to hand:

- your username and password supplied by your IAP
- the names of your incoming and outgoing mail servers.

Task 1 Using Outlook Express for email

1 To connect to Outlook Express, if your current IAP is not Microsoft, then complete this step and step 2.

Open Outlook Express and click the **Read Mail** button.

If this is the first time you have used this option a 'Wizard' will prompt you either to set up a new account or use an existing one. Make sure that the second option is selected; Windows 98 should already have detected who your IAP is; Figure 13.1 shows an example of this – your IAP name may obviously be different to the one shown.

Click the **Next** button and complete the rest of the Wizard; you will normally be able to accept all the default options suggested.

When completed you will be returned to the main email window.

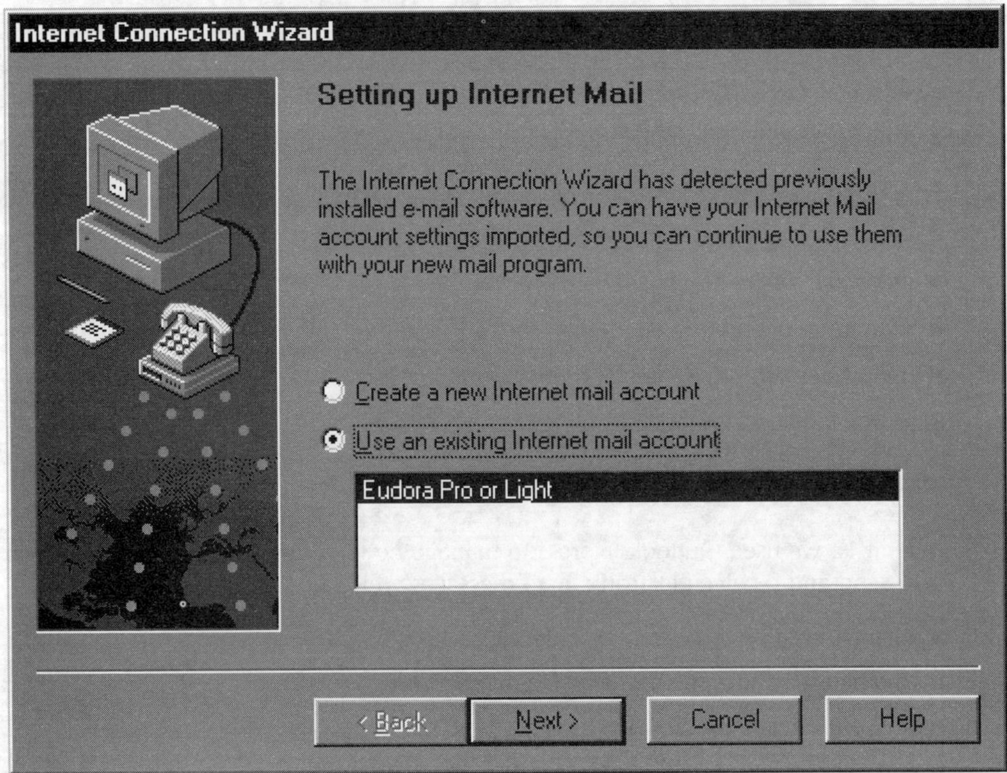

Figure 13.1

2 If you have been using another email service you can usually import your messages into Outlook Express – the originals and any new messages will continue to be stored on your original mail service. Select the **Inbox** icon at the top left of the window.

Open the **File** menu and select **Import** then the **Messages** option. Follow the instructions provided by the Wizard.

3 To compose a new message, click the **Compose Message** button on the toolbar (use the **View** menu if the toolbar is not visible). A blank message form appears.

As a test you can send an email to yourself as I have done in the example shown in Figure 13.2; the message will be sent to and stored on the mail server at your IAP's host computer in the normal way. When you go online (connect to your IAP) then the server automatically sends it to the recipient's email address – in this case you!

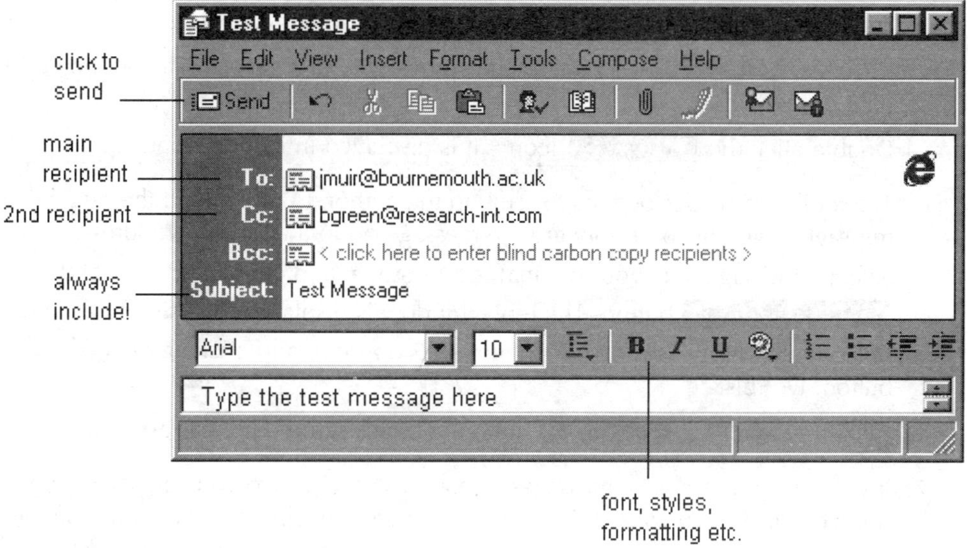

Figure 13.2

Tips for composing an email message

- Email addresses may be in upper or lower case and must be exactly correct, e.g. no spaces and the correct dashes and slashes.
- Recipients in the **to:** and **cc:** sections will see a list of all the other recipients of the message; recipients in the **bcc:** section will not.
- You can enter more than one recipient in the **to:**, **cc:** or **bcc:** sections by separating the email addresses with commas, e.g. jmuir@bournemouth.ac.uk, jwilson@poole.co.uk.
- You can format your email message using the features on the formatting toolbar and **Format** menu – experiment with these now if you wish.
- Use the *F7* function key or the **Spelling** checkon the **Tools** menu to check your spelling.

- You can use the **Insert** menu either to attach a file to the email message or to insert text from an HTML or text file.
- You can use the **Tools** menu to set the priority of your message to low, medium or high.

4 To send an email message, click the **Send** button now – it will normally send the message automatically. If you are offline, i.e. *not* connected to your IAP's mail server, then you may be prompted to connect straight-away. If the message is not sent, open the **Tools** menu and select **Options**. Click the **Send** tab and check that the option **Send messages immediately** is selected. Close the dialog box.

5 To check for new messages, click the **Send and Receive** button on the toolbar and connect if prompted to do so; click the **Inbox** icon if necessary to display the contents of the inbox folder. Depending on the speed of your mail server your test message should now be displayed in the list. Notice any open and closed 'envelope' icons to denote read and unread messages.

Click the **Message** icon once – it is previewed in a special pane at the bottom right of the window.

Double click the **Message** icon – it is displayed in its own window.

6 The toolbar provides buttons to reply to the author, to reply to all the original message recipients or to forward the message on to a new email address.

Select a message, e.g. your original test message, and click the **Reply to Author** button. The reply window is displayed; it is simply a matter of typing the reply as shown in Figure 13.3 opposite and clicking the **Send** button. Do this.

Click the **Send and Receive** button to check if the reply has arrived.

7 If you have a number of messages to compose or reply to you can save connection charges by working offline. If you are currently connected then disconnect. Open the **File** menu and make sure that **Work Offline** is selected, i.e. ticked. (This option is only available from the main Outlook Express window, not from the In box window.)

Compose a new message or reply to an existing one.

While the message window is still open select **Send Later** from the **File** menu.

A dialog box may ask you to confirm that you wish to store the message in the Outbox. Do this and open your outbox – you will find that the message is stored.

Now send the message by clicking the **Send and Receive** button and going online when prompted.

Remember to disconnect again when you are finished.

You can save a copy of any of your email messages for future reference: select the message, open the **Edit** menu, select **Copy to Folder** and select the destination folder.
You can delete a selected message using the **Edit** menu or by right clicking it.

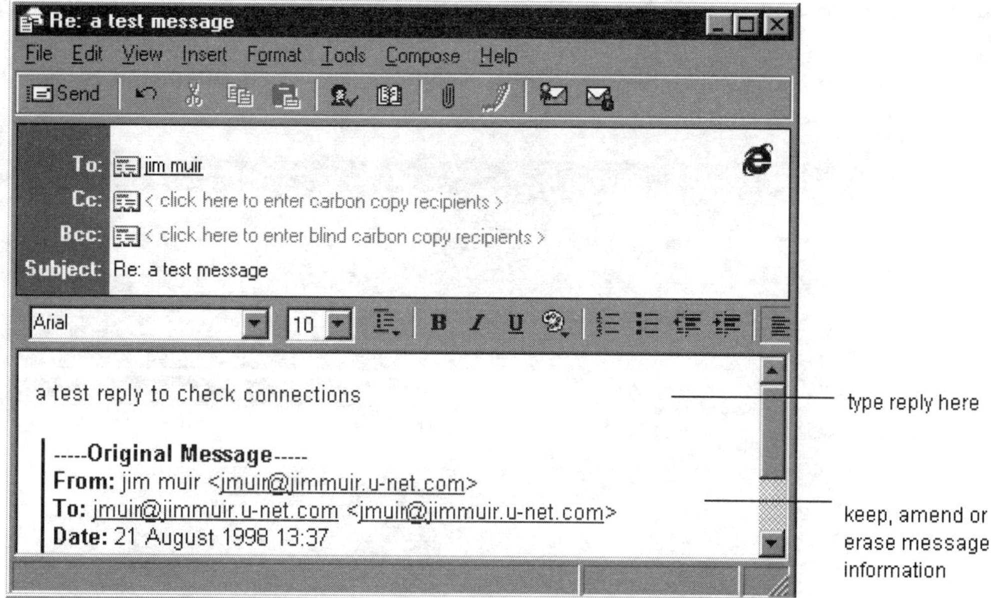

Figure 13.3

8 Open the **Tools** menu and select **Options**. The **Options** dialog box has seven tabs allowing you to select different mail handling options.

- Click the **Send** tab and review the standard settings; you will see that Outlook Express will automatically save a copy of sent messages, include the original message in a reply and so on. You can also select plain text or HTML format for your email messages.
- Review the settings on the other tabs too; you should be aware of these settings.

Task 2: Stationery and signatures

In this task we will try out some of the ways in which you can customise your email messages. You can either format messages individually or use an Outlook Express 'stationery' style. You can also use HTML – the formatting language used for Web documents (see Unit 11).

1 Make sure that the main Inbox window is displayed; if not open Outlook Express and click the **Read Mail** button.

2 To choose a stationery style, click the **Down arrow** next to the **Compose Message** button. A number of stationery options are displayed (see Figure 13.4 on the following page).

Choose one, e.g. **Holiday Letter**. You may have to enlarge the message window to view the stationery style.

Close the message window and try some other styles.

You can set a style as the default for all your new messages using the **Tools - Stationery** option.

You can apply a stationery style to an email message you are in the process of composing using the **Format – Apply Stationery** option.

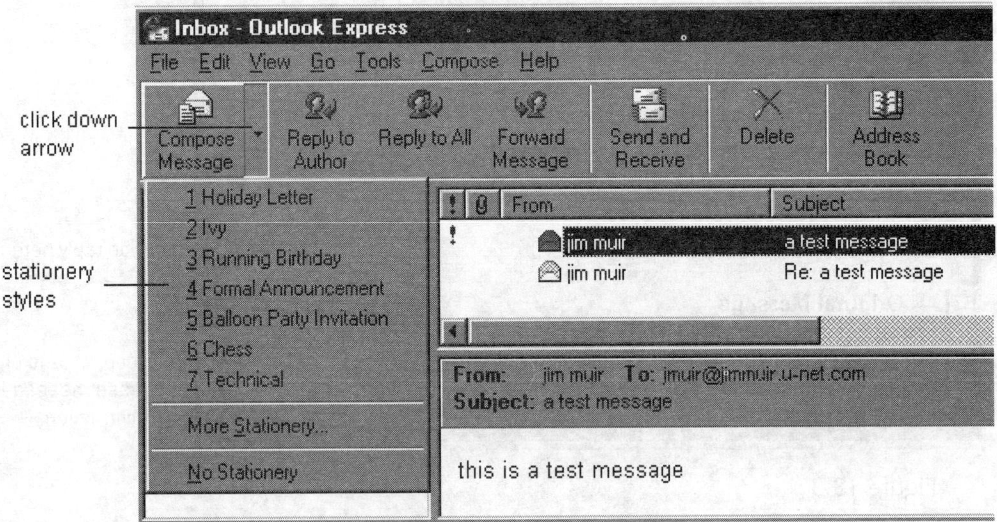

Figure 13.4

3 A signature is a short message, often about you, that you can include at the bottom of your email messages.

Close any new message windows then open the **Tools** menu and select **Stationery**.

Click the **Signature** button on the **Stationery** dialog box – the **Signature** dialog box is displayed (see Figure 13.5 opposite).

Click the **Text** button and type a suitable message about yourself, e.g. an item of concern to a number of your email contacts (if you select the **File** button instead then you can select a file that contains a message).

Leave the dialog box open and continue with the next section.

4 A business card is an email attachment that contains personal information, e.g. address, phone, fax etc. It is stored in the Outlook Express Address Book which contains a list of your contacts.

Click the **New** button on the **Signature** dialog box – the **Properties** dialog box opens; make sure that the **Personal** tab is selected.

5 Complete some details about yourself; see Figure 13.6 opposite for an example.

Click the **Add** button to add your details to the Address book. You can use the other tabs on the **Properties** dialog box at this stage, e.g. home/business, to complete details about you.

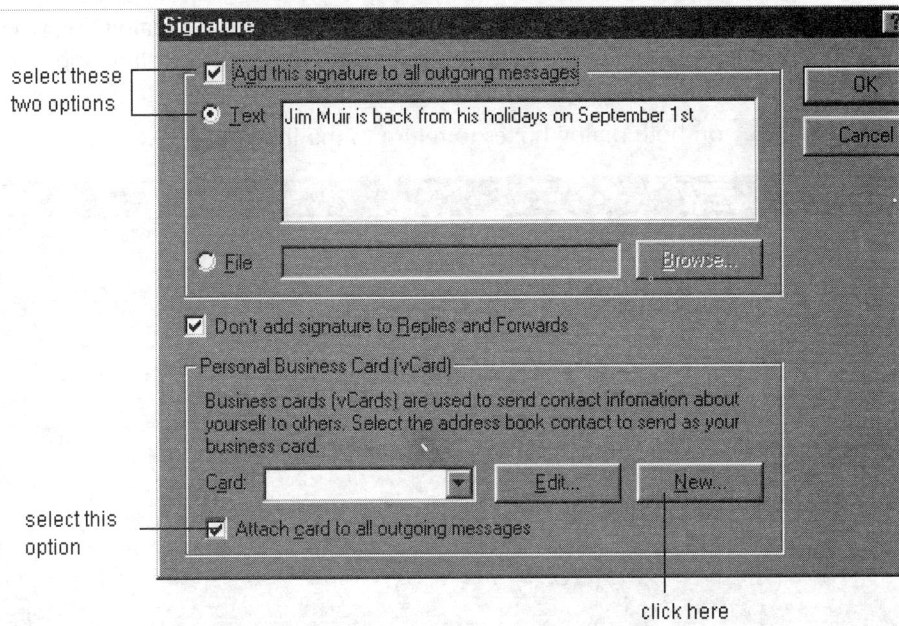

Figure 13.5

Figure 13.6

6 Click the **OK** button and you are returned to the **Signature** dialog box where you have the options to add a new business card or edit an existing one – see Figure 13.7.

Click **OK** on both dialog boxes to return to the Inbox window.

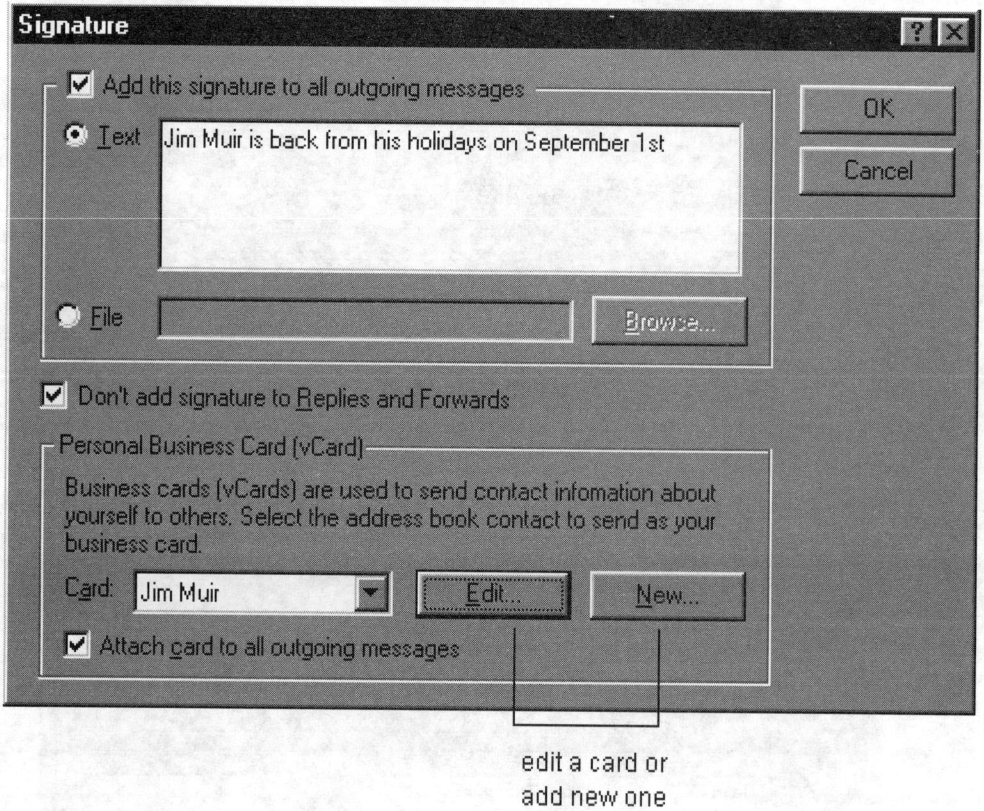

Figure 13.7

7 Click the **Address Book** button on the Inbox toolbar; your details are listed in the Address Book. You can use the Address Book to edit details of existing contacts or to add new ones.

Close the Address Book.

8 Now click the **Compose Message** button on the Inbox toolbar. The New Message window opens showing both the signature and an icon for the business card at the top right of the window.

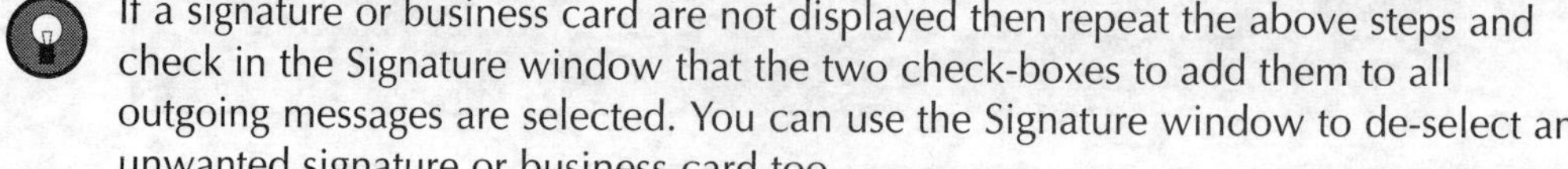

If a signature or business card are not displayed then repeat the above steps and check in the Signature window that the two check-boxes to add them to all outgoing messages are selected. You can use the Signature window to de-select an unwanted signature or business card too.

Task 3: Formatting email messages

In the previous task we tried out some of Outlook Express' standard formats; in this task we will use the Formatting toolbar to add some useful formats of our own. You will find it very straightforward, particularly if you have used a word processor or a Web page editor.

1 Make sure that the main Inbox window is displayed; if not open Outlook Express and click the **Read Mail** button.

Click the **Compose Message** button to open a new message window.

Now try creating the email message using Figure 13.8 as a guide. First you will need to locate the cursor on the part of the email window where the message will be typed.

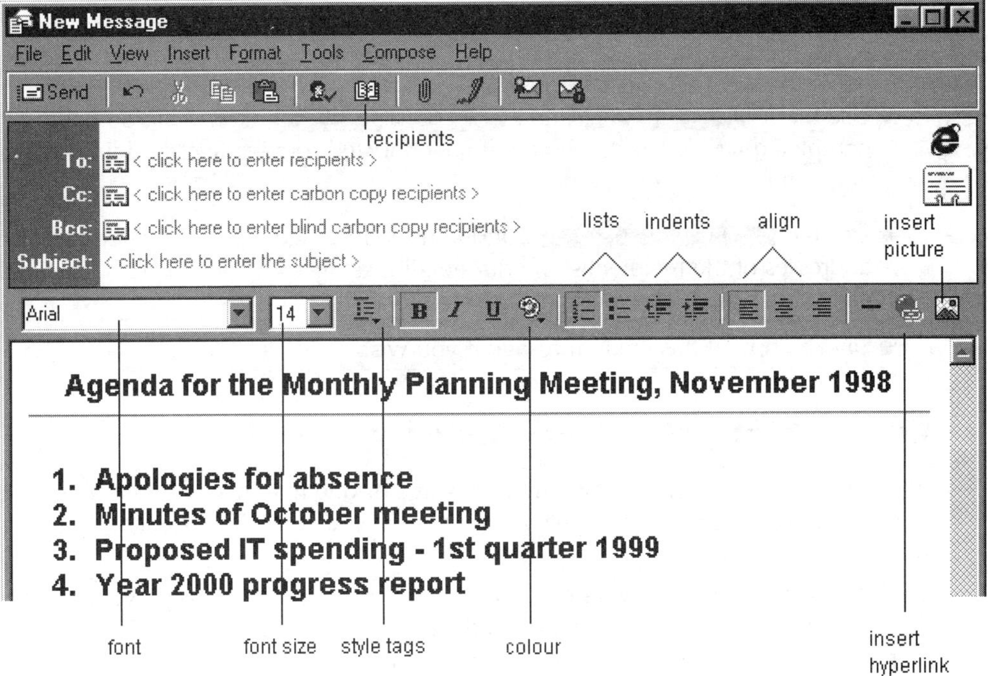

Figure 13.8

2 To set styles, click the **Style Tag** button on the formatting toolbar and select **Heading 3** from the menu. Now type the first line of the message ***Agenda for the monthly Planning Meeting, November 1998***.

3 Styles, fonts and colours can be amended either using the formatting toolbar or by opening the **Format** menu and selecting **Font**.

Make sure that the first line of text is selected, i.e. highlighted.

Click the down arrow on the **Font** and **Font Size** boxes (see Figure 13.8) and experiment with various font combinations.

Use the other buttons on the Format toolbar to alter the text colour, underlining etc.

Centre the title and insert a horizontal line underneath it.

Use the **Edit-Undo** command (or **Edit-Undo** button) to reverse unwanted changes. You can also use the *Delete* and *Backspace* keys to delete.

4 To select a list style, press the *Enter* key to insert a line space after the heading and click the **Align Left** button.

Click the **Style Tag** button on the toolbar and select **Numbered list**. Now type the list of agenda items shown in Figure 13.8.

Now highlight the entire list and experiment with other list styles, e.g. bulleted and indentation.

5 Keep the message window open and try out the following.

- Use the **Insert Picture** and **Insert Hyperlink** buttons – if you have completed Unit 12 Task 4 you will have located some images and links which you can use.
- Use the **Select Recipients** button on the message toolbar to select the addresses of the recipient(s) of your email message. Outlook Express automatically stores all your email message recipients.
- Save a copy of this email message if you wish.

Outlook Express and security

If you are sending a confidential email message or one that involves a commercial transaction (such as ordering or paying for goods) you want the message to be secure.

Outlook Express provides ways of securing your electronic mail; to prevent unauthorised individuals intercepting and reading email messages they can be encrypted. To prove that an email message really does come from a particular sender you can provide a digital ID to prevent forgery.

Digital ID's are issued by special third parties known as certificate authorities – in the case of Windows 98 by the organisation Verisign.

Task 4: Email security

1 Make sure that the Inbox window is displayed; if not, open Outlook Express and click the **Read Mail** button.

Close any open email messages. Open the **Tools** menu and select **Options**.

Click the **Security** tab on the dialog box that appears.

Click the **More Info...** button to find out more about digital ID's.

2 When you have finished close the Help window and click the **Get Digital ID** button to connect to the appropriate Microsoft Web site. When you have completed the registration with Verisign a digital ID will be emailed to you.

Storing email

Once you start to accumulate a large number of email messages it is useful to sort them into folders. You are most likely to want to sort your inbox messages in this way, especially if you receive a large number of newsgroup messages that you wish to store and read later.

Task 5: Organising your email

1 To create a folder, make sure that the Inbox window is displayed; if not open Outlook Express and click the **Read Mail** button.

Close any open email messages then open the **File** menu and select **Folder**.

Choose the **New Folder** option; a dialog box appears (see Figure 13.9).

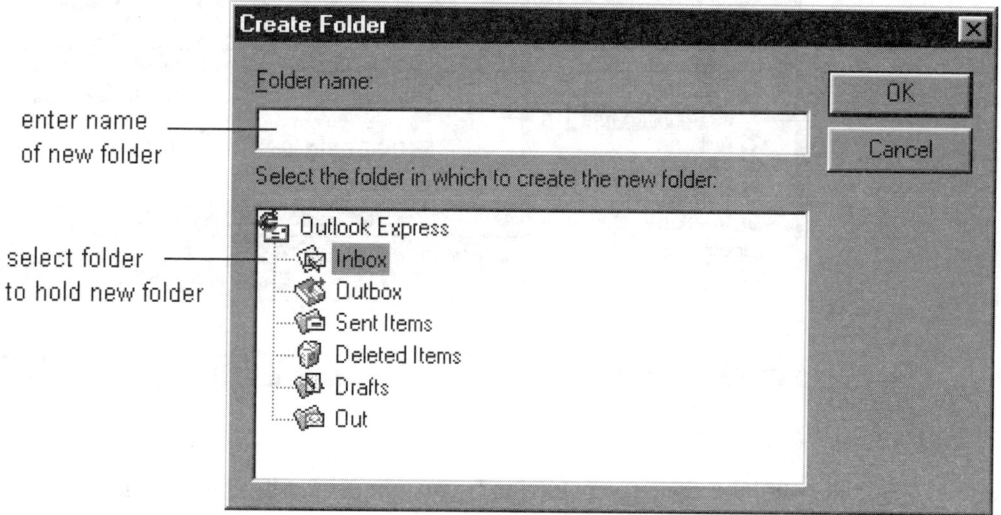

Figure 13.9

Type the name of the new folder, then select the folder that will hold this new folder, e.g. **Inbox** (to create a new folder at the top level highlight Outlook Express)

Click the **OK** button and check that the new folder is located in the correct folder.

Any of the main folders – Inbox, Outbox etc. – that contain other folders are marked with an open/close box in a similar way to Windows Explorer – see Figure 10. Click this box, a + sign indicates closed, a – sign indicates open.

2 Now use the **Edit** menu or the 'drag and drop' technique to move messages to the new folder, e.g. copy one of the messages from your inbox folder to the new folder.

Figure 13.10 shows a new folder **Pending Reply** created in the Inbox folder; it holds three messages, one of them unread.

You can copy or move multiple messages by holding down the *Ctrl* key, selecting the files, then opening the **Edit** menu and selecting either **Move to Folder** or **Copy to Folder**.

If you wish to save a message permanently open the **File** menu and select **Save as**. The message can then be deleted from the email folder if you wish.

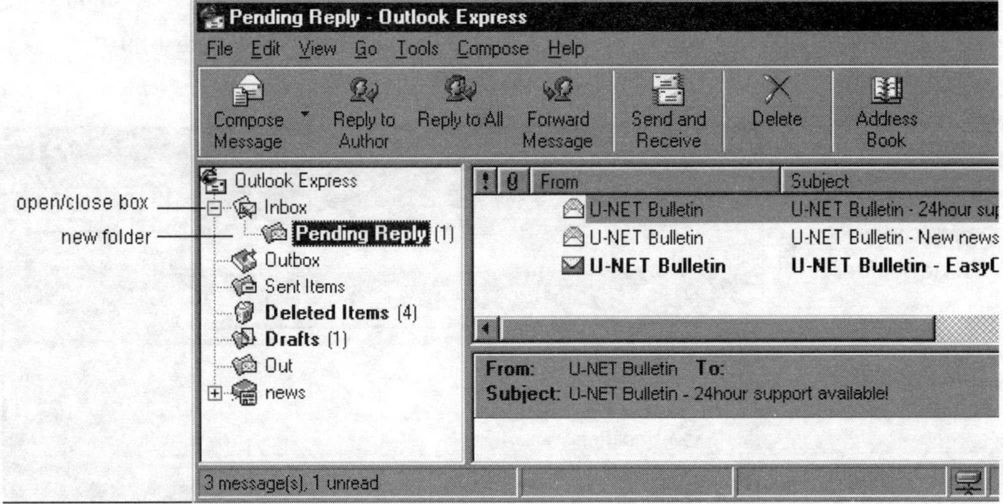

Figure 13.10

3 Not all your Inbox messages need to be read immediately. Rather than reading all your Inbox messages and then moving them to the relevant folder, you can route them automatically; some can even be deleted or blocked. This is called *filtering*.

Open the **Tools** menu and select **Inbox Assistant**; when the dialog box appears click the **Add** button.

Figure 13.11 opposite shows an example of filtering in action – all messages to the recipient jmuir@poole.co.uk from the sender jwilson@bournemouth.ac.uk on the subject of overtime are automatically routed to my folder **Pending Reply**.

- The top half of the dialog box allows you to choose a number of filtering conditions; the lower half lets you specify various courses of action – copying, moving, deleting or not downloading at all.
- To fill out the lower half of the dialog box you must select an action first, e.g. move to, copy to, etc.

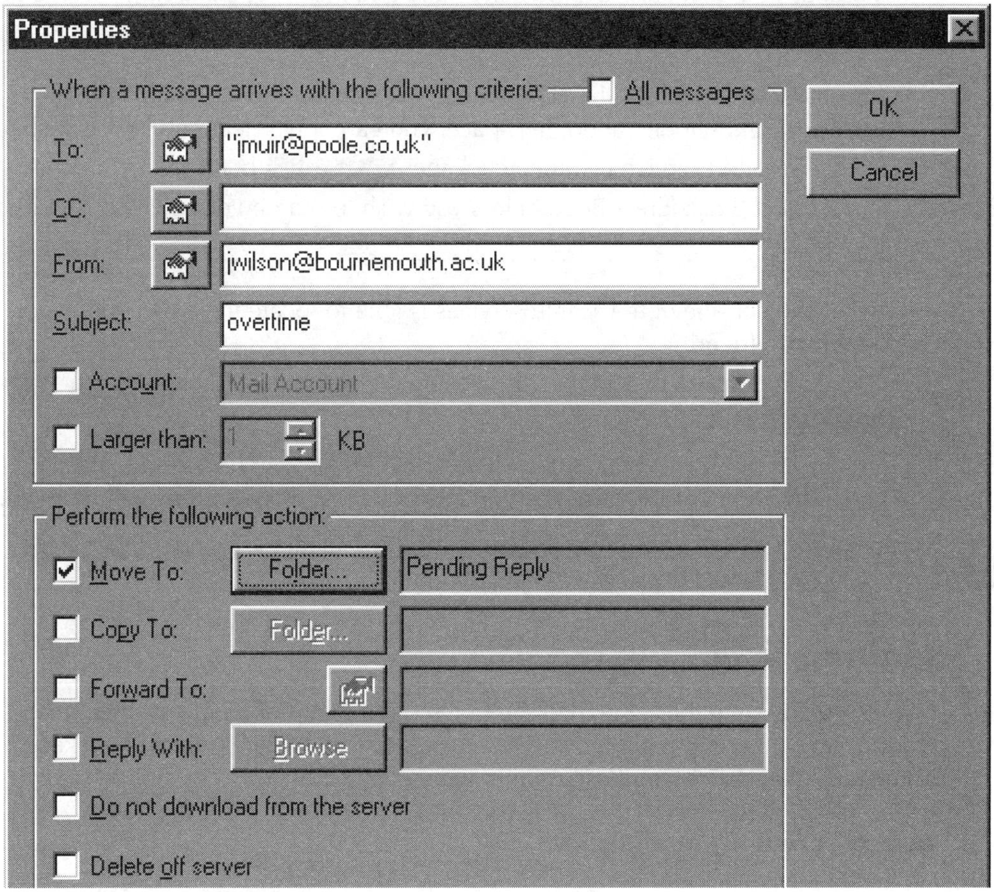

Figure 13.11

4 Create a suitable filter as above then compose a message to yourself that meets the filter conditions. Send the message and check that the Inbox Assistant has taken the appropriate action.

5 To find messages, open the **Edit** menu and select **Find Message**.

The **Find Message** dialog box allows you to search by one or more criteria – sender, recipients, subject heading, message body or date.

Select a folder to search, e.g. Inbox, include subfolders if necessary and try a search.

If successful a list of messages are displayed and can be opened and read.

6 Outlook Express also lets you locate individuals who have an email address on the Internet. Open the **Edit** menu and select **Find People**.

The **Find People** dialog box opens allowing you to locate individuals by name, email, address etc. The more details you can supply the better, providing you are sure of them; searching on, for example, a common surname can yield a list of thousands of individuals. On the other hand one incorrect detail may mean that the relevant person is not located, even if the other details are correct.

7 Click the down arrow on the **Look in:** box – a number of Net search services are displayed, e.g. Bigfoot, Yahoo, Infospace; you can only select one. If you wish to review a selected service first then click the **Web Site** button.

Do not select the Address Book unless you wish to search your own contact list (see Task 2).

8 Check whether one of the search services is able to locate the email address of yourself or a friend.

Fill in appropriate details in the **Find People** dialog box and then click the **Find Now** button.

You may be prompted to go online to connect to the search service's Web site. Do so and eventually a list of possible individuals or organisations will be listed.

You can also conduct a people search without using Outlook Express. Open the **Start** menu and select the **Find - People** option.

Mailing lists

If you regularly send the same message to the same group of recipients then it is worth creating a group mailing list. The recipients' email addresses can be taken from your Address Book and/or keyed in individually.

Task 6: Creating mailing lists

1 Make sure that the Inbox window is displayed; if not open Outlook Express and click the **Read Mail** button.

Click the **Address Book** icon – when the Address Book window opens click the **New Group** button.

The **Group Properties** dialog box opens; enter a name for the mailing list.

2 To add recipients to the mailing list click *either*,

- the **Select Members** button to choose an existing contact from your Address Book

  or,

- the **New Contact** button to add a new name to your address book.

3 Figure 13.12 shows the dialog box for a mailing group called 'IT Committee' which contains three members. You can add, remove or change the details of a recipient.

Click **OK** on both dialog boxes to return to the main Outlook Express email window.

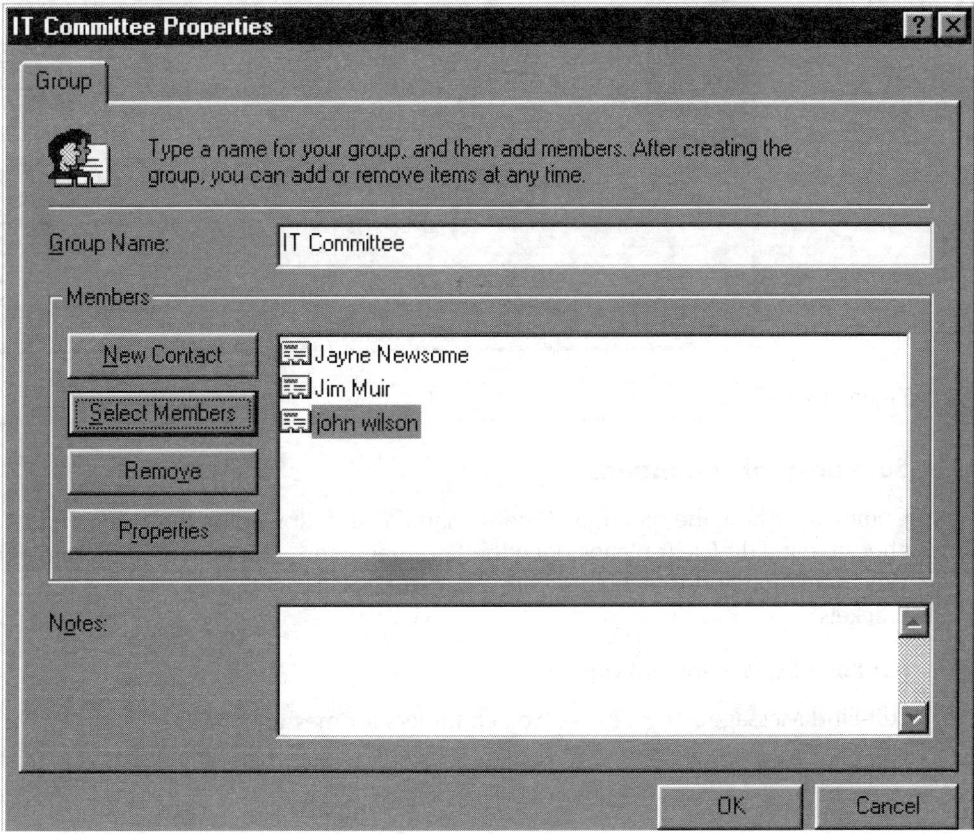

Figure 13.12

4 To see how the mailing list would work click the **Compose Message** button.

Click the card icon next to the **To:** section in the New Message window – see Figure 13.13 on the following page.

The **Select Recipients** dialog box opens; select the name of your mailing list, click the **To:** button then **OK**.

The name of the mailing list now appears in the **To:** section of your email message.

Send the email message if appropriate or cancel it.

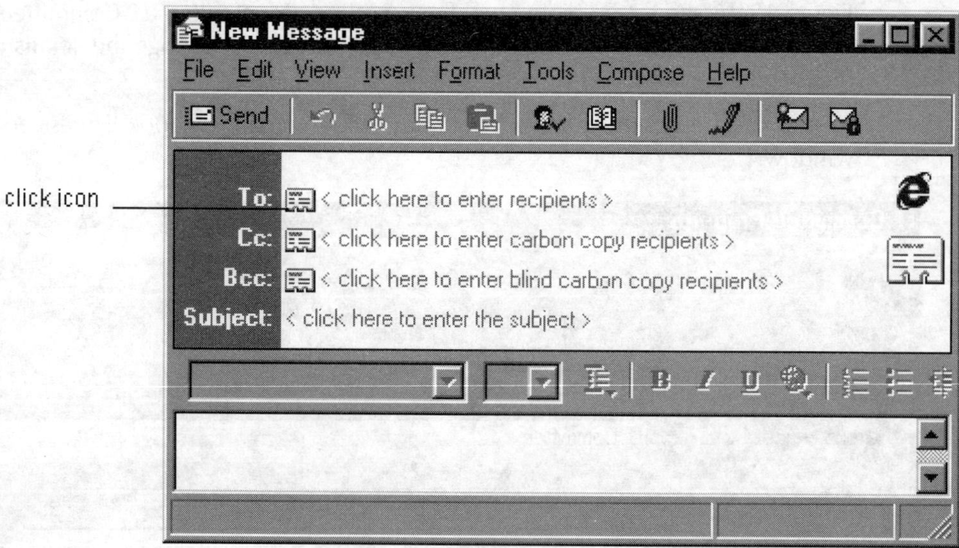

Figure 13.13

Summary of commands

Commands show the menu or Window name first, followed by the command to choose, e.g. Edit-Clear means open the **Edit** menu and select the **Clear** command. Where a command is available from a particular window this is indicated in brackets.

(Outlook Express Inbox Window)

Edit-Find Message	Search folders for messages
Edit-Find People	Search Net for an email address
Edit-Move/Copy to Folder	Move or copy email messages
File-Folder-New Folder	Create new email folder
File-Import Messages	Import email from another email service
File-Save as	Save email message to disk
File-Work Offline	Compose email offline
Tools-Inbox Assistant	Filter incoming email
Tools-Options	Set various email option
Tools-Stationery	Select Stationery, Signature or Business card

(Outlook Express New Message Window)

Format-Font	Select message font

Glossary

Active Desktop	displays information channels on the World Wide Web that you can subscribe to – news, entertainment etc.
Application	any program or set of programs that carries out a particular job such as word processing or Web browsing
Business card	an email attachment that contains personal information, e.g. address, phone, fax etc. It is stored in the Outlook Express Address Book
Defragmenting	moving data around on the disk until all parts of the same file are stored together
Desktop	the background area of the screen which may be plain or patterned. It is used as a working area to open windows, work with them and close them when no longer needed. Nearly all your tasks – viewing documents, running programs, using the Internet or email – start from the desktop
Dialog box	a window that contains a message or asks you to supply some information
Drive	used to read information from or write information to a diskette or hard disk
Embedding	copying an object from a source document to a destination document
File	anything created on the computer – a letter, report, spreadsheet, digitised sound or images etc – has to be saved as a file i.e. copied into the computer's memory
Folder	used to store group of files; folders can be 'nested' inside each other as subfolders
Icons	small pictures or graphic images of programs, files or computer hardware etc.
In-place editing	automatically returning to the home application of an image in order to edit it (the image itself being incorporated into a document in another application)
Newsgroup	a number of email messages on a related topic stored on a central computer or server
Pop-up menu	a menu that appears, letting you perform actions on an object
Signature	a short message, often about you, that you can include at the bottom of your email messages
Taskbar	always visible at the bottom of the screen while Windows 98 is running. It shows the Start button, plus a button for every task that is running, e.g. program or open document

Title and Title Bar	every window has these. Depending on the type of window the title can be the name of an application (program), a file or a group of resources, as in the case of My Computer. If there are several windows open then the title bar of the active window – the one that you are using – appears as a deeper colour than the others, usually blue
Toggle option	an option that can be selected or deselected by clicking
Toolbar	displays various buttons - Back, Forward, Up etc. These are extra commands and supplement those on the menu bar
WebBot	a small program or application that automates a task such as saving e.g. Timestamp updates the date and time on a Web page
Window	a rectangular area that displays information – icons, folders or files
Wizard	a series of dialog boxes guiding you through the steps of a process

Index